# *WebKit*

## FOR

# DUMMIES®

# by Chris Minnick

**WILEY**

John Wiley & Sons, Inc.

**WebKit For Dummies®**

Published by
**John Wiley & Sons, Inc.**
111 River Street
Hoboken, NJ 07030-5774

www.wiley.com

Copyright © 2012 by John Wiley & Sons, Inc., Hoboken, New Jersey

Published by John Wiley & Sons, Inc., Hoboken, New Jersey

Published simultaneously in Canada

For general information on our other products and services, please contact our Customer Care Department within the U.S. at 877-762-2974, outside the U.S. at 317-572-3993, or fax 317-572-4002.

For technical support, please visit www.wiley.com/techsupport.

Wiley publishes in a variety of print and electronic formats and by print-on-demand. Some material included with standard print versions of this book may not be included in e-books or in print-on-demand. If this book refers to media such as a CD or DVD that is not included in the version you purchased, you may download this material at http://booksupport.wiley.com. For more information about Wiley products, visit www.wiley.com.

Library of Congress Control Number: 2011946308

ISBN 978-1-118-12720-9 (pbk); ISBN 978-1-118-22490-8 (ebk); ISBN 978-1-118-23835-6 (ebk); ISBN 978-1-118-26293-1 (ebk)

Manufactured in the United States of America

10 9 8 7 6 5 4 3 2 1

WILEY

# About the Author

**Chris Minnick** has been a Web developer and Web entrepreneur since the mid-90s. He is the genius behind several successful Web start-ups, including ContentBoxer.com and Minnickweb.com. He is also the genius behind several not-so-successful start-ups, including StickOfButterOnAStick.com, CelebrityAgeMachine.com, and Texas-Shaped.com.

He writes, speaks, teaches, and consults on the Mobile Web and works with businesses to maximize their online revenue. Chris has written numerous books and articles on a wide range of Internet-related topics including mobile app development, e-commerce, e-business, Web design, XML, and application servers.

When he's not working or writing, Chris enjoys swimming in San Francisco Bay and making wine. More information can be found on his blog: www.chrisminnick.com.

# Dedication

To Margaret, who has been on this journey with me from the beginning and never stopped believin'.

# Author's Acknowledgments

Thank you to everyone at Wiley who made this book happen, including Katie Feltman and Pat O'Brien; to Ed Tittel for technical editing, general guidance, and support over the years; and to my agent Carole Jelen. You're all the best ever.

Huge appreciation to all of my friend and family, who encouraged me and "liked" my Facebook status, even at 1:00AM when I was exhausted from another marathon writing session, including: Margaret Minnick, Jeff Schwarzschild, John "Spurious" Lewis and Molly "Superlativa" Lewis, Maya Wallace, Stephanie and Pat Howse, Sam Hubbard, Brandon McGowen, Gae Reck, Vicente Lozano, Deanne Brooks, Ben Drake, Savanna Bohlman, Tina Knop, Jeremy and Amy Duncan, Jim Vanderveen, Michele Vandenbergh, Kristen Brunton, Maureen Brunton, Marilyn Steinheiser, Sara Stapleton ("grr"), Jesse James, Steven Cranston, Dave Kalman, Carl Landau, Shelly Rentz, Carmen Isias, Mike Burkhart, Carol Hachey, Paul and Jonna Stebleton, Paul and Elizabeth Jackson, Carol and Sondre Skatter, Lujuana Treadwell, Don Treadwell, Ruth Minnick, Mom and Dad, Beth and Geoff and Eliza Burkhart, Kathy and J Elliot, David and Kelly and the girls, Ken Byers, Meg and Emily Mann, Mr. Jones and Sparky.

A very special thank you to my colleagues at Minnick Web Services, Mara Shank and Priscila Ibarra, who put up with me every day and help me keep it together.

## Publisher's Acknowledgments

We're proud of this book; please send us your comments at http://dummies.custhelp.com. For other comments, please contact our Customer Care Department within the U.S. at 877-762-2974, outside the U.S. at 317-572-3993, or fax 317-572-4002.

Some of the people who helped bring this book to market include the following:

*Acquisitions, Editorial, and Vertical Websites*

**Project Editor:** Pat O'Brien

**Acquisitions Editor:** Katie Feltman

**Senior Copy Editor:** Barry Childs-Helton

**Technical Editor:** Ed Tittel

**Editorial Manager:** Kevin Kirschner

**Editorial Assistant:** Amanda Graham

**Sr. Editorial Assistant:** Cherie Case

**Cover Photo:** © iStockphoto.com / Cary Westfall

**Cartoons:** Rich Tennant (www.the5thwave.com)

*Composition Services*

**Project Coordinator:** Patrick Redmond

**Layout and Graphics:** Lavonne Roberts, Corrie Socolovitch

**Proofreaders:** Jessica Kramer, Toni Settle

**Indexer:** BIM Indexing & Proofreading Services

---

**Publishing and Editorial for Technology Dummies**

    **Richard Swadley,** Vice President and Executive Group Publisher

    **Andy Cummings,** Vice President and Publisher

    **Mary Bednarek,** Executive Acquisitions Director

    **Mary C. Corder,** Editorial Director

**Publishing for Consumer Dummies**

    **Kathleen Nebenhaus,** Vice President and Executive Publisher

**Composition Services**

    **Debbie Stailey,** Director of Composition Services

# Contents at a Glance

# Table of Contents

# Introduction

. . . . . . . . . . . . . . . . . . . . . . . . . . . . . . . . . . . . . . . . . . . . . . . . . . . . . .

Mobile apps are the rocket fuel powering the growth of the web today. Everything is going mobile. If you're starting a web business today without a mobile strategy, or if you have a mobile strategy but it isn't the center of your business, you're going to have a hard time gaining any sort of traction.

Ever since Apple released the browser engine behind its Safari Web browser as open source, WebKit and the mobile web have been joined at the hip. In the last few years, WebKit has advanced the state of the art for the Mobile Web by aggressively adopting new web standards, such as HTML5 and CSS3, and by pushing the performance of existing standards like JavaScript.

By itself, WebKit is interesting. When combined with the mobile Web, it's powerful. When it's the heart of almost every smartphone browser coming out today, it's revolutionary. That's what this book is about.

# Why I Love WebKit, and You Should Too

The smartphone and tablet markets today are split between several different operating systems — including Apple's iOS, Google's Android, Research in Motion's Blackberry, Microsoft's Windows Mobile, and several other players. Each of these different operating systems has its own way of developing and deploying "native" apps (the ones you download from an "app store") — and none of them works with any of the others.

If you're developing a mobile app, then, and you want it to run on as close to every smartphone and tablet as possible, you can spend many thousands of dollars to develop the iPhone version, then spend many thousands of dollars more to develop the Android version, then the Blackberry version, and so on. And, you haven't even started to work on the tablet versions yet.

The requirement to essentially rewrite your app for every mobile platform just doesn't seem right or necessary — and it isn't.

Right now, WebKit-based browsers run on nearly all of the major smartphone and tablet operating systems. This makes WebKit the cross-platform mobile app standard. Industry leaders such as Google, Twitter, and Facebook have made the decision that it makes more sense to focus on writing one incredible mobile web app, rather than to create multiple native apps. The rest of the mobile development world is rapidly coming around to the same conclusion.

If you're a business owner who wants to take your business mobile, WebKit means that you can likely leverage your existing web presence in developing your mobile app.

If you're a web developer who wants to make the shift to mobile, WebKit means you can develop apps using many of the same skills that you already know, including HTML, CSS, and JavaScript.

If you're a user of mobile devices, WebKit means that your data and apps don't need to be tied to your device. You can access the same apps on your desktop computer that you use on your phone. Your apps will update themselves without you doing anything at all. And — perhaps best of all for those of us who love to get our hands on the latest gadgets — you won't be locked into using just one mobile operating system.

# Who Should Read This Book

This is a beginner's guide to developing mobile web apps for devices with WebKit browsers. I don't assume that you have any prior web development or mobile app development experience.

I've distilled my own years of web development experience, along with thousands of pages of documentation, articles, blog posts, and technical manuals into this book (and boy are my arms tired!).

I designed this book to be hands-on, because that's how I learned everything I know about the web and because I believe that's the best way to really get to know anything new.

I've written and included several mobile web apps, and numerous code snippets throughout the book. These are designed to make you curious and to be jumping off points for your own experimentation with the mobile web. I've also provided links to a large number of resources for learning about the mobile web and for seeing some examples of apps that others are creating.

I've attempted to provide as complete a picture of mobile web development for WebKit browsers as I can without going off onto highly technical explanations of concepts that aren't central to the matter at hand (well, at least not unless it was absolutely necessary, or at least fun).

I hope that my efforts, along with the efforts of the hundreds of people who have contributed to my knowledge or the examples and demos I cite in this book, will inspire you to work with us to push the limits of the web and the mobile web.

If you have no experience with web or mobile development, but you want to learn to do mobile development, you should read this book. If you're a web developer who wants to shift to developing mobile apps, you should read this book. If you're a native app developer who wants to create cross-platform apps, you should read this book. If you're starting a web business, or if you already own one, you should read this book. If you're one of my friends or family members and you want to find out if you're mentioned in here, you should read this book.

# Conventions Used in This Book

This book guides you through learning to use and to develop mobile web apps for WebKit browsers. Throughout the book, I'll be including code written in HTML5, CSS3, XML, and JavaScript.

Code examples in this book appear in a monospaced font so that they'll stand out. That means the code you see will look like this:

```
<meta name = "viewport" content = "width = device-width"/>
```

All of the URLs in this book (and there are a lot) are also in a monospaced font:

```
www.dummies.com/go/webkit
```

I've posted all of my example apps to the above website, and you can check them out if you have any questions about anything in the code (is that a 1 or a lower-case "L"?) I'll provide updates to the code at that website as well as at www.webkitfordummies.com.

# Foolish Assumptions

I don't assume much, and I've tried at every step of the way to be there to give you a hand with some of the trickier parts of your journey to mobile web-app guru-land.

I expect you to have a computer and an Internet connection. The operating system on your computer doesn't matter too much. Mac, Windows, and Linux users will all be able to complete the examples.

I use all three of these operating systems in my daily life, but I tended to skew toward the Mac OS X side of things while writing this book (as you'll detect in the screenshots). This isn't meant to imply that your experience of this book will be any worse if you use Windows. I, and my trusty technical editor, have gone over all of the examples to make sure they work correctly on at least Mac and Windows. You may need to get a little creative in parts if you use Linux for your primary desktop operating system.

Furthermore, you should at least be familiar with smartphones or tablet computers and apps. Maybe you've tried your buddy's iPhone. That's good enough.

All of the software used in this book can be downloaded for free. In addition, you can try all of different smartphone operating systems on desktop computers by using emulators.

# How This Book is Organized

_WebKit For Dummies_ has six main parts. You can read the book from start to finish, or just find what you want in the Table of Contents or the Index.

## Part I: Introducing WebKit

Part I introduces you to WebKit and the big picture of mobile web-app design. I'll also get you set up with a shiny new browser that you'll use throughout the book.

## Part II: Your First Mobile Web App

In Part II, you'll dive head-first into mobile web-app development. We'll make one app that will display and organize some of the links I gathered while writing this book. The second app will be the foundation for a little cookbook app featuring a few of my favorite (extremely basic) recipes. We'll round out this part by talking about testing and then an increasingly important aspect of mobile web-app development: offline apps.

# Part III: Mobile Web Fundamentals

Part III is where I go into details about some of my favorite topics: things like HTML5, CSS3, JavaScript, and much more. From how to start planning and thinking about an app, to how to write some pretty nifty code to make it all go — this is where you'll find the real meat and potatoes (or perhaps you'd prefer our vegetarian option: delicious portabella mushrooms marinated in garlic and balsamic vinegar and grilled. Served with buttered noodles and grilled asparagus).

# Part IV: Optimizing Your Apps

In Part IV, we go a step further and look at how you can take your HTML5 app and make it really shine. I'll tell you some details about each of the major mobile platforms that use a WebKit browser, and get into some nitty-gritty details of how to tweak your app for optimum compatibility with each platform.

I'll also go into the all-important topic of optimizing for performance and then wind up this part with the ultimate platform-specific optimization — creating a native app from your web app.

# Part V: Advanced Topics

Part V is a really exciting one. In this part, you'll learn about some next-level techniques and tools. Many of them are available to be used right now. Others are so new and cutting edge that you may have to wait a little bit after you learn them before you can use them in a real-world app. This is the part where we talk about how to take pictures from your WebKit browser, use a phone's location to show the user on a map, create animation without plugins, and even dive in to 3D graphics.

# Part VI: The Part of Tens

Part VI is about lists of things I think every mobile web developer and WebKit user ought to know. You'll see some of my favorite HTML5 demos, learn some shortcuts and tricks for WebKit, and find out how you can make WebKit even better by using extensions.

# Icons Used in This Book

This icon indicates a useful pointer that you shouldn't skip.

This icon represents a friendly reminder. It describes a vital point that you should keep in mind while proceeding through a particular section of the chapter.

This icon signifies that the accompanying explanation may be informative (and maybe even interesting), but it isn't essential to understanding the core concepts in the chapter.

This icon alerts you to potential problems that you may encounter along the way. When I give you a warning, it's to prevent you from making a mistake that will have big implications. (I don't continually remind you that typos in programming code will keep you from getting the job done, but it's true.)

# Where to Go from Here

It's time to dig in and get your hands dirty with WebKit! Turn the page and have some fun. If you have questions or comments about the material, or if you just want to drop me a line to say that you got the book and to ask how I'm doing (just fine, thanks!), or if you want to invite me to your family picnic (I love family picnics, and us writer types don't get out in the sun much) you can reach me at chris@minnick.com.

# Part I
# Introducing
# WebKit

The 5th Wave                    By Rich Tennant

SOMEWHERE IN THE CITY, SASQUATCH, BIGFOOT AND ELVIS SPEND ANOTHER WARY NIGHT.

"Look—all I'm saying is every time they come out with a new browser with an improved search function, it's just a matter of time."

# In this part . . .

Hello, my new friend! Meet WebKit. Maybe you've heard of it. It counts among its best friends both Apple and Google, and has also been known to hang out with Research in Motion, Nokia, and a whole bunch of those hippy-dippy open source types. Not only is it popular, it's also super-modern, light-weight, fast as a bullet, and probably already installed on your phone. Sounds like someone you want to know, right? Well, read on!

This part of the book starts out with an overview of how WebKit fits into the world of browsers and Mobile apps. You'll learn just enough history to be able to know who to blame when something doesn't work right. After that, we'll dive into the guts of WebKit and talk about the nitty-gritty of how it puts together Web pages and does the magic it does. Finally, you'll download the very latest version of WebKit and get yourself set up to do some serious browsing, app development, and debugging.

# Chapter 1

# Opening for Business

*W*ebKit is an open-source web browser engine that's installed on a very large percentage of the latest smartphones and tablet computers. As a result, it's rapidly becoming much more than a way to view web pages — it's turning into the common denominator of the Mobile Web.

In addition to mobile browsers, WebKit also is the power behind several popular desktop browsers, an operating system (Google's ChromeOS), and an increasing number of other applications.

The stars have aligned in WebKit's favor, and the Mobile Web is ready for takeoff. But before I get to that, here's a look at what exactly a browser and a browser engine do.

At the end of this chapter, I show you how to install the latest version of WebKit and take it for a test drive. If you're already familiar with how web browsers work and the difference between a web browser and a web browser engine, you can skip to "The Parts of WebKit" and dive in to the deep end of the pool.

## What Is a Web Browser Engine?

Glad you asked (You *did* ask, right?) A *web browser engine* is a highly complicated piece of software that has one main task: to make your web browsing experience as seamless and as fast as possible. The browser engine does the low-level (basic, unglamorous, but essential) work of a browser — including loading web pages and other documents, figuring out how a page should be displayed, running scripts in the web page, and much more.

## *Corvette or clunker: Every browser has one*

Engine, that is. Every web browser (such as Internet Explorer, Mozilla Firefox, and Google Chrome) has a *browser engine* (sometimes also called a layout engine or a rendering engine) at its core. Think of a web browser engine as similar to the engine of a car: It's the part of the software that does the actual work behind the scenes. Just as automakers wrap their engines with vehicle bodies, tires, transmissions, and seats, different web browsers build different features and user interfaces around the browser engine that give them their special look or extra capabilities.

Table 1-1 lists the most common web browser engines, along with the web browsers that use them. As you can see, just three or four browser engines power the vast majority of web browsers in use today.

| Table 1-1 | Browsers and Their Engines |
| --- | --- |
| **Browser** | **Engine** |
| Internet Explorer | Trident |
| Firefox | Gecko |
| Safari | WebKit |
| Chrome | WebKit |
| Arora | WebKit |
| Midori | WebKit |
| OmniWeb | WebKit |
| Shiira | WebKit |
| Epiphany | WebKit |
| iCab | WebKit |
| SRWare Iron | WebKit |
| Konqueror | KHTML |
| NetSurf | NetSurf |
| Novell Evolution | GtkHTML |
| Opera | Presto |

# Moving pages through the browser stack

It's useful to think of a web browser's functionality as a stack of layers, all of which build upon each other and interact with each other. The web page you see onscreen passes through each of these layers on its way to your monitor and your eyeballs.

At the bottom layer is the engine, which handles low-level chores that are pretty similar from browser to browser. At the top level of the stack are more sophisticated tasks and features specific to particular browsers — for example, the way Google Chrome lets you search Google by entering keywords into the address bar.

Figure 1-1 shows what the browser stack looks like for Google's Chrome web browser. Web pages in this model are processed from the bottom up. You can read more about each of the different components in this stack at

```
http://dev.chromium.org/developers/design-documents/
            displaying-a-web-page-in-chrome
```

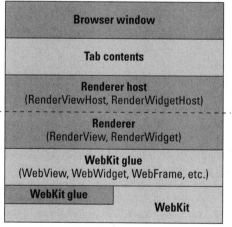

**Figure 1-1:**
Web pages
are
processed
through
a number
of layers
before being
displayed to
you.

# A little history lesson

In 1993, I was in my second year of college when a friend showed me the Mosaic web browser. I had spent the better part of my teenage years happily typing away in mostly text-based computer bulletin board systems — the predecessor to the Internet. The web was like someone had just dropped a color TV into my Neanderthal cave.

A few weeks later, I had built my first web page. It was notable only in that it didn't contain any blinking text. I won a "best of the web" award for my efforts, and I was hooked.

I couldn't locate this particular site, but the picture on the left shows one of my earliest efforts, which is almost (okay, it pretty much is) laughable today.

The earliest "graphical" web browsers were pretty simple pieces of software. They could render the newly invented HTML markup language, complete with links, and could display some types of images and multimedia if you had the right plug-ins.

To find out how primitive things were back before you were knee high to a grasshopper, check out `www.dejavu.org` (*not* `www.dejavu.com`), where you can surf the web using emulators of ancient browsers. The figure in the center shows what a typical web page from 1994 looked like. The figure on the right shows the emulator of the Mosaic Netscape 0.9 browser (circa 1994) attempting to render Facebook.com. We've come a long way.

When Mozilla, and later, Netscape were the only graphical browsers around, there were no browser compatibility issues. Furthermore, mobile devices were only just starting to emerge, and weren't fancy enough for surfing the Web. Everything was either a text-based browser (such as Lynx), or a graphical browser running on a desktop computer. Centering and an occasional table were about as complicated as the layouts got.

It wasn't long before the "browser war" erupted: Netscape and Microsoft competed to build the coolest features into their browsers. Compliance with Web standards suffered greatly as outdoing the competition became the standard by which browsers were judged.

The result of the browser wars was confusion and stagnation in web development. The most popular web browsers didn't fully support the standards and weren't compliant with each other, so a generation of web developers learned to either dumb down their sites or to do all sorts of strange tricks to give the user experience a minimal level of consistency with different browsers.

Out of the browser wars, we got many of the headaches web developers have been putting up with for the last 10 years. But we also got some of the greatest features, including JavaScript — which, you'll see in this book, is probably the second most important thing to happen to the Web (after HTML).

# What Does a Browser Do?

At its core, a web browser is a program that reads and interprets web pages, and then displays them onscreen. At a deeper level a web browser is a program for requesting and receiving files using the HyperText Transfer Protocol (HTTP) and interpreting HyperText Markup Language (HTML).

On top of this most basic function of a web browser, many layers of complexity and additional features have been built. The web browser has enabled the Web to become a universal computing platform; it's making installable software and monolithic desktop operating systems a thing of the past.

## Behind the scenes

In your day-to-day life, you may interact with one or more web browsers without even thinking or comprehending what it is they're doing. In this part, I'll quickly step through the processing that happens in the background when you click on a link to your favorite website.

Scene: Your office. You've just started your computer, and you want to check the news before diving in to your work. You click your desktop icon for your favorite web browser, and the browser starts. This is where the fun begins. The next series of events, which may only take a second or two, go something like this:

1. **Requesting.** The browser checks whether it has a default home page set. It does. Say your default page is `news.google.com`. The web browser will use this information to send a request through your local connection to the Internet. In plain English, it may say something like, "Hi, I'd like the file at `news.google.com`."

2. **DNS resolution.** Your browser's request will typically pass through several routing points on its way to `news.google.com`, where a web server will interpret the request and send back a document.

You can see an example of how many different points your request goes through on its way to the final destination by performing what's called a `traceroute`. Try this:

Open the console window (on Mac OS X) or the command-line interface (in Windows), and type in the following:

- On Mac OS X (or Unix):

```
traceroute www.wiley.com
```

- In Windows:

```
tracert www.wiley.com
```

You'll see a series of numbered lines of text fly by. Each of these represents a different node (that is, computer on the network) that your computer hops through (visits briefly) on its way to finding the address you requested. Your `traceroute` results may look something like the following. Note: The final step, with the asterisks, is most likely the final destination, but the server hosting wiley.com is configured to ignore `traceroute` requests.

```
traceroute wiley.com
traceroute to wiley.com (208.215.179.146), 64 hops max, 52 byte packets
 1  10.0.1.1 (10.0.1.1)  1.679 ms  0.739 ms  1.017 ms
 2  [my home network's address]  1.288 ms  1.404 ms  1.233 ms
 3  172.22.4.5 (172.22.4.5)  1.018 ms  0.950 ms  1.479 ms
 4  172.21.1.9 (172.21.1.9)  4.862 ms  1.558 ms  1.540 ms
 5  172.21.0.254 (172.21.0.254)  1.782 ms  2.321 ms  1.556 ms
 6  te-4-1.car1.sacramento1.level3.net (4.53.200.9)  7.195 ms  6.543 ms
        6.627 ms
 7  ae-11-11.car2.sacramento1.level3.net (4.69.132.150)  7.056 ms  7.054 ms
        8.013 ms
 8  ae-4-4.ebr2.sanjose1.level3.net (4.69.132.158)  7.046 ms  7.368 ms
        7.644 ms
 9  ae-62-62.csw1.sanjose1.level3.net (4.69.153.18)  6.759 ms  5.958 ms
    ae-92-92.csw4.sanjose1.level3.net (4.69.153.30)  7.313 ms
10  ae-3-80.edge2.sanjose3.level3.net (4.69.152.145)  44.113 ms
    ae-2-70.edge2.sanjose3.level3.net (4.69.152.81)  7.604 ms
    ae-4-90.edge2.sanjose3.level3.net (4.69.152.209)  7.480 ms
11  192.205.32.205 (192.205.32.205)  17.387 ms  17.349 ms  17.328 ms
12  cr1.sffca.ip.att.net (12.122.86.90)  79.150 ms  79.372 ms  78.698 ms
13  cr1.cgcil.ip.att.net (12.122.4.122)  77.725 ms  78.639 ms  77.657 ms
14  cr2.cgcil.ip.att.net (12.122.2.54)  76.990 ms  76.681 ms  77.127 ms
15  cr1.n54ny.ip.att.net (12.122.1.1)  80.434 ms  80.396 ms  80.775 ms
16  cr81.nw2nj.ip.att.net (12.122.105.30)  76.866 ms  75.886 ms  76.650 ms
17  12.122.115.105 (12.122.115.105)  75.429 ms  74.989 ms  75.171 ms
18  12.94.29.178 (12.94.29.178)  81.303 ms  81.196 ms  81.357 ms
19  * * *
```

3. **Loading.** When your browser finds the correct server, it receives the document from the remote server along with any associated files. This process is called *loading*.

4. **Parsing.** After all the files needed to put the page together are loaded, the browser goes through your document and breaks it up into parts that it can understand — specifically a Document Object Model (DOM) tree (for more about the HTML DOM, flip over to Chapter 11). This process is called *parsing*.

5. **Script execution.** After parsing, the browser will execute any scripts it finds in your document (generally JavaScript).

6. **Style resolution.** Style resolution is where the browser figures out what everything should look like on the page.

7. **Painting.** After everything is loaded, the document has been parsed, and the rest of it, your browser will "paint" the web page to the screen for you to see.

8. **Event handling.** After the document is painted, the browser sits and waits for you to do something else so it can react in a way that the just-loaded page instructed it to. This reaction to an event is *event handling*.

These steps aren't just nice to know for the next time you play Web Browser Pub Trivia. It's actually quite helpful to know (for example) that script execution happens before style resolution. For example, if you write a script that prints a line of text to the browser, you can be sure that any formatting (using CSS) that you also write to make that text look good will be applied after the text has been written.

## *Meet the current crop of web browsers*

Thousands of different types and versions of web browsers are in use today, but it's safe to say that for most people, there are just a few basic types, which I list here in their current order of total global browser market penetration (including mobile and desktop browsers):

✔ **Internet Explorer (IE):** IE browsers currently account for about 43 percent of browsers.

✔ **Mozilla:** Mozilla is the name used to refer to browsers that are based on the Gecko layout engine, which is developed by the Mozilla Foundation. The list of Mozilla browsers includes Firefox, Netscape, Flock, Camino, and Epiphany. They account for about 29 percent of browsers as of this writing.

- ✔ **WebKit:** WebKit-based browsers make up about 25 percent (and rising) of all browsers today.

- ✔ **Opera:** Opera maintains approximately a 2-percent share of the total browser market.

At this point, the general trend on the Web as we know it is that WebKit is rising in market share (thanks to mobile browsers and Google Chrome), IE and Firefox are declining, and Opera is staying steady. On mobile devices, however, the picture is vastly different: WebKit browsers account for at least 70 percent of all mobile browsing. The rest (around 25 percent) is primarily Opera Mini.

Things are changing so fast with Mobile browsers that any numbers I list here are sure to be obsolete by the time this book is published. Figure 1-2 (courtesy of StatCounter) shows trends in mobile browser usage for a recent one-year period. Opera has the largest share of mobile browser usage, but WebKit-based browsers lead total market share.

---

## Who's going to the Opera?

Opera, which has only a 2-percent share of total browser usage, has a significant share of mobile browser usage. This is because of Opera Mini, which is a very popular *proxy browser* for mobile devices, although not necessarily for smartphones.

A *proxy browser* is a browser designed to reduce the amount of data that must be transferred to a mobile device and the amount of processing that the mobile device is required to do to the data. It does this by having the fetching of data and the initial processing of that data be done on a remote server.

For people with less powerful phones, or who get charged by the amount of bandwidth they use, a proxy browser is very useful.

Opera Mini and WebKit browsers aren't in direct competition. Tablets and smartphones with WebKit browsers are generally powerful enough and used on fast enough networks that the additional performance gained from using a proxy browser isn't currently worth the limited functionality. This may be changing, however. Amazon's Silk browser, which is included with newer Kindle tablets, is an example of a WebKit-based proxy browser that combines the best of both worlds — the functionality of WebKit with the benefits of a proxy browser.

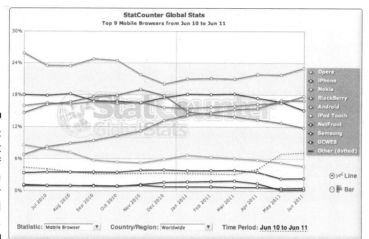

**StatCounter Global Stats**
Top 9 Mobile Browsers from Jun 10 to Jun 11

**Figure 1-2:**
Market
share of
mobile
browser
usages and
total market.

For the latest browser usage statistics, visit `http://gs.statcounter.com`.

More important than just the percentage of mobile devices that include WebKit browsers is the actual list of devices and mobile operating systems that use WebKit. As of this writing, this list includes the latest versions of the following:

- Android
- iOS
- HP/Palm webOS
- BlackBerry
- Amazon Kindle
- Nokia

Although some of these devices have different levels of support for WebKit's features, WebKit now dominates the smartphone and tablet browser market.

# Understanding Browser Quirks and Incompatibilities

But, why should it matter what browser engine a device uses? Isn't a web page the same web page no matter how you view it?

Uh, no. But things are improving.

## Changing standards for browser engines

In a perfect world, every web browser engine would adhere strictly to well-written and specific standards about how to render web pages and do the other jobs of a web browser, and it would be possible to view any web page in any web browser and see the exact same thing.

This has never been the case, however. Starting with the so-called "browser wars" I mention earlier, web browser vendors added proprietary functionality on top of some pretty unspecific specifications (such as HTML and CSS). In other cases, browsers were purposefully designed to render web pages differently from other browsers as a way to get a competitive edge. The thinking seems to have been something like the following:

> If we, [name your browser warrior from the 1990s], have a large enough share of the web browser market, people will need to design their web pages to work in our browser. Therefore, it's not in our interest to adhere strictly to standards because then anyone could use any browser.

So the situation that arose over the years forced web designers to test their work in multiple browsers, and write workarounds for the bugs and differing capabilities of various browser engines. It was common practice to put `Best viewed on` text on web pages similar to the notice seen in Figure 1-3.

**Figure 1-3:** You wouldn't put a "best driven on with" sign on a high-way, would you?

The good news is that in recent years, desktop computer browser makers have switched their focus from trying to make their browser unique to trying to be the most standards-compliant browser.

All the latest versions of the major web browsers have great support for Web standards. We're rapidly approaching a time when you'll be able to create web pages that work the same on the vast majority of the thousands of different types of desktop computer web browsers in use today simply by following the standards.

Now, I'm known for being a very optimistic guy. I realize that that last sentence may have caused some grumbling among some of the seasoned veterans out there, and I admit that my prediction may turn out to be wrong. But if we all work together (and encourage users of Internet Explorer 6 to upgrade), I strongly believe that we can make this dream a reality. Why does it matter? Well, read on. . . .

## Moving to mobile: Compatibility headaches everywhere

Web browser usage is rapidly shifting away from desktop computers and toward mobile devices. Unfortunately for web developers, the compatibility problem in the mobile world has been much worse than it was in the heyday of desktops.

Not only have web designers had to work with a very wide variety of web browsers, which each support a different set of features — they also have had to work with widely different screen sizes and platform capabilities.

### Mobile web nightmares

Whereas on desktop browsers, you can pretty much count on being able to display pictures and run JavaScript, these features were not at all standard on mobile phones.

Mobile phones were — and still are — stuck with a huge mess of browsers and layout engines that all did their own thing, and a variety of different standards for Mobile app development that not many people have taken the time to learn.

### Enter the native app

As a result, when mobile devices became powerful enough to run serious applications, application developers decided to forgo trying to make good web apps, and they built apps that were tailor-made for specific devices or device operating systems. These are knows today as *native apps*.

Native apps became the new competitive edge for vendors of mobile phones and mobile operating systems — think about Apple and its App Store, or Google and its Android Market. Developers of native apps, unlike the developers of websites or web apps, don't need to worry about how their apps will work on different operating systems. They just build an app to work on the iPhone, for example, and then build a separate version that works on Android devices, and a separate version for Palm, and a separate version for BlackBerry, and . . . you get the picture.

This solution has worked well for years, and has resulted in some great apps. The problems, however, are many. Here are a few of the greatest hits (or misses), which get a more detailed look later on:

- ✔ It's expensive and time-consuming to build multiple versions of an app. It can't be done by one person working alone in his spare time.
- ✔ After you do build your app and get it into the app stores, someone else controls the availability of your app and takes a large cut (30 percent in the case of the Apple App Store).
- ✔ Releasing a new version of a native app requires you to get your app reapproved.

Table 1-2 lists several popular mobile operating systems and the languages that are used to develop native apps for each. Table 1-3 shows the languages used to develop mobile web apps on each of these operating systems.

### Table 1-2      Mobile Operating Systems and Languages

| Operating System | Native App Platform |
|---|---|
| Android | Dalvik |
| Blackberry | Java |
| iOS | Objective-C |
| webOS | HTML5 |
| Windows Mobile 7 | XNA/Silverlight |

### Table 1-3      Mobile Web App Languages

| Operating System | Web-App Platform |
|---|---|
| Android | HTML5 |
| Blackberry | HTML5 |
| iOS | HTML5 |
| webOS | HTML5 |
| Windows Mobile | HTML5 |

## Return of the mobile web app

While native apps have been grabbing all the headlines, the mobile browser situation has improved dramatically over the last couple of years. The way that this has been achieved is completely different from how it was done on the desktop. Rather than vendors competing with each other to make their browser engines be the best and to support the latest standards, many smartphone and tablet operating systems have decided to use the same browser engine — WebKit.

The phenomenal agreement among nearly all mobile device makers to switch to WebKit as their browser engine is an event nearly as groundbreaking as if suddenly the world's tweens stopped liking bad pop music and started listening to Charlie Parker or classic 1980s punk rock (in my opinion, anyway; you may choose your own analogy here).

What this means for anyone who wants to create a mobile app is that you no longer need to write native code for each platform you want to support. You can write code that runs in WebKit, and it will pretty much work on any device with an A-Grade browser.

Not only is WebKit revolutionary because of its ubiquity, it's also revolutionary because it's really good. What's more, it also happens to be free (as in "free beer," yes, but more importantly, as in "free speech").

The concept of *graded browser support* divides all web browsers into several categories, according to how capable and common they are. WebKit-based browsers are both highly capable and highly common. This puts them solidly in the A-Grade browser world.

### What makes mobile web apps so great?

A good mobile web app that will run on any WebKit-capable device can be built cheaply, quickly, and with just a small team or no team at all. If you have a great idea and a bit of knowledge about web technologies — and this book, naturally — there's nothing at all stopping you from taking your shot at creating the next smash hit app!

Just as desktop applications are being replaced by online applications, the mobile web app is now poised to take over on the small screen. In this book, you get the lowdown on how to use standard web development technologies, such as HTML, CSS, and JavaScript, to write sophisticated and powerful mobile apps that will impress your friends and colleagues, will run on a wide variety of smartphones and other mobile devices, and will give you a competitive edge over all those suckers who are still writing native apps.

Before I get to that, let me back up and zoom in on WebKit.

# The History of WebKit

WebKit grew out of the KHTML browser engine, which powered the Konqueror web browser back in the day. KHTML was developed starting in 1998 by the KDE open-source community to be a browser for use mostly on Unix and Linux operating systems. Because KHTML is open-source and free software, anyone is free to download the source code, modify it, and create their product from it (as long as they comply with the terms of the GNU Lesser General Public License). Konqueror for Windows is shown in Figure 1-4.

## Enter Apple

In 2001, Apple adopted the KHTML engine and the KDE JavaScript Engine (KDE) to use as the base for its Safari web browser. Apple called its Mac OS version of these two engines WebCore and JavaScriptCore. The combination of WebCore and JavaScriptCore, along with the Apple-specific code written to tie everything together, became known as WebKit.

From the time that Apple first announced WebCore and JavaScriptCore, they were open source. It wasn't until 2005, however, that Apple released the entire WebKit project as open source.

**Figure 1-4:** Konqueror was the first browser based on the KHTML engine.

WebKit basically started as a way for Apple to save time in creating its own web browser. The choice to use KHTML, rather than another browser engine, was made for three reasons: KHTML was small (in terms of lines of code), the code was clean and well-written, and the browser was standards-compliant.

In short, KHTML was the best available foundation for building the next-generation browser engine now known as WebKit.

## WebKit spreads

Shortly after Apple announced the open-sourcing of WebKit, mobile phone operating system developers started announcing versions (also known as *ports*) specific to their devices.

Mobile phones from Nokia, Samsung, LG, and others were suddenly using browsers based on WebKit. When the iPhone was announced, it too featured WebKit. Android, Palm, and even the Amazon Kindle have followed in subsequent years with their own WebKit browsers.

## Development continues

WebKit is being continually developed and improved thanks to the WebKit open-source developer community — a group of hundreds of developers, some of whom are purely volunteers and some of who work for companies like Apple and Google that have a stake in the development of WebKit.

With so many different companies working on WebKit and on their own WebKit browsers, things are not as harmonious as you may think. From the very beginning, when Apple first announced WebCore, there has been a certain amount of chaos and tension in the community.

In the early days, the relationship between the WebKit open-source community and Apple was particularly rocky. Prior to releasing WebCore, Apple made numerous changes to its branch of KHTML in secret. At the same time, KHTML development was continuing in the KDE community. When Apple finally did release WebCore, there were accusations that Apple was taking more than it was giving back, which is generally regarded as a negative among open-source developers.

The fact is, this is a very fast-moving area. It's not always in the best interests of vendors such as Apple, Google, HP/Palm, and others to fully release their customizations of WebKit back to the open-source community *(upstreaming)*. This clash between the idealism of the open-source community and the profit motives of companies that rely on the open-source project is inevitable. Somehow, though, WebKit is managing to navigate these waters.

Over time, the relationship between KDE, the WebKit team, and Apple has improved. One indicator of this is that even KDE has made the decision to adopt WebKit as the browser engine for Konqueror.

According to the terms of the GNU Public License, anyone who modifies WebKit for his or her own use is required to make the changed version freely available as well. However, the terms of the Lesser GNU Public License that WebKit uses has a kind of loophole: It's permissible not to release the source code for products you create that only *link* to code that's covered under the GNU Public License. In this way, Apple and other browser makers can keep some of the details about their browsers a secret.

# The Parts of WebKit

WebKit is made up of three components:

- ✔ **WebKit:** Handles talking to the operating system
- ✔ **WebCore:** The real "engine" behind the browser
- ✔ **JavaScriptCore:** The JavaScript parser

Here comes the skinny on each component.

## WebKit

Confusingly enough, one of the components of the WebKit browser engine is also called WebKit. This component is a library of code that "sits on top" of the other components and handles interactions between them and the operating system.

# WebCore

WebCore is the biggest slice of the WebKit pie. It handles all core functionality of the browser engine (thus the name), in the following order:

1. Loading web pages and other assets.
2. Parsing HTML and XML markup and creating a tree structure of the data
3. CSS style resolution
4. Layout of web pages
5. Painting the page to the browser window

In addition, WebCore also handles

✔ Listening for *events* (such as mouse clicks or pointer motions)

✔ Enabling HTML editing (which lets WebKit provide editing capabilities for many applications on the Mac OS, such as the default Mail client, Microsoft Entourage, and Yahoo! Messenger)

# JavaScriptCore

JavaScriptCore handles the execution of JavaScript code in the browser.

This part of WebKit has been replaced by Google in its Chrome browser with Google's own custom JavaScript engine (called V8). As a user of the Chrome browser, this is completely transparent to you except that V8 is capable of running JavaScript much faster than JavaScriptCore. It accomplishes this primarily by compiling JavaScript code to the (much faster) machine code prior to running it.

Modern web apps contain a lot of JavaScript code. The speed with which the browser can handle this code has a large impact on the user experience of the app.

For my purposes here, I don't need to go into great detail about WebKit's internal workings. If you're interested in getting involved with WebKit development or you just want to know more about how it works, I recommend visiting the Surfin' Safari blog at www.webkit.org/blog. Google also has a number of videotaped lectures on YouTube that explain how different components of WebKit work.

# Getting Started with WebKit

Because WebKit is open-source and free software, anyone can download it, and even mess around with the source code that makes it run if they want to. The first part of this chapter gives you the quick tour of WebKit; the rest of the chapter shows you how to download WebKit and (oh, yeah) install it.

Chapter 2 shows some useful tweaks to the user interface after you install it.

## Downloading WebKit

WebKit is in a constant state of improvement and change. As new features and bug fixes are added to the code, the latest versions are posted to WebKit.org. These incremental releases are called *nightly builds*.

Three versions of the nightly build/s are available for download:

✔ **Mac OS X**

The Mac OS X build should run on any version of Mac OS X.

✔ **Windows**

The Windows build will run on any version of Windows.

✔ **Source**

The Windows and Mac OS X builds are *binary builds,* meaning that the code has been compiled and is ready to run. Unless you're using an operating system besides Mac OS X or Windows (such as Linux), the binary build for your Mac or Windows development system is the build to download.

---

## Source build

The source nightly build is the complete source code for WebKit. There are detailed instructions at WebKit.org for how to work with the source. I'm not going to go into it here, as it's beyond the scope of this book.

If you're proficient in C++, you may want to have a look at the section of WebKit.org called "Working With the Code". For the rest of us, just download a nightly build in this chapter and take it for a ride.

WebKit is not a browser. Rather, it's a browser engine that runs *inside* a browser. The Mac OS X and Windows nightly builds, therefore, include WebKit running within the Safari web browser. For the sake of simplicity, however, I refer to the nightly build of Safari + WebKit as just WebKit, or the WebKit nightly build.

To download a nightly build for Windows or Mac OS X, follow these steps:

1. **Go to** `www.webkit.org` **in a web browser.**

2. **Click the Download Nightly Builds button or the Download the Latest Nightly Build link.**

3. **Select either the Windows or Mac OS X Build, according to the operating system that you use.**

   • *Mac OS X:* A `.dmg` file will download to your computer.

   • *Windows:* A `.zip` file will download to your computer.

   After the file downloads, it's ready to install. Read on!

## Installing WebKit

WebKit installation is simple. The steps depend on your operating system:

✔ **Mac OS X**

   1. *Double-click the* `.dmg` *file to open the disk image.*

   Inside the folder, you'll see a WebKit icon.

   2. *Drag the WebKit icon into your Applications folder.*

   To create a shortcut to WebKit in Mac OS X, find WebKit.app (the WebKit application) and drag it to your dock.

✔ **Windows**

   1. *Double-click the file and then click Extract All Files.*

   Windows asks you to select a location for the extracted files.

2. *Choose a location that you'll be able to find easily, such as your desktop, and proceed to extract the files by clicking OK.*

After the files are extracted, you have a folder named WebKit followed by a dash and then the revision number of the nightly build, like this: WebKit r97524.

3. *Rename the extracted folder to just WebKit and then drag it into your Program Files folder.*

If you're using a 64-bit version of Windows, you should drag the WebKit folder into the Program Files (x86) folder.

To create a shortcut to WebKit in Windows, find WebKit.exe (the WebKit application) and drag it to your toolbar.

If you already have Apple Safari installed on your computer, you'll notice that the nightly build of WebKit has a similar icon as Safari, except that the outside of the compass is gold instead of silver.

Nightly builds are meant to be used for testing purposes only. They are *not* fully tested and ready-for-release software. Don't freak out if you see some functional instability and, um, *unexpected* results while you're working with a nightly build. To minimize such hassles, I recommend that you also install the latest released versions of both Google Chrome and Apple Safari to use while working with this book.

## Staying up to date

Because WebKit is constantly changing, it is a good practice to update regularly. Even if you don't enable the automatic update checking, you should still periodically update WebKit. Every two or three weeks, download the latest nightly build for your system and install it, just as this chapter shows. Don't worry about losing any settings or bookmarks that you create in WebKit as a result of upgrading. These are stored elsewhere on your computer and won't be affected by upgrading to the latest version.

Sitting through the daily WebKit update process can be frustrating — it will download, then extract, then update, then relaunch. It takes my iMac about 3 to 5 minutes, depending on whether I just turned it on.

Think of this time as your "me time" — a chance to spend a quiet moment meditating, or organizing your desk, or get another cup of coffee.

# *Launching WebKit*

After WebKit is installed, you're ready to launch it: Just double-click the application file. There you have it — the very latest version of WebKit running on your computer, as shown in Figure 1-5. There should be nothing too surprising to you here; on the surface, WebKit runs works just like any other Web browser. It's what's inside that matters.

**Figure 1-5:** Launching WebKit for the first time opens the browser and takes you to a page that thanks you for testing WebKit.

On Mac OS X, the first time you launch WebKit, you're asked whether you want to update WebKit automatically. If you select Check Automatically, WebKit will ask you every day whether you want to update to the latest build. Before you answer that question, consider: The update typically takes a few minutes, and can be slightly annoying if you're in a hurry.

Before you move on to the next chapter, take some time and try surfing your usual sites with WebKit and see whether you notice any differences between how WebKit works and what you're used to.

Take a look also at www.webkit.org, which contains some demos that showcase some of the advanced features of WebKit.

# Chapter 2

# Configuring WebKit

* * * * * * * * * * * * * * * * * * * * * * * * * * * * * * * * * * * * * * * * * * * * *

*In This Chapter*

▶ Customizing WebKit for web-app development

▶ Enabling the Develop Menu

▶ Inspecting WebKit's Web Inspector

▶ Using some time-saving WebKit tricks

* * * * * * * * * * * * * * * * * * * * * * * * * * * * * * * * * * * * * * * * * * * * *

*W*ebKit is not only a cutting-edge browser, it's also a world-class tool for building and debugging web apps. In this chapter, you get a first look at some of WebKit's advanced functionality for web-app developers. I start with a little configuration.

## Customizing Your WebKit Interface

After you start WebKit, you need to enable a few options to optimize the browser for developing web apps. To customize your WebKit, follow these steps:

1. **If you have the Windows version, click the gear-shaped icon at the right side of the browser, as shown in Figure 2-1.**

   Doing so enables the standard main menu bar and makes many WebKit options and tools easier to find later.

**Figure 2-1:**
Enabling
the menu
bar in the
Windows
WebKit
version.

After you enable the menu bar, you need to enable the Develop Menu, which gives you access to a variety of tools for developing and debugging your apps.

2. **Choose Edit⟹Preferences (Windows) or Safari⟹Preferences (Mac OS X) from the main menu.**

   The WebKit Preferences dialog box opens.

3. **Click the Advanced tab and then select the Show Develop Menu in Menu Bar check box.**

4. **Close the Preferences dialog box.**

   The Develop Menu appears in the menu bar.

To make a few adjustments to the WebKit toolbar, follow these steps:

1. **Choose View⇨Customize Toolbar from the main menu.**

2. **Drag the Web Inspector, Add Bookmark, and Report Bug icons to your toolbar, next to the gear icon on the right.**

You use the various features of the Web Inspector throughout this book, and it's always handy to have access to it right in front of you.

I point you to some great sites throughout this book, and you'll no doubt want to bookmark a few. I like to clear out the default bookmarks from the book-marks bar in my development browser and put in only bookmarks that are related to the task at hand. You can remove bookmarks from the bookmarks bar by right-clicking them and choosing Delete. Or, you can simply click and drag bookmarks off the bookmarks bar into the main browser window to delete them. I recommend that you bookmark www.webkit.org and www.webkitfordummies.com now and add them to your bookmarks bar.

Figure 2-2 shows what the toolbar of my optimized version of the WebKit nightly build looks like at this point.

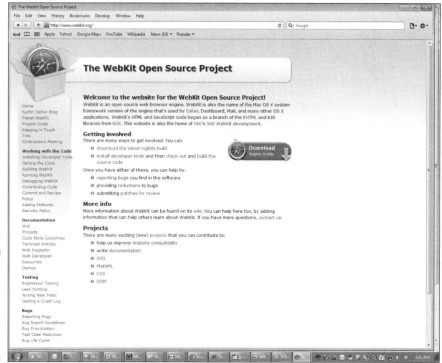

**Figure 2-2:**
WebKit is start-ing to get developer-optimized!

The Report Bugs icon you added to the toolbar allows you to give back to the WebKit project by reporting any bugs you encounter while working with the nightly build. The beautiful thing about the WebKit nightly build is that you get to use the most cutting-edge browser available, and the WebKit developers get access to an enormous group of people testing their code on the widest possible range of websites and computers. If you do your part, it's a win-win scenario.

WebKit.org has a guide to reporting bugs, which you can find at `www.webkit.org/quality/reporting.html`.

# Getting Started with the Develop Menu

The Develop Menu that you set in your menu bar (see the preceding section) contains a wealth of built-in features that are well worth your time to really get to know.

If you're familiar with the Firebug extension for Firefox, some of these tools will look familiar. The difference with WebKit is that these tools are built into the browser and don't require an extension.

## Opening a page with another browser

The first option in the Develop Menu is Open Page With Another Browser. Now here's a feature I never dreamed I'd see back in the cutthroat browser-war days of old: It provides a list of the browsers installed on your computer and lets you select one to open and load the current web page — a neat little trick that can save you a couple clicks and maybe a copy-and-paste while you're testing web apps.

The Open Page With Another Browser feature is shown in Figure 2-3.

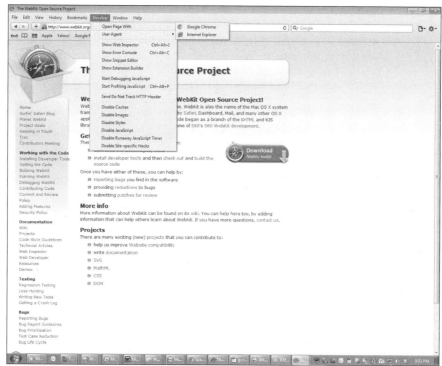

**Figure 2-3:**
Here's
something
you're
unlikely to
see in a cer-
tain browser
from
Redmond,
Washington.

Even though this book focuses on WebKit as a Mobile Web app platform, I still firmly believe that it's important to test your apps in as many browsers as possible. Testing and fixing problems in a wide variety of browsers makes your app more accessible and teaches you new skills. You may even discover that you prefer another browser to your standard go-to browser.

## User agent

The next choice down in the Develop Menu is the User Agent Selection menu. *User agent* is another name for any software that accesses web content — for example, a desktop web browser, a mobile browser, a search engine crawler, or a host of other specialty devices.

Each user agent has a unique identifying name, also known as a *user agent string,* that it reports to every web site or web app that you visit. The user agent string contains information about the version of the browser, the operating system, and more.

For example, here's a sample user agent string:

```
Mozilla/5.0 (Macintosh; Intel Mac OS X 10_6_7)
        AppleWebKit/535.1+ (KHTML, like Gecko)
        Version/5.0.5 Safari/533.21.1
```

This happens to be the string reported by the nightly build of WebKit running on Mac OS X. You can see the user agent string for the version of WebKit you're using by selecting Other from the User Agent menu.

User agents are not only useful for identifying a browser, they're also pretty interesting from a historical perspective. Notice that the user agent string for Chrome contains identifiers for Mozilla, WebKit, KHTML, Gecko, and Safari. It all seems like a big confusing mess, and it sort of is. But here's a quick look at each part of the user agent string just given:

- ✔ **Mozilla/5.0**: This indicates that the browser is compatible with the Mozilla rendering engine. This is not all that useful anymore, but when IE and Mozilla duked it out back in the day, it was helpful to know which side a browser was on.

- ✔ **Macintosh; Intel Mac OS X 10_6_7:** This provides information about the computer and operating system the browser is running on.

- ✔ **AppleWebKit/535.1+:** The platform, or browser engine, the browser uses, along with the build number.

- ✔ **KHTML, like Gecko:** Details about the browser engine. If you weren't familiar with WebKit, you might recognize KHTML. If you're not familiar with that, you might understand that it's "like Gecko." In other words, it's compatible with Mozilla.

- ✔ **Version/5.0.5:** This shows the browser's version number.

- ✔ **Safari/533.21.1:** The browser and the browser build number.

The user agent string provides a boatload of data about the browser and computer — and web developers commonly use that information to customize the user experience of a web app.

For example, if your Mobile Web app detected that a user was accessing your site with an Android browser, you could show that user a web page optimized for Android, or just display a message specific to Android users.

In effect, the User Agent menu in WebKit lets you impersonate web browsers of various types so you can see how your app works in them.

To impersonate a web browser, try this:

1. **Visit** www.youtube.com **using WebKit.**

2. **Choose Develop➪User Agent➪Safari iOS 4.1-iPhone.**

   Notice that the page reformats to a mobile-friendly single-column view, and an iPhone-specific message appears asking you to add YouTube to your Home screen, as shown in Figure 2-4. Notice that, even though I'm viewing this page with a desktop browser, YouTube is displaying the iPhone version.

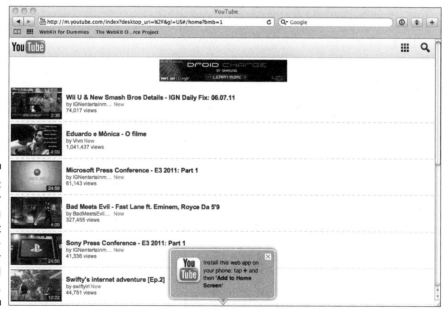

**Figure 2-4:**
The User Agent menu lets WebKit impersonate other devices and browsers.

3. **Change your user agent to some of the other options, such as one of the iPad choices.**

4. **Just for fun, drag the lower-right corner of your browser window to resize it while you have the iPad user agent selected.**

   Notice how the layout of the page changes when your browser window gets smaller.

## The Error Console

The Error Console is a text-based window that often reveals information about errors generated when your web page loads.

We revisit the Error Console later in this chapter in the "Console" section, for a look at its capabilities in conjunction with the Web Inspector.

## Using the Web Inspector

The Web Inspector is WebKit's all-in-one front-end tool for debugging web apps. The more you develop web apps, the more useful you'll find the Web Inspector.

Some of Web Inspector's functionality is beyond the scope of this book at this point. I only touch upon some of its components right now and return to them later (see Chapter 5) when they become relevant. Other parts of this powerful set of tools can be described and appreciated right now.

Click the Web Inspector menu item or the icon that you just added to the toolbar. A pane opens at the bottom of your browser window, as shown in Figure 2-5.

Many of the tools of the Web Inspector aren't currently available in mobile browsers. However, you'll most likely be doing most of your mobile development on a desktop computer, so it's important to know your way around this powerful set of tools.

**Figure 2-5:**
The Web
Inspector
windows
opens as a
pane at the
bottom of
the browser
by default.

### Elements panel

Click Elements in the Web Inspector. The Web Inspector panel changes to show you an outline-style view of the current web page's code, with different types of content highlighted in different colors.

These colors are

- ✔ Violet for HTML tags
- ✔ Orange for attribute names
- ✔ Blue for attribute values

If you don't yet know what tags, attributes, and attribute values are, don't worry. You find out in Chapter 4.

Continuing the tour of the Elements panel of the Web Inspector window, moving counterclockwise, you come to the buttons at the bottom of the window, as shown in Figure 2-6.

**Figure 2-6:**
A couple of
very handy
links are
available
at the bot-
tom of the
Elements
panel.

- Undock opens the Web Inspector in a separate window. If Web Inspector is currently in a separate window, this button docks Web Inspector as a pane in the Web browser.

- Show Console opens a Console window, which is useful for debugging JavaScript.

- The magnifying glass puts your browser into Inspect Mode.

TIP

Inspect Mode is the component of Web Inspector that I use most. It lets you see very quickly exactly what's going on with a web page — especially with regard to layout and style. If something isn't working the way I expect with a page, a couple of quick clicks in Inspect Mode usually help me track down and fix the problem.

### Using Inspect Mode

While you have the Elements panel selected, click the magnifying glass icon, and then hover your mouse over different parts of the web page, as shown in Figure 2-7. Notice that blocks of text and images become highlighted as you move your mouse, and text appears along with the highlighting.

The text that appears when you hover your mouse over different things on the page tells you the HTML tag that is used to render that element, followed by any additional identifying information that may be available for it (such as a class or ID). After the tag and identifying information, the size of the element (in pixels) is displayed in square brackets.

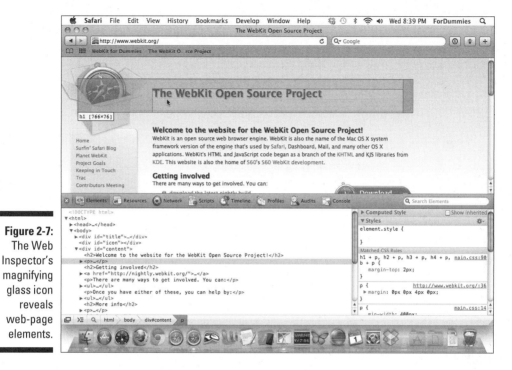

You'll also notice that regions around elements are highlighted in different shades of blue as you move your mouse around. These different shades indicate different properties of the selected element.

✔ The lightest blue color indicates the space taken up by the element itself — whether it's an image or a piece of text.

✔ The next darker shade indicates the padding around an element.

✔ The next darker shade shows the margin.

✔ The darkest shade shows any border around an element.

All these shades of blue can help you make visual distinctions in your code when you're working with Cascading Style Sheets (CSS).

After you've explored the current page with the magnifying glass, find somewhere that seems interesting on the page and click it. Several things will happen as a result.

- ✔ The magnifying glass icon becomes deselected.
- ✔ The element you clicked in the page is highlighted in the code outline.
- ✔ The window on the far right of the Web Inspector, the Styles window, changes.

Being able to click something on a web page and see instantly where it is in the code saves you a lot of time while you're debugging. That advantage, along with being able to see all CSS rules that apply to that particular element, as well as how the browser interprets and applies them, may well revolutionize the way you work with web pages.

If you're lucky enough to be new to HTML and CSS development as they are today, getting handy with just these tools in the Elements panel will catapult you into a level of control over and understanding of your site layouts and designs that web developers previously never even dreamed about. Okay, but enough talk.

### Using the Styles pane

The Styles pane will show you all the styles applied to the currently selected element, followed by all the CSS rules that match this element.

You may notice that some of the rules are crossed out. This is because of the *Cascading* in Cascading Style Sheets. As I explain in Chapter 10, CSS code is interpreted according to a *Cascading order:* If two rules both specify that a certain type of text — say, first-level headers — should be a different color, the rule that was declared most recently (or that takes precedence for another reason) cancels older, less important rules.

You can use the Styles pane to edit the style properties of the currently loaded web page. This is useful for figuring out how to fix a nagging problem or for experimenting with style settings. For example, follow these steps:

1. **Browse to** www.webkit.org, **and open the Elements panel in the Web Inspector (if it's not already open).**

2. **Use the magnifying glass to find a block of text or a headline, and then click that text to view the style rules that affect it.**

3. **Double-click the value of one of the rules.**

   For example, find a font-size property and change it to something much larger. If it's set to 12px, change it to 24px.

4. **Deselect one of the check boxes next to a style rule.**

   Deselecting a check box allows you to see how the page is rendered without that style rule.

5. **Deselect as many check boxes in the Styles pane as you like.**

   Notice how different combinations of enabled and disabled styles have different effects on the page.

You're working only with a local copy of the web page, so no one else sees your changes. Feel free to experiment and try anything at all. Have fun with it. To return the page to how it looked before you started editing styles, just refresh the page.

Figure 2-8 shows my re-styled version of the WebKit.org home page. Although I've changed the look of the site fairly substantially, the content of the site remains the same. Content is generally outside the control of CSS.

**Figure 2-8:**
The Styles pane is useful for trying new styles without making them live on the server.

Separation of content from design is one of the classic, indispensable principles of good web and application design.

### Resources panel

Click the Resources button in the Web Inspector to open the Resources panel.

The Resources panel shows information about the files and different types of storage used by your web page, as shown in Figure 2-9.

**Figure 2-9:**
The Resources panel shows all the files that make up a web page.

*Resource* doesn't mean oil or minerals under the ground. When used in the context of a web browser or in relation to web standards, *resource* refers to any file accessed by the browser — HTML files, XML files, JavaScript files, CSS files, images, audio, video, Flash files, you name it.

### Network panel

The first time you open the Network panel, as well as a couple other panels, you get a message telling you that you need to enable that panel and warning you that it will slow down your browser. Because you're using this browser primarily for development, and not for your day-to-day surfing needs, go ahead and select Always Enable.

After you enable the Network panel and reload your page, you see a window with bars of different colors laid out on a timeline, as shown in Figure 2-10.

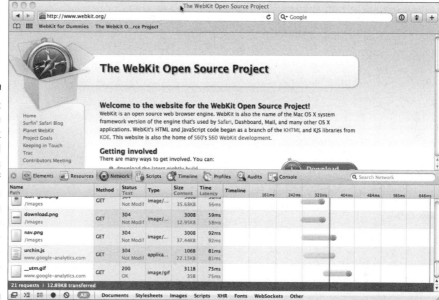

**Figure 2-10:**
The Network panel displays a chart of how the resources that make up the current page were downloaded.

The Network panel is much more than just a pretty picture; it shows all the resources that make up a web page and tells you when the resource was requested, how long it took the server to respond *(latency),* when the first byte of the resource arrived on your computer, and when the resource finished loading.

To take the Network panel for a spin, follow these steps:

1. **With the Network panel open in the Web Inspector, load your favorite website, such as** www.wiley.com**.**

2. **While the page loads, notice all the activity in the Web Inspector.**

   It goes pretty quick, so don't blink! When the page is done loading, you see a list of files (or *resources)* along the left side. You need a lot of files to make a modern web page.

3. **Click some of these resources.**

   You can see details about the file, or the contents of the file itself, in the main part of the panel.

As of this writing, the Macintosh and Windows versions of the nightly build Web Inspector interface are different in a number of ways. However, the nature of the nightly build is that it's constantly changing. If things don't look exactly like the images in this chapter in your future WebKit, feel confident that you can't do any damage to anything by just clicking buttons and seeing what happens.

### Scripts panel

The Scripts panel is a JavaScript debugging tool. Before you take a more detailed look at JavaScript (see Chapter 11), take a quick look at this panel.

For now, what I can say is that JavaScript has been called the "best and worst programming language in the world" and is a vital part of programming Mobile Web apps.

Having a handy tool for figuring out how a JavaScript program works, or doesn't work, is something that becomes more useful the more experienced you get.

### Timeline panel

The Timeline panel (shown in Figure 2-11) allows you to record detailed information about what happens when a web page loads and then monitor it in real time as events trigger actions.

The Timeline panel is where you can really see the different parts of a web browser engine doing its thing. The Timeline panel gives you a complete rundown on what it takes to load a web page along with how long each part took and what the sequence of events was.

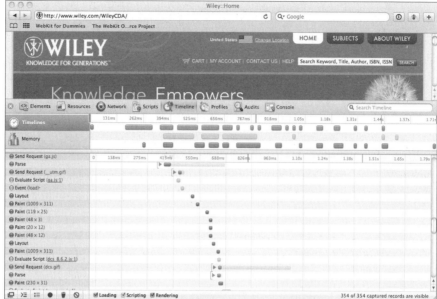

**Figure 2-11:**
The
Timeline
panel shows
how your
page was
loaded,
parsed, and
painted.

To get started with the Timeline panel:

1. **Click the Record button at the bottom of the panel.**

   This is the round button to the left of the trashcan icon. The button turns red when you click it to show that it's recording.

2. **Open a web page you've never visited before —** www.weirdal.com, **for instance.**

   You see a burst of activity in the Timeline panel as the various parts of the page are requested, loaded, parsed, laid out, and painted.

3. **When the page is done loading, click the Record button again to stop recording.**

   The Record button turns back to black.

You see a lot of data in the Timeline panel. Each line is a separate thing that had to happen to show the web page at www.wierdal.com.

Some of the lines have an arrow next to them. If you click the arrow, it expands to show sub-items. A simple example is the process that happens every time your web browser shows an image. This process is one component of the bigger picture of how a web browser functions (as described in Chapter 1):

1. The browser gets instructions from an HTML page to display an image in a certain place in the document.

   Most commonly this instruction comes in the form of an HTML img tag.

2. If the browser doesn't already have the image saved in its browser cache, it sends a request to the web server for the image.

   An HTTP request does this job.

3. The web server responds and begins sending the image to the browser.

   This is known as the *HTTP response*. If the requested resource exists on the server, this response will be HTTP/1.1 200 OK along with various other bits of data.

   The first part of the response (HTTP/1.1 200 OK) is the *response code*. If the resource doesn't exist, or if there's some other problem with getting hold of it, the server sends a different response code.

4. The browser finishes loading the image.

   For most of the resources on a typical website, you'll probably notice that the actual loading and parsing of the resource is one of the fastest parts of the Timeline. The part that really gets you is *latency* — waiting for the server to respond to a request.

5. The browser waits for the rest of the resources that are required in order to show the image.

   The way an image is displayed usually depends on how other objects on the page are displayed. For example, a CSS file may specify the positioning of the image.

6. When everything has been loaded from the server, the process of pars-ing and laying out the HTML and other resources begins.

A model of the page is created in memory before you actually see any-thing.

7. The page is painted.

The rendered web page is painted to the browser window so you can see it.

The most common HTTP response codes are shown in Table 2-1.

| Table 2-1 | The Most Common HTTP Response Codes |
|---|---|
| *Response Code* | *Meaning* |
| 200 OK | The request was successful. |
| 301 Moved Permanently | This and all future requests should be sent to a new URL. This is used when a file or a web site has been moved to a new URL. |
| 401 Unauthorized | The resource is password-protected, and you either didn't supply a password or you supplied an incorrect one. |
| 404 Not Found | The resource isn't available, but it may be avail-able again in the future. |
| 500 Internal Server Error | This error simply indicates that something went wrong on the server, which prevented the request from being fulfilled. |

The Timeline is especially useful for monitoring and tracing back through events that happen in the background of sophisticated web applications where there may be processes happening that the user isn't even aware of.

For example, click the clear button at the bottom of the Timeline (the circle with the line through it). Everything will disappear from the Timeline. Now, click record and then go to www.google.com. You'll notice there's a flutter of activity when the page is first loaded, followed by a regular change to the Timeline as the web page does some sort of counting or timing.

If you have a Gmail account, you can try the same thing. You'll notice that Gmail has a lot of complicated things going on the background that the user doesn't necessarily know or need to care about.

This sort of complex and ongoing activity in the browser wasn't possible until new ways of using JavaScript, CSS, and HTML were refined (and later came to be known as *AJAX*).

Looking at the complex interactions and fast-paced events of a modern web app really gives you a feeling for why it's helpful to be able to record what's happening.

A relatively simple web page makes following the entire Timeline through to the end much easier. For example, Figure 2-12 shows the result in the Timeline when you visit WebKit.org.

**Figure 2-12:** The process of loading a pretty simple web page, as shown in the Timeline panel.

If you're trying this at home, don't stop the recording just yet. Try moving your mouse pointer around the screen. You'll notice that when the pointer passes over a link, the Timeline changes as the link becomes underlined.

What's happening here is that your mouse triggers an event that the web page listens for. The browser has been instructed, using JavaScript or CSS, to do something in response to this event. In the case of WebKit.org, an underline is placed below linked text when your mouse is over the link. The Timeline shows you exactly what goes on inside the browser engine when it detects a mouse-over event.

Upon inspection, you see that the Timeline panel shows a Recalculate Style message, followed by a Paint message. Because the browser already has everything it needs in order to calculate the style and paint in its memory, it doesn't need to load anything when it detects an event. This is a very simple example of client-side processing. It results in much faster web applications, which are much more pleasant to use because they seem more seamless.

Mobile Web apps make extensive use of client-side processing and storage in order to eliminate the performance gap between web apps and native apps.

### Profiles panel

The Profiles panel is great for digging deeper into performance problems. You can record script activity (run a profile), then sort by how long each activity took to execute, and then focus your energy on the parts of your code that take the longest or that are repeated most frequently.

### Audits panel

The Audits panel is another tool in your arsenal for improving your web app's performance. Unlike the Resources and Timeline tools, however, the Audits panel focuses on identifying specific ways you can improve your site's performance:

✔ Before you run an audit, you can select whether to audit

- The network utilization of your app

- The performance of your app in the browser

✔ After you choose what you want to audit, you can choose whether to

- Audit the web app in its current state (which may be completely still, or which may be quite active)

- Reload the page and audit the process of loading and running the app

Whatever options you select, you're presented with a sobering list of items identified mostly by red dots (with some yellow ones mixed in):

✔ The red dots are big problems that cause significant performance slow-downs on your site.

✔ The yellow dots are recommendations to consider for maximum performance.

Web app design always involves tradeoffs and compromises among functionality, design, and performance. Almost every web app has areas in which it could improve performance. It's up to the developer to decide whether the cost of enhancements is worth the benefit.

Figure 2-13 shows the Audits panel for Apple.com. Notice that even Apple has areas in which it could improve.

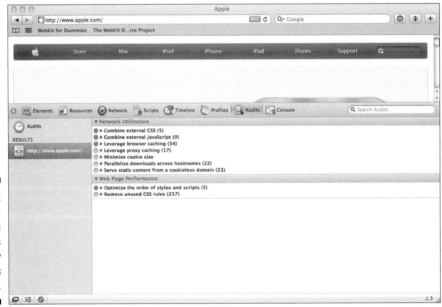

**Figure 2-13:**
Apple.
com has
many items
flagged by
the Audits
panel.

Expanding each item reveals details about the different recommendations. For example, an audit may reveal that you have a large number of external CSS files, or that your site isn't taking advantage of browser caching.

### Console

This is the same window as the Error Console that I mention earlier.

Most often, you interact with the Console in conjunction with another tool. For example, if you're debugging a bit of JavaScript that contains an error, the Console is where you go to see what the error was.

Because of its nature, the Console window can be opened either by itself or at the bottom of any of the other Web Inspector panels.

The Console can also be used to execute JavaScript commands, to run functions in the current web page, or to find out the current values of variables. For example, type each of these commands into the Console, followed by Enter (or Return).

```
Date()
document.write("Hi")
```

The command runs immediately — and any output from the command is printed in the Console window. If the command results in an error (for example, if you typed `date()` (with a lowercase d) instead of `Date()`, the error is printed to the Console.

# Using the Extension Builder

Browser *extensions* are computer programs that add functionality to a browser. They are not originally part of WebKit and are not supported by it. Such support is viewed as more appropriate for each individual web browser to handle.

Initially, Apple didn't include the capability to run extensions in Safari. In fact, it wasn't until version 5 that they first appeared.

*Extensions* are add-ons to the browser that can be developed by anyone. They can be used to modify how the browser works or to add functionality to the browser.

You can view your installed extensions, and install new ones, in the Extensions tab of the Preferences window.

The Extensions Builder is below the Develop Menu. Although outside the scope of this book, if you're adventurous and want to try your hand at creating an extension of your own, you can do so here.

## Using the Snippet Editor

To view the Snippet Editor, choose Develop⇨View Snippet Editor from the main menu (or choose Develop⇨Show Snippet Editor in Windows). The Snippet Editor looks simple, but it's actually quite powerful and useful.

Entering HTML, CSS, and JavaScript into the top window allows you to see instantly how the browser renders your code in the lower window.

For now, you can get a feeling for what the Snippet Editor can do by opening it and entering the following code into the upper window.

```
<html>
<body>
<canvas id = "test" width="400" height="300"></canvas>
<script>
var canvas=document.getElementById('test');
var a = canvas.getContext('2d');
a.fillStyle='#000000';
a.fillRect(20,20,40,20);
</script>
</html>
```

If you typed everything correctly, you see a black rectangle in the lower window. Change the values in the parentheses next to fillStyle and fillRect, and notice how the changes are reflected instantly in the lower window.

Canvas is one of the new elements included in HTML5. I detail Canvas in Chapter 19. If you're as excited by this demo as I was the first time I saw it, feel free to skip ahead now or check out www.canvasdemos.com to see some great examples of what's possible.

# Uncovering Hidden Features of WebKit and Safari

In this section, I show you some tips and tricks for using WebKit and the Safari browser in which it runs. These range from neat little tricks to shortcuts that will save you many minutes or even hours (over the long haul, of course).

## Useful keyboard shortcuts

Learning a few keyboard shortcuts and freeing yourself from the tyranny of the mouse are always worthwhile investments. Here are a few of my favorites. Note that some of these don't work on Mac OS X, or they do work but with the Command key instead of Control.

- **Ctrl+Enter:** Adds www. before and .com after what you type in your address bar.

  If you didn't already know about this one, try it now. Type just **google** into your browser's address bar, and then press Ctrl+Enter. Watch out, however, because this trick always adds .com, which may get you in some hot water at work or at home if you're trying to visit the browser emulation site I mention in Chapter 1.

- **Ctrl+l (Command-L on Mac OS X):** Puts your cursor in the address bar and selects the contents of the address bar.

- **Ctrl+k (Windows only):** Puts your cursor in the browser quick search box.

- **Ctrl+/ (Command-/ on Mac OS X):** Toggle the bottom (status) bar on and off.

- **Ctrl+, (Command-, on Mac OS X):** Opens the Preferences.

- **Ctrl+m (Command-M on Mac OS X):** Minimizes the browser window.

- **Ctrl+n (Command-N on Mac OS X):** Opens a new window.

- **Ctrl+h (Windows only):** Opens the browser history in a new window.

✔ **Ctrl+f (Command-F on Mac OS X):** Opens the browser window search box.

✔ **Ctrl+d (Command-D on Mac OS X):** Bookmarks the current page.

✔ **Ctrl+w (Command-W on Mac OS X):** Closes the window.

✔ **Ctrl+r (Command-R on Mac OS X):** Refreshes the window.

✔ **Ctrl+Alt+I (Command-Alt-I on Mac OS X):** Opens the Web Inspector.

## Handy menu shortcuts to remember

In this chapter, you saw each of the items in the Develop Menu. You'll likely make such frequent use of some of them that it's helpful to have alternative ways to access them.

### Easy access to the Web Inspector

To easily inspect any element on a web page, follow these steps.

1. **Highlight that element in the browser window, the same way you would highlight text in a word-processing program, and right-click your mouse.**

   The contextual menu appears.

2. **Choose Inspect Element.**

   The Elements pane in the Web Inspector opens with the text or other object that you highlighted.

### View Source

As helpful as the Web Inspector is for debugging and figuring out what's going on with a web page, sometimes you just need to see all the HTML that makes up a page. Viewing the source can also be a great learning tool — when you see a page that you really like, you can simply view the source and get an idea for how that page was built.

I encourage you to use view source often, especially as you work your way through the next part of this book, to see what's going on with various web pages and web apps.

You can also go to www.dummies.com/go/webkit and find all the code examples and example web apps in this book. Use View Source to see and then copy the source code for these apps, and save yourself some typing.

The keyboard shortcut for View Source is

- ✔ **In Mac OS X:** Command-Option-U
- ✔ **In Windows:** Ctrl+Alt+U

# Part II
# Your First Mobile Web App

The 5th Wave                    By Rich Tennant

"It's web-based, on-demand, and customizable.
Still, I think I'm going to miss our old sales
incentive methods."

## *In this part . . .*

**I** don't believe in going slow. In this part, you're going to dive right in and write some mobile Web apps. In a few short chapters, you go from zero to mobile Web app hero. Able to leap tall buildings, or at least more able to leap them than you were when you were still considering developing Web apps for heavy old desktop computers.

We start out by developing a little app for browsing my personal collection of bookmarks from writing this here book. Next, you shift gears and build a nice little cook-book app that we'll use at various places throughout the book. You'll learn about Web app frameworks, some JavaScript, how to find and solve problems when they come up, and finally we'll dive into making your Web apps run without the Web. Get ready to have your ideas about the Web blown away!

# Chapter 3

# Building Your First Mobile Web App

*W*ith your own copy of the nightly build installed, you're ready to get practical. I don't believe in having to slog through all the preliminary steps before I get down to business (this may explain why I'm such a bad dancer). I think there's more to be learned by getting your hands dirty with some sort of useful app and then explaining what's going on later.

In this chapter, you'll set up your Mobile Web app development environment and get up and running with your first Mobile Web app in much less time than you ever imagined possible.

## Setting Up Your Development Environment

Before you begin developing your app, you need to spend just a few minutes setting up your Mobile Web app development environment.

### Choosing a code editor

Mobile Web app development can be done with very simple tools — all of which can be acquired for free, and many of which may be on your computer already.

For the most basic Mobile Web development, all you really need is a text editor — and pretty much anything will do. The available options range from stripped-down editors like Notepad (in Windows) or TextEdit (in Mac OS X) to complete What You See Is What You Get (WYSIWYG) editors that let you write complete apps without seeing a line of code.

Between these two extremes is a group of tools known as "code editors." These are mostly text-based tools that also contain features such as project organization tools and code completion. Code editors are designed to make your life easier without removing you too far from the actual code that makes your app work. This is the type of tool that I (and most web developers I know) prefer.

This book walks you through installing and setting up Komodo Edit — a good free code editor from ActiveState software. It provides a good balance between ease of use and sophisticated features.

It's always beneficial to try new code editors and integrated development environments (IDEs). If you're new to web development or mobile development, you'll learn a lot from the experience. If you're a seasoned pro, a new code editor can give you a new perspective on things you thought you knew pretty well.

Examples of other editors or development environments that you may want to check out include

- ✔ Adobe Dreamweaver
- ✔ BBEdit (in Mac OS)
- ✔ TextPad (in Windows)
- ✔ Eclipse
- ✔ NetBeans

## Installing Komodo Edit

To get started with Komodo Edit, follow these steps:

1. **Go to** `www.activestate.com/komodo-edit` **and click the link to download Komodo Edit.**

   Komodo Edit is the free editor. Komodo IDE is a more full-featured product that is available as a trial but requires payment to continue using past the trial expiration date.

2. **Choose the correct version for your computer and download it to your computer.**

The website will detect your operating system automatically and show you a large button to click to download the most recent version, as shown in Figure 3-1.

**Figure 3-1:**
Click the big button to download the right version of Komodo Edit.

After the download is complete, double-click the downloaded file and follow the instructions to install Komodo Edit.

## Adding WebKit as your default browser

In this section, I show you how to set up Komodo Edit to preview your web apps using WebKit. Follow these steps:

1. **Launch Komodo Edit.**

   • If you're using Mac OS X, it may be a good idea for you to add a shortcut to Komodo Edit to your Dock.

   • If you're working on a Windows computer, you'll find the shortcut to launch Komodo Edit in your Start menu.

2. **Choose Edit➪Preferences from the main menu.**

3. **Select Web & Browser under the Category list on the left.**

4. **Click Browse Next under Which Browser Should Komodo Use when Opening URLs.**

   The file browser window opens.

5. **Locate `WebKit.exe` (on Windows) or `WebKit.app` (on Mac OS X) and select it.**

6. **Select Preview in External Browser (specified above) in the Preview in Browser section.**

   Figure 3-2 shows what your Web & Browser preferences should look like now.

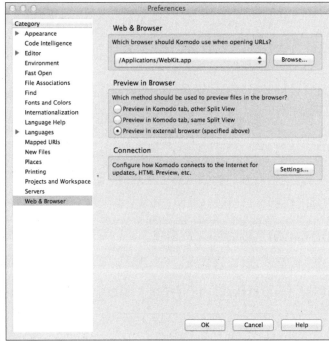

7. **Close the Preferences window.**

## Creating a project

All your files in Komodo Edit will be organized into *projects*. A project normally contains a single web app or website.

To get started on your first project, open Komodo Edit and then either

✔ Choose File➪New➪New Project from the main menu (for Mac OS X).

✔ Choose Project➪New Project (for Windows).

Komodo Edit prompts you to create a project file. To keep things clean in the future, follow these steps:

1. **Choose a location that's easy for you to remember — for example, your My Documents folder (in Windows) or your Documents folder (in Mac OS X).**

2. **Use the New Folder button to create a subfolder for this project. Name the folder MyFirstMobileProject.**

3. **In the Save As text box, change the name of the project file to MyFirstMobileProject.**

4. **Click Save.**

    The Projects sidebar appears at the left in the Komodo Edit window, showing your new project listed there, as in Figure 3-3.

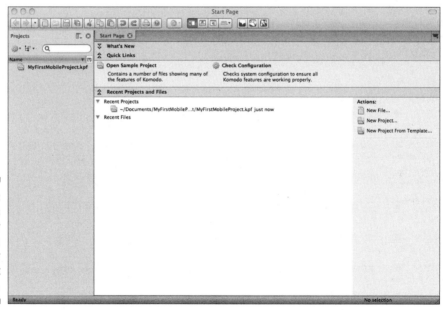

**Figure 3-3:**
The Projects Sidebar shows a list of your Komodo Edit projects.

If you're using Mac OS X, choose View➪Tabs & Sidebars➪Projects from the main menu to see the Project sidebar.

You use this blank project to put together a Komodo Edit template from which you create your first Mobile Web app. Many elements of Mobile Web apps stay the same from app to app. For example, all apps have a homepage and an icon used to launch the homepage. The homepage and the icon likely won't be the same for all your apps, but the fact that they have them will remain a constant.

Any time you have a situation where more than one website or app will have things in common, it's a great opportunity to reduce the amount of work you'll have to do in the future. Most times, the little bit of effort you put into creating and using a template will result in much greater time savings and better apps in the future.

# Starting Your Mobile Template

Mobile Web app design is complicated because there are hundreds of different devices out there, each with their own capabilities and screen size. In this book, I narrowed the range of devices to discuss by focusing on those with a WebKit-based browser. However, this still leaves me with a huge range of possibilities for inconsistencies and device-specific quirks that can wreck the user experience of our app.

Fortunately, someone else (many people, actually) have already dealt with the difficult problems of Mobile Web app compatibility, and some of them have been brilliant and generous enough to document and publish the best solutions they've found for various problems. One such effort to create highly cross-platform compatible Mobile Web apps is the Mobile Boilerplate. Created by Shi Chuan, Paul Irish, and Divya Manian, this set of files and documentation provides a solid foundation for mobile developers to build upon.

In this section, you'll create a Komodo Edit template that uses Mobile Boilerplate.

## Getting started with Mobile Boilerplate

To become familiar with what Mobile Boilerplate is, follow these steps:

1. **Navigate to** `http://html5boilerplate.com/mobile` **in your WebKit browser.**

While you don't *have* to use WebKit to view this site, you should get into the habit of using it. Your browser screen should look similar to Figure 3-4. Look this page over for a moment. Notice the fancy headlines and text styling, along with the cool star icons. If you're familiar with the pre-HTML5 way of developing web pages, you're about to get a surprise.

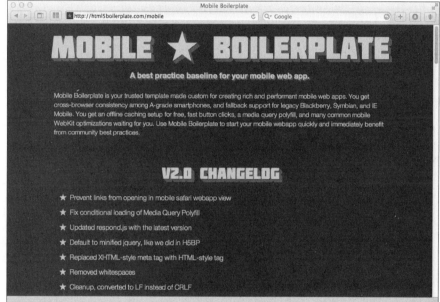

**Figure 3-4:**
The Mobile Boilerplate homepage viewed using the WebKit on a desktop computer.

2. **Choose View⇨View Source from the main menu.**

   A text file will open up, which will contain the source code for the Mobile Boilerplate, as shown in Figure 3-5. This page itself uses Mobile Boilerplate. Note all of the different commands and tags in the header of this page (between <head> and </head> in the source code). Each one of these serves a specific purpose in helping to provide a great mobile user experience to the largest number of users.

3. **If you have a mobile phone with a web browser, try opening this site with that device.**

   Yes, I realize that this URL is a bit long to be easily typed into many phones, so I've taken the liberty of creating a short URL for you: http://bit.ly/wkfdmbp.

Doing anything for mobile requires you to be very concerned with eliminating clutter and unnecessary bulk wherever possible. By creating a shortened link, I cut the number of characters almost in half and created an easy to remember link for you too (the letters after bit.ly stand for **W**eb**K**it **f**or **D**ummies **M**obile **B**oiler**p**late).

```
○ ○ ○                Source of http://html5boilerplate.com/mobile/
<!doctype html>
<html lang="en" class="no-js">
<head>
  <meta charset="utf-8">
  <meta http-equiv="X-UA-Compatible" content="IE=edge,chrome=1">
  <title>Mobile Boilerplate</title>
  <meta name="HandheldFriendly" content="True">
  <meta name="MobileOptimized" content="320"/>
  <meta name="viewport" content="width=device-width, initial-scale=1.0">
  <!-- For iPhone 4 with high-resolution Retina display: -->
  <link rel="apple-touch-icon-precomposed" sizes="114x114" href="images/h/apple-
  touch-icon.png">
  <!-- For first-generation iPad: -->
  <link rel="apple-touch-icon-precomposed" sizes="72x72" href="images/m/apple-
  touch-icon.png">
  <!-- For non-Retina iPhone, iPod Touch, and Android 2.1+ devices: -->
  <link rel="apple-touch-icon-precomposed" href="images/l/apple-touch-icon-
  precomposed.png">
  <!-- For nokia devices: -->
  <link rel="shortcut icon" href="images/l/apple-touch-icon.png">

  <meta name="apple-mobile-web-app-capable" content="yes">
  <meta name="apple-mobile-web-app-status-bar-style" content="black">
  <link rel="apple-touch-startup-image" href="images/l/splash.png">
  <meta http-equiv="cleartype" content="on">
  <link rel="stylesheet" href="css/style.css?v=4">
  <link rel="stylesheet" href="css/shCore.css">
  <script src="js/libs/modernizr-custom.js"></script>
</head>
```

**Figure 3-5:**
There's a
lot going on
in Mobile
Boilerplate.

If you don't have a mobile phone with a web browser, or if you just
don't feel like bothering with it right now, scroll down about half way on
mobileboilerplate.com/mobile, and you'll see a screenshot showing what it looks like on various devices, as shown in Figure 3-6.

**Figure 3-6:**
Mobile
Boilerplate
looks good
on many
different
devices.

4. **Click the Boilerplate Documented link to start the download of Mobile Boilerplate.**

   Two versions of Mobile Boilerplate are available:

   - Boilerplate Documented contains copious notes about everything it's doing so you can see exactly how it works.

   - The "stripped" version (just plain Boilerplate) is designed for use with live Mobile Web apps and is reduced to a much smaller file size.

5. **Unzip the file you just downloaded.**

   - On Mac OS X, you can extract the files by double-clicking the zip file.

   - On Windows, you can extract them by double-clicking the zip file and then selecting Extract from the options in the left the folder window that opens.

The next step is to import the Mobile Boilerplate into your project. The directions for doing this depend on your version of Komodo Edit and operating system.

## Importing Mobile Boilerplate in Mac OS X

If you're using the Mac OS X version, follow these steps:

1. **In Komodo Edit, make sure that your new project is selected in the Projects sidebar; then choose Project⇨MyFirstMobileProject⇨ Properties.**

   The Project Properties window for your project opens.

2. **Select Directory Import from the Categories menu in the left pane.**

3. **Under Directory to Import From, use the browse button to locate the folder containing the unzipped Mobile Boilerplate files.**

4. **Click OK.**

5. **Double-click the name of your project in the Project Sidebar to see the list of Mobile Boilerplate files that you just imported.**

## Importing Mobile Boilerplate in Windows

If you're using the Windows version, follow these steps:

1. **Right-click your project in the Projects sidebar and choose Add⇨ Existing File.**

   A file browser window will open.

2. **Browse to the Mobile Boilerplate folder that you unzipped earlier, select all the files inside it, and click OK.**

   Note that you can only add files, not folders, in this step. Figure 3-7 shows what your Projects sidebar should look like now.

**Figure 3-7:**
The files
from the
root of the
Mobile
Boilerplate
have been
added to the
project.

3. **Right-click your project in the Projects sidebar and choose Add⇨ Existing Folder.**

   The file browser will open again.

4. **Select the folder named build inside the Mobile Boilerplate folder and click OK to add it to your project.**

   The build folder and all its subfolders and files will be added to your project.

5. **Repeat Step 4 to add all the folders inside the Mobile Boilerplate to your project.**

   When you're finished, your Projects sidebar should look something like Figure 3-8.

   The Mobile Boilerplate contains a couple of hidden files, including one called .htaccess, which is used to configure some settings when your site is copied to the Internet. If your computer isn't configured to show hidden files, you won't see these files if you open your project folder by navigating to it through the Mac OS X Finder or Windows Explorer. Komodo Edit will display the hidden files in your project, however.

6. **Choose File⇨Save All from the main menu.**

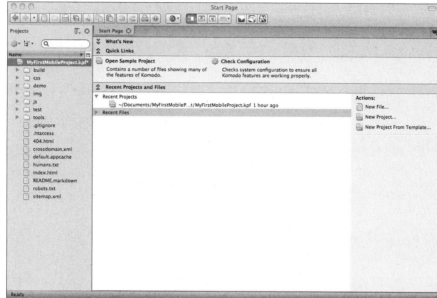

**Figure 3-8:**
Your first
mobile
project, with
the Mobile
Boilerplate
files added.

# Creating a Komodo Edit template

After you import the Mobile Boilerplate into a Komodo project, the next step is to save this project as a template so you can easily start with the Mobile Boilerplate for future apps.

To save your project as a template, follow these steps:

1. **Select your project in the Projects Sidebar.**

2. **Choose Create Template From Project.**

   • Choose Project⇨Create Template from Project from the main menu (in Mac OS X).

   • Choose Project⇨New from Template⇨Create Template from Project (in Windows).

3. **Change the name of the template to MobileBoilerplate.kpz and save it in the My Templates directory**

   The My Templates directory is the default location when you create a template.

That's all there is to it. You now have a rock-solid foundation for building your first Mobile Web app.

## Creating a new project from a template

Before you start your new project, you should get rid of that old dusty one from a couple pages back. Follow these steps:

1. **Select the project named `MyFirstMobileProject` in the Projects Sidebar.**

2. **Choose Project⇨Close Project from the main menu.**

With that out of the way, now you can get down to business and see what this Boilerplate can do!

1. **Start a new project:**

   • Choose File⇨New Project from Template from the main menu (in Mac OS X) and select the Mobile Boilerplate template that you just created.

   • Choose Project⇨New from Template⇨Mobile Boilerplate (in Windows).

   If the Mobile Boilerplate template that you just created isn't listed as an option in the New from Template menu, close Komodo Edit and restart it.

2. **Name your new project `WKFDbookmarks`, choose a new folder inside your Documents folder in which to store it, and then click Save.**

   When everything is done, you should have a window that resembles Figure 3-9 (with the path to your folder reflecting the directories on your computer, of course).

**Figure 3-9:**
With your new Mobile Boilerplate template, you can create infinite mobile projects.

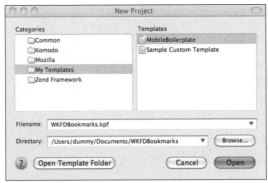

3. **Click Open to create your new project.**

Figure 3-10 shows the result. A new project will appear in the Projects Sidebar with the name `WKFDBookmarks`, and it will have the standard Mobile Boilerplate files already.

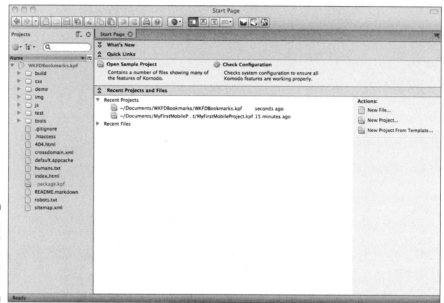

If you've followed all the steps in the book since the beginning of Chapter 1, here's what you've done:

1. You installed WebKit and optimized the interface for web-app development.

2. You installed Komodo Edit and set some preferences.

3. You downloaded Mobile BoilerPlate and created a Komodo template with it.

4. You used your Mobile BoilerPlate template to create a new Mobile Web app project.

You're ready to make an app!

## Finally! Meet your first app!

It's time to test your work and bask in the glory and beauty of your first mobile app.

1. **In the Projects sidebar, double-click the file named `index.html` to open it in the editing window.**

   You'll see a lot of code and explanations of the code, as shown in Figure 3-11.

   Nearly each line of the file has a URL that you can visit to find out more information about why that line is there.

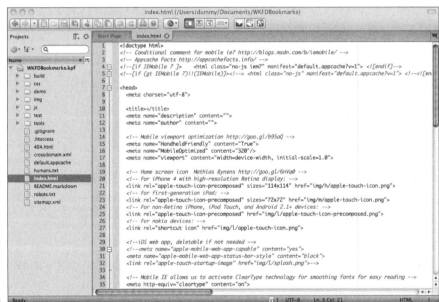

**Figure 3-11:**
The Mobile
BoilerPlate
`index.
html` file
contains
a lot of
informative
comments.

2. **Choose View⇨Preview in Browser from the main menu, or click the icon in the toolbar of Komodo Edit that looks like a globe.**

   A pop-up window appears, asking you how you want to preview the document, as shown in Figure 3-12. If you were previewing a JavaScript file or another file that needs to be viewed from within an HTML file, you would use this feature to select the file that includes the file you're working with. Because you're just viewing an HTML file, you can just leave Preview with This File selected, select the Remember This Selection for This File check box, and then click Preview.

**Figure 3-12:**
Komodo
Edit gives
you the
opportunity
to preview
your file
using
another file.

Your WebKit browser will launch (or come to the front if it's already running), and you'll see your very first Mobile Web app, which should look very much like Figure 3-13. Yes, it's completely blank.

**Figure 3-13:**
Surprise!
It's a cross-
platform-
capable
"flashlight"
app!

So there it is. Right now, you're probably saying something like, "I did all that work to get a blank page?"

Yes, you did. It's a fantastically mobile-ready blank page, however.

# Building the WKFDBookmarks app

Time to make a few more changes in order to make this page actually display something. The WKFDBookmarks app provides you with a list of links I compiled during the writing of this book. The results are then displayed in a mobile-friendly format.

This app is a seemingly simple little thing, but it makes use of a number of different languages and techniques that you'll be able to use over and over in developing Mobile Web apps. You get the added benefit of having an app that links to all the sites I mention in this book, along with a bunch of other sites and articles that I just find useful or interesting.

Here's a brief explanation of how this app will work:

1. I created lists of bookmarks for this book using the free web bookmarking service, Delicious.com.

   Delicious.com publishes bookmarks using RSS feeds, which are a standard way to syndicate data on the web.

2. This app uses a free service provided by Google — the Google Feed API — to retrieve a list of bookmarks from Delicious.

3. Our app then formats the list of bookmarks as HTML links.

## Using web APIs to make your life easier

An *application programming interface* (API) is a set of rules and specifications for a piece of software that tells how other programs can interact with it programmatically. In this case, you'll be making use of Google's Feed API, which handles all the details related to fetching an RSS feed and parsing it for displaying a web page. All this app needs to do to use it is to issue a couple of pretty simple commands.

You'll make use of Google APIs and other freely available third-party code and services throughout this book to create powerful and useful apps while requiring as little coding as possible.

The APIs, templates, and libraries that I chose to include here are currently widely used among professional mobile and web developers, and I expect them to be supported and maintained well into the future. However, it is important when you use third-party code to keep up to date with updates as they are released. You can find links to documentation and downloads for all of the libraries and APIs used in this book in the WKFDBookmarks app that you're about to build.

### Getting your Google API key

Websites that make their APIs freely available to be used by other websites usually require some sort of unique identifier and authentication to prevent abuse of their services.

Although it's not required by Google, it is a good practice to use an API key to access Google APIs. An *API key* acts as both a username and a password when you request code or services from Google.

If you already have a website where you'll be posting your web apps, visit `http://code.google.com/apis/loader/signup.html` to read more about why you would want to use an API key.

To sign up for a Google API key, follow these steps:

1. **Go to** `http://code.google.com/apis/loader/signup.html` **and enter the URL of your website into the form.**

   If you don't have a website, sign up for a free web hosting account.

   You need access to a web hosting account to get the most out of many of the exercises in this book. There should be no need to pay for hosting for doing any of the exercises, however. Here's a good list to get you started on your search for a free web host:

   ```
   www.makeuseof.com/tag/top-7-easy-and-free-web-hosting-
                services
   ```

   If you aren't logged in to a Google account, you're shown a form where you can log in. If you don't yet have a Google account, follow the directions to create one.

2. **After you're logged in and have entered your website address, copy the API key (it's a long string of numbers and letters) and save it to a text file on your computer.**

   If you forget to do this step, you can just go back to this page at any time and enter your website address again to retrieve the API key.

3. **In your WKFDBookmarks project in Komodo Edit, open** `index.html` **and put your cursor on an empty line, just below the line that reads:**

   ```
   <!--! end of #container -->
   ```

4. **Type in this code:**

   ```
   <script type="text/javascript" src="https://www.google.com/jsapi?key=YOUR
            KEY HERE"></script>
   <script type="text/javascript">
   ```

```
    google.load("feeds", "1");
    function initialize() {
      var feed = new google.feeds.Feed("http://feeds.delicious.com/v2/rss/
          cminnick/webkit book");
      feed.load(function(result) {
        if (!result.error) {
          var container = document.getElementById("feed");
          var html = '<ul>';
          for (var i = 0; i < result.feed.entries.length; i++) {
            var entry = result.feed.entries[i];
            html += '<li><a href="' + entry.link + '">' + entry.title + '</
            a></li>';
          }
            html += '</ul>';
            container.innerHTML = html;
        }
      });
    }
    google.setOnLoadCallback(initialize);
</script>
```

**5. In the first line, replace** `"YOUR_KEY_HERE"` **with your actual API key.**

**6. Find the line in** `index.html` **that reads:**

```
<div id="main" role="main">
```

**7. Type in the following on the next line:**

```
<div id="feed"></div>
```

**8. Save your file and choose Choose View⇨Preview in Browser from the main menu, or click the preview in browser icon.**

Your page opens in WebKit, as shown in Figure 3-14; you should see a list of four links.

**Figure 3-14:**
The very
first version
of WKFD-
Bookmarks
is pretty
basic.

If you have a web hosting account, publish your project to it, and test it using any mobile device with a web browser.

## Taking it up a level

Obviously, this app is pretty dull so far. But if you've got it up and running now — congratulations on creating a Mobile Web app that works! But onward and upward: Here's a rundown on a few adjustments that make this app something you can really use and be proud of.

The code you'll be changing starts with the JavaScript line that includes your Google API key and ends with

```
google.setOnLoadCallback(initialize);

</script>
```

Simply having a list of the four most recent things I've bookmarked isn't very helpful. In this next iteration of the WKFDBookmarks app, you'll modify it to list the bookmarks by how they're tagged, and you'll link each tag to a list of bookmarks.

Here's what that code block looks like after this first round of adjustments. The new additions and modifications are in bold.

```
<script type="text/javascript" src="https://www.google.com/
          jsapi?key=ABQIAAAAFIjo-DIGjBtkPUQWUf5mCBStazoUw9vSvxlew7ls7o8LQtGM
          OBTvOCjUruPMcDAUwb_gq1UnywMsxQ"></script>

<script type="text/javascript">
google.load("feeds", "1");
function initialize() {

          var feed = new google.feeds.Feed("http://feeds.delicious.com/v2/
          rss/tags/cminnick/webkit book");
  feed.setNumEntries(30);

          feed.load(function(result) {
    if (!result.error) {
      var container = document.getElementById("feed");
      var html = '<ul>';
      for (var i = 0; i < result.feed.entries.length; i++) {

                  var entry = result.feed.entries[i];
        html += '<li><a href="' + entry.link + '">' + entry.title +  '</a></
              li>';

                  }
      html += "</ul>";
      container.innerHTML = html;
    }

                });

          }

google.setOnLoadCallback(initialize);
</script>
```

Notice that this new code only has two lines that are different from the origi-nal code. To see what the new app looks like, click the preview in Browser button or refresh your browser window. You should see a page similar to Figure 3-15. All the magic was done by simply changing the Delicious RSS feed that you're using and increasing the number of items that the Google Feed API fetches.

**Figure 3-15:** After mak-ing a couple changes to the app, it's starting to become useful.

Take a look at the differences between the Delicious RSS feed in the first iter-ation of the app and the feed in the second. If you knew any other Delicious. com username, you could retrieve that user's public bookmarks by using this same format. This URL is another great example of a web API.

## Mobilize those links

If you've tried using this app on a smartphone, you've probably noticed that it's rather difficult to press those individual chapter links.

With just a little bit of CSS, the links can be made much more press-able:

1. **In Komodo Edit, open the file named `style.css`.**

You can find this file inside the css folder in the WKFDBookmarks project.

2. **Put your cursor at the very end of this file and enter the following CSS code:**

```css
/* Button style for BWKFDBookmarks App */

    ul {
    list-style-type: none;
    margin:0;
    padding: 0;

    }

    ul a {
    text-decoration: none;
    border: 1px solid #ccc;
    padding: 10px 60px 6px;
    color: #999;
    font-size: 18px;
    line-height: 45px;
    background: #ddd;
    -webkit-border-radius: 8px;
    -webkit-box-shadow: 1px 1px 2px rgba(0,0,0,.5);
    text-shadow: #fff 0px 1px 1px;
    background: -webkit-gradient(linear, left top, left bottom,
    from(#eeeeee), to(#cccccc));

    }

    ul a:active {
    -webkit-box-shadow: 0px 0px 0px rgba(0,0,0,.5);
    position: relative;
    top: 1px;
    left: 1px;

    }
```

3. **Save** style.css.

   If you're uploading your files to a web server for testing, upload the new style.css, too.

4. **View** index.html **in your WebKit browser or on a smartphone.**

   You should see something similar to Figure 3-16.

   I've done a little bit of CSS3 magic to transform the once-boring bulleted list of links into a less-boring bunch of touch-friendly buttons — complete with rounded corners and gradients.

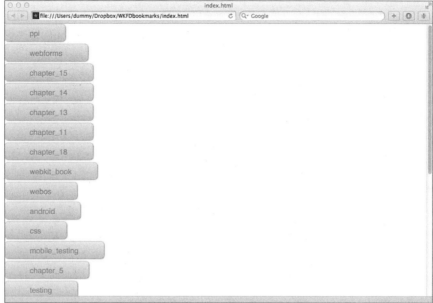

**Figure 3-16:**
The
Bookmarks
app starts to
take shape!

# Chapter 4

# jQuery Mobile

. . . . . . . . . . . . . . . . . . . . . . . . . . . . . . . . . . . . . . . . . . . .

. . . . . . . . . . . . . . . . . . . . . . . . . . . . . . . . . . . . . . . . . . . .

*O*ne persistent fact of life is that a Mobile Web app has to work correctly on many different mobile devices. Mobile Boilerplate (introduced in Chapter 3) is a great tool for handling those details. It gives you a solid foundation on which to build your app — but it's just a foundation. The real work of making your app look good is still up to you.

In this chapter, I talk about Mobile Web frameworks — in particular, jQuery Mobile.

As the name implies, a *framework* is more than just a foundation for an app. It actually provides pre-built functionality and interface elements that you can use in putting together your apps.

# Developing with Frameworks and Libraries

In software, the terms "framework" and "library" are used to describe packages of computer programs that can be used by programmers to reduce the work that they need to do while creating other computer programs.

Programmers and marketers may draw distinctions and argue over whether something is a framework or library, but for the purposes of this course, the terms are interchangeable, and I'll use whichever term the creators of the library or framework use.

The idea behind frameworks and libraries is that there are common components of any app, which can be "abstracted." *Software abstraction* is the process of creating a generic program to accomplish a task so that the programmer doesn't need to worry about the details of that task. By abstracting common functionality, you (as the developer) no longer need to worry about the code that makes these things happen and can instead focus on the functionality that makes your specific app unique.

For example, the framework that you'll be examining — jQuery Mobile — contains (among many other things) a set of smartphone-optimized buttons, bars, and icons that you can use in your apps. If you don't mind giving up some control over what your buttons and bars look like, you can use the jQuery Mobile standard buttons so you don't need to worry about designing your own.

Even better, you don't even need to worry about placing individual buttons or icons if you don't want to. If you're using jQuery Mobile, you can just tell it what the parts of your app's user interface are (header, body content, link, or footer for example), and it just takes care of styling them for you. You may choose to go with the default settings, or you can customize them.

Before I go into details about how to use jQuery Mobile, I want to give you a brief introduction to its roots. jQuery Mobile is so cool, in large part because it's built upon the shoulders of a (very clever) giant: jQuery.

## What is jQuery?

*jQuery* is a very popular free and open-source JavaScript library that is used by more than 40 percent of the most popular websites today. Its slogan pretty much sums up why it's so popular: "The Write Less, Do More, JavaScript Library."

Developed, incredibly enough, by one person, John Resig, jQuery is so widely used today that it's become the *de facto* standard for creating what are known today as AJAX applications on the web.

In the midst of such complexity, jQuery simplifies handling many different types of JavaScript problems. It also works across a wide variety of web browsers *and* allows the creation of plug-ins that extend its capabilities.

One such plug-in is jQuery Mobile.

## The pause that refreshes

AJAX — short for Asyncronous JavaScript and XML — is a name given to a programming technique that allows web browsers to send and retrieve data and update your browser window without refreshing the whole web page.

However, the words behind AJAX don't fully describe the technology:

✔ AJAX applications aren't necessarily asynchronous.

✔ Most developers don't use XML in their AJAX applications, opting instead for a technique called JavaScript Object Notation (JSON).

# *What is jQuery Mobile?*

jQuery Mobile (jQM) is a "Touch-optimized Web framework for smartphones and tablets." With very little work required on your part, it reformats your web app to work (and look great) on nearly every popular mobile device platform in use today, including

✔ iOS

✔ Symbian S60

✔ BlackBerry OS

✔ Android

✔ Windows Mobile

✔ webOS

✔ bada

✔ MeeGo

To support all these devices with your Mobile Web app, all you need to do is make use of jQuery Mobile. Everything else is taken care of by the framework. Ain't life beautiful?

To see some examples of sites built with jQuery Mobile, visit the jQuery Mobile Gallery at www.jqmgallery.com. It's really pretty remarkable what's been done with this framework so far, and how far it's come.

Figure 4-1 shows the jQuery Mobile Gallery on a desktop browser. Figure 4-2 shows the same site when viewed with a mobile browser.

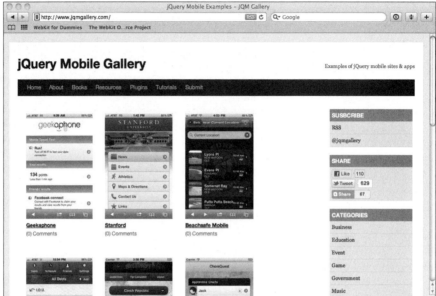

**Figure 4-1:**
jQuery
Mobile
Gallery
shows off
some of
the best
apps built
with jQuery
Mobile.

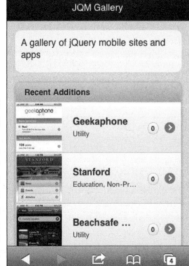

**Figure 4-2:**
Surprise!
The mobile
site for
jQuery
Mobile
Gallery was
built using
jQuery
Mobile.

# Introducing the Mobile Cookbook App

Without further ado, it's time to look at some code. In this section, I show you how to use jQuery Mobile to create a simple cookbook app containing a few of my favorite recipes. (Develop apps first, eat later.)

## Cooking up a cookbook app

In designing a mobile cookbook app, you have many of the same concerns that are common to any mobile app — in particular, these:

- ✔ It should be usable by someone who is busy doing something else.
- ✔ It should be attractive and logical so that users can quickly grasp how the user interface works.

In addition to these challenges, a cookbook needs to have the following features:

- ✔ **It should be easily updatable as recipes are improved or changed.** I'm constantly improving my favorite recipes. By releasing them as a Mobile Web app, I can make sure that you always have the latest versions.

- ✔ **It should be available offline.** Chances are good that you'll be connected to the Internet most of the time when you're using the cookbook, but there may be times when you're camping in the remote wilderness and need one of my recipes.

- ✔ **It shouldn't be limited by the amount of storage space on your mobile device.** Because the actual app lives on the web, the cookbook can be much larger than if it were a native app that was stored completely on your phone.

## Setting out the ingredients: HTML basics

Before you get cooking with jQuery Mobile, it's wise to check the HTML ingredients before they go into the pot. If you're not yet fluent in HTML, don't worry — it's very simple to pick up. I cover HTML — and HTML5, in particular — in Chapter 9. For now, here's what you need to know:

- ✔ HTML is a *markup language*. That is, it uses beginning and ending tags to designate ways to display content; the web browser then interprets and displays the marked-up content.

✔ Beginning tags are surrounded by less-than and greater-than symbols (< and >). Ending tags have a forward slash (/) after the less-than symbol. For example, in the following snippet of code, the HTML h1 tag is used to mark the text HTML Basics as a level-one header:

```
<h1>HTML Basics</h1>
```

This complete snippet of code — including the beginning tag `<h1>`; the content, HTML Basics; and the ending tag `</h1>` — is called an *element*.

✔ Web browsers interpret and display HTML elements according to rules defined in the HTML specification. For example, a web browser will display an h1 element in a larger size than an h2, which will be larger than an h3. Figure 4-3 demonstrates this.

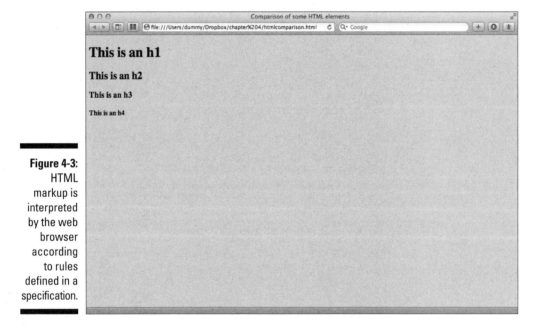

**Figure 4-3:**
HTML markup is interpreted by the web browser according to rules defined in a specification.

Figure 4-3 was created using this HTML code:

```
<!DOCTYPE html>
<html>
<head>

<title>Comparison of some HTML elements</title>

</head>
<body>
```

```
                         <h1>This is an h1</h1>

                         <h2>This is an h2</h2>

                         <h3>This is an h3</h3>

                         <h4>This is an h4</h4>
        </body>

        </html>
```

✔ Beginning and ending tags can be combined within a single set of brackets when an element doesn't contain content. For example, the HTML `img` element is used to display an image. It doesn't need to surround text content, as the `h1` does.

```
<img src="puppy.jpg" alt="picture of a puppy" width="100" height="100" />
```

✔ Values within a beginning tag — for example, `src`, `width`, and `height` in the previous `img` element — are called *attributes*. Attributes serve many useful functions, including these:

- Uniquely identifying an element

- Changing the default behavior of an element

- Triggering JavaScript code when an event happens to an attribute

To get a more substantial taste of HTML, check out *HTML, XHTML & CSS For Dummies* by Ed Tittel and Jeff Noble (John Wiley & Sons, Inc.).

## Sinking your teeth into jQuery Mobile

The basics of jQuery Mobile are pretty simple. Here's all you need to do to get started:

1. **Launch Komodo Edit and start a new project without using a template.**

2. **Name your project `MobileCookbook` and save it in a new folder.**

3. **Create a new blank file in your project and save it as `index.html`.**

   This will be the homepage for your app.

4. **Create a basic mobile HTML5 template for your app by entering the following code into** `index.html`:

```
<!DOCTYPE html>
<html>

<head>
```

```
<meta charset="utf-8">

<meta name="viewport" content="width=device-width,
        minimum-scale=1, maximum-scale=1">

<title></title>

</head>

<body>


</body>

</html>
```

**5. Add jQuery Mobile to your app by placing the following code in the header (between `<head>` and `</head>`) of your HTML document.**

```
<link href="http://code.jquery.com/mobile/latest/jquery.mobile.min.css"
        rel="stylesheet" type="text/css" />
<script src="http://code.jquery.com/jquery-1.6.1.min.js"></script>
<script src="http://code.jquery.com/mobile/latest/jquery.mobile.min.js">
        </script>
```

Note that I'm simply linking to the hosted versions of the jQuery Mobile files. You may also download jQuery Mobile and put it on your server if you wish.

At the time of this writing, jQuery Mobile is still in Beta testing. If that sounds like Greek to you, essentially, the developers don't yet feel that jQuery Mobile is quite ready for production use, but it's getting close. I expect that the version you (future reader) are using will be far better than the one I have access to right now. For this reason, the links to the hosted version of jQuery Mobile that I include in this chapter will point to the absolute latest build.

Note that, as with the nightly build of WebKit, the nightly build of jQuery Mobile is not fully tested; use it only for development and experimentation. I encourage you to visit `http://jquerymobile.com` right now and find out what the latest released version is and use that instead of the above links for anything that you may actually want someone besides yourself to see.

**6. Give your page a title.**

Enter Mobile Cookbook between the title tags, like this:

```
<title>Mobile Cookbook</title>
```

7. **Type the following HTML5 code into the body (between `<body>` and `</body>`) of your page to create a section in your page:**

```
<section>
  <header></header>

  <article></article>

  <footer></footer>

</section>
```

HTML5 elements simply describe the structure of the document. It's pretty clear what the purpose of the code between the `<section>` and `</section>` tags is.

8. **Copy from `<section>` to `</section>` and paste it into your document twice more, so that you now have three sections.**

Now you have three sections in your document. Each section will be a separate recipe in your cookbook. The next step is to add the jQuery Mobile code and the content that transforms this web page into a Mobile Web app.

9. **Add `data-role="page"` to each `<section>` tag.**

jQuery Mobile uses a the value of an attribute called `data-role` to identify the different parts of an app. For this app, each recipe should appear on a separate page. Be sure to begin each section with the following code:

```
<section data-role="page">
```

10. **Add a unique ID to each section so that jQuery Mobile can tell them apart.**

Because each section becomes a separate recipe, you can just number them `"recipe1"`, `"recipe2"`, and `"recipe3"`, like this:

```
<section data-role="page" id="recipe1">
  <header></header>
  <article></article>
  <footer></footer>
</section>
<section data-role="page" id="recipe2">
  <header></header>
  <article></article>
  <footer></footer>
</section>
<section data-role="page" id="recipe3">
  <header></header>
  <article></article>
  <footer></footer>
</section>
```

11. **Put the name of each recipe into the `header` of each section, using the `h1` element.**

    These names become the titles of three separate pages in your app.

    ```
    <header><h1>Lemonade</h1></header>
    ...
    <header><h1>Soup</h1></header>
    ...
    <header><h1>Tortillas</h1></header>
    ```

12. **Give each page a footer, by putting the following inside the `footer` element:**

    ```
    cooking is fun
    ```

13. **Enter recipes into the article elements of each of the recipe pages.**

    I formatted each of the recipes as a numbered list by using the HTML ordered list element (`ol`) and the HTML list item element (`li`).

    • *Recipe 1: Lemonade*

    ```
    <ol>
        <li>Mix and heat 1 cup of water and 1 cup of sugar
            until the sugar is dissolved.</li>
        <li>Add 1 cup of lemon juice.</li>
        <li>Add 2-3 cups of water, and lots of ice.</li>
        <li>Enjoy!</li>
    </ol>
    ```

    • *Recipe 2: Soup*

    ```
    <ol>
        <li>Chop and saut&eacute; 1 onion, 1 stalk celery,
            and 1 carrot for a few minutes.</li>
        <li>Add 5 cups vegetable stock and 1 can diced
            tomatoes.</li>
        <li>Wash and then stir in 1 cup lentils.</li>
        <li>Add 1 bay leaf, salt and pepper.</li>
        <li>Add chopped serrano peppers to taste.</li>
        <li>Cook until lentils are soft.</li>
        <li>Enjoy!</li>
    </ol>
    ```

    • *Recipe 3: Tortillas*

    ```
    <ol>
        <li>Stir together 2 cups of instant corn masa mix
            and 1/4 teaspoon salt.</li>
        <li>Add 1 1/4 cups water and mix together well.</li>
        <li>Form balls of dough from the mix.</li>
        <li>Press balls of dough into tortillas with a
            tortilla press.</li>
        <li>Cook tortillas on a comal.</li>
        <li>Enjoy!</li>
    </ol>
    ```

14. **Add jQuery Mobile data-role attributes to the `header`, `article`, and `footer` elements for each section.**

    These data roles are

    - `<header data-role="header">`
    - `<article data-role="content">`
    - `<footer data-role="footer">`

15. **Add** `data-role="listview"` **to the** `ol` **beginning tags, as follows:**

    ```
    <ol data-role="listview">
    ```

16. **Save `index.html` and your project, and click the Preview in Browser button in Komodo Edit to see your app so far.**

    If you entered everything correctly, a page should open in WebKit and show the lemonade recipe.

    Notice that the different elements of the page have been formatted to look like a mobile app, but there doesn't seem to be a way to get to the other two recipes. The next step shows you how to add a table of contents, or a home page, to the app.

17. **Enter the following section before the section containing the lemonade recipe.**

    ```
    <section data-role="page" id="toc">
    <header data-role="header">
       <h1>WKFD Recipes</h1>
    </header>

    <article data-role="content">

       <ul data-role="listview">

          <li><a href="#recipe1">Lemonade</a></li>
          <li><a href="#recipe2">Soup</a></li>
          <li><a href="#recipe3">Tortillas</a></li>
       </ul>
    </article>
    <footer data-role="footer">cooking is fun</footer>
    </section>
    ```

    In this section, I use the unordered list element (`ul`) rather than the ordered list (`ol`) that was used in the recipes. Also, I put the anchor, or link element — `a` — around each recipe names and then linked to them by the values in their `id` attributes.

18. **Save your file, and click the Preview in Browser icon. This time, you should see a table of contents.**

    Figure 4-4 shows how it looks in iOS.

**Figure 4-4:**
The table
of contents
page links
to each of
the recipes
in the
cookbook.

If you click one of the recipe names, that recipe scrolls into place, as
shown (on Android) in Figure 4-5. Notice that, except for the built-in
functions of the two phones (such as the look of the address bar and the
bottom toolbar on iOS), the iPhone and Android versions have a consistent look and feel.

**Figure 4-5:**
Clicking a
link from the
table of con-
tents makes
the app
open the
correspond-
ing recipe.

# *Spicing up your cookbook app*

Now that you have a basic cookbook app, it's time to add a little more excitement to it — or at least make it more useful.

### *Getting back to basics*

Right now, the functionality for navigating to a recipe is in place, but there's no way to get back to the table of contents except by using the browser's Back button. Because the goal here is to provide a native-like experience, that just won't do.

Fortunately, jQuery Mobile has a built-in command for adding a Back button to the head of any page that has a parent page. The command is (drum roll, please): `data-add-back-btn="yes"`. To enable the Back button, just add this command to the element in your document that has the `data-role="page"` attribute. In this case, add it to the `section` elements for each of the recipes.

Your `section` elements should now look like this:

```
<section data-role="page" id="recipe1" data-add-back-btn="yes">
```

When jQuery Mobile sees this attribute, it inserts a nice-looking Back button that returns the user to the page most recently visited.

### *Converting the footer into something we can use*

Next: Okay, that footer is pretty corny. Make it useful by adding a link to a basic unit-conversion table. Then the table can pop up in a dialog box so you can access it anytime without leaving the current recipe.

1. **Open `index.html` in your Cookbook app.**

2. **Replace the `cooking is fun` text in each section's footer element with the following:**

   ```
   <a href="conversions.html" data-rel="dialog" data-transition="pop">
           Conversions</a>
   ```

   This is just a standard HTML link element, but with these two jQuery Mobile attributes added in:

   - `data-rel="dialog"` tells jQuery Mobile to open the link as a dialog box.

   - `data-transition="pop"` adds a cool little transition effect that happens while the dialog box is opening.

Some other possible values for the `data-transition` attribute are `flip`, `slidedown`, and `slideup`.

**3. After you change all the `footer` elements, save `index.html`.**

If you preview your app now and try to click the Conversion button in the footer, what you see looks something like Figure 4-6. The nice error message is completely generated by jQuery Mobile with no work on your part (well, except for having left a broken link).

**Figure 4-6:**
You added a link to the footer, but it doesn't go any-where yet.

The next thing to do is to create the actual page that becomes the dialog box:

**1. Choose File⇨New File from the main menu, create a new HTML file, and add it to your project.**

**2. Save the file as `conversions.html`.**

**3. Replace any pre-entered content in your new page with the following HTML5 / jQuery Mobile code:**

```
<!DOCTYPE html>
<html>
<head>
  <meta charset="utf-8">
  <meta name="viewport" content="width=device-width, minimum-scale=1,
        maximum-scale=1">
```

```
    <title>Conversions Dialog Box</title>
    <link href="http://code.jquery.com/mobile/latest/jquery.mobile.min.css"
         rel="stylesheet"  type="text/css" />
    <script src="http://code.jquery.com/jquery-1.6.1.min.js"></script>
    <script src="http://code.jquery.com/mobile/latest/jquery.mobile.min.js">
         </script>
</head>
<body>
  <div data-role="page">
    <div data-role="header">
    <h1>Conversions</h1>
    </div>
    <div data-role="content">
    <p>1 gallon = 4 quarts</p>
    <a href="index.html" data-role="button" data-rel="back">OK Got it!</a>
    </div>
  </div>
</body>
</html>
```

Figure 4-7 shows the dialog box opened in iOS. Although this is just a normal page, it's styled as a dialog box because it was linked that way.

**Figure 4-7:**
jQuery
Mobile
applies
styling to
dialog-box
pages so
they look
like the
native dia-
log boxes.

## *Presentation, presentation, presentation*

Creating a successful Mobile Web app is like cooking — presentation matters. jQuery Mobile's default look is actually pretty tasty. It's obvious that a lot of work has gone into getting every pixel and every animation as right as possible in order to give the most solid-feeling user experience possible.

By default, jQuery Mobile makes the header and footer bars black and uses blue and grey in different places for contrast. But, maybe black and blue aren't your favorites. Or, maybe you'd just like to have something a bit more sunny.

### *Changing colors*

jQuery Mobile uses a Theme system to make the look and feel of an app easy to change. In this chapter, you're just looking at the default theme, which features an iOS-like look with rounded corners and large buttons.

Within the default theme are five color swatches that you can use for each different `data-role`. These swatches are named using the letters *A* through *E*. The main (background) colors of the five swatches are listed in Table 4-1.

| Table 4-1 | jQuery's Default Theme Color Swatches |
|-----------|----------------------------------------|
| *Swatch* | *Color* |
| Swatch A | Black |
| Swatch B | Blue |
| Swatch C | Gray |
| Swatch D | White |
| Swatch E | Yellow |

Figure 4-8 shows what a button looks like with each of the five swatches. (Okay, if you're reading this in black-and-white hard copy, use your imagination.) If you select one of these swatches, jQuery Mobile also adjusts everything that's affected by that change so that you don't end up with something like white text on a yellow background, for instance.

Themes swatches are applied to elements using the `data-theme` attribute. Jazz up your cookbook by applying some different swatches.

 1. **If it's not already open, open `index.html` from your Cookbook app in Komodo Edit.**

**Figure 4-8:**
jQuery
Mobile's
default
theme has
five different
swatches
to choose
from.

2. **Add** `data-theme="e"` **to each of the** `header` **elements, like this:**

```
<header data-role="header" data-theme="e">
```

3. **Add** `data-theme="e"` **to each of the** `footer` **elements.**

4. **Preview your app.**

   Now it looks something like Figure 4-9.

**Figure 4-9:**
The cook-
book app
doesn't look
so dreary
with bright
yellow
headers
and footers
applied to it.

The Conversions dialog-box page can also be modified to match the new
yellow theme of the app. Apply the `"e"` color swatch to the `header`,
`content`, and `button` elements on the dialog-box page:

```
<div data-role="header" data-theme="e">
...
<div data-role="content" data-theme="e">
...
<div data-role="button" data-theme="e">
```

### Adding icons and images

jQuery Mobile comes with a standard set of icons you can apply to any button. They run the gamut of your standard mobile app icons, including forward, backward, home, delete, search, and alert.

You add icons to links by using the data-icon attribute. For example, add an "info" icon to each of the Conversions dialog buttons:

```
<a href="conversions.html" data-rel="dialog" data-
        transition="pop" data-icon="info">
```

Each of the icons is a white image on a dark background and is designed to work well with any of the five button colors. If the standard set of icons doesn't have what you need, you can create your own icons and use those instead.

## Images on buttons

Putting images on buttons is a simple matter of putting an image tag within the button's link element. Here's the code to put a photograph of a glass of lemonade on the button that links to the lemonade recipe.

```
<li><a href="#recipe1">Lemonade<img src=" http://www.
        webkitfordummies.com/MobileCookbook/images/
        lemonade.jpg" /></a></li>
```

Here's the new code for the table-of-contents block, with an image added for each of the menu items.

```
<section data-role="page" id="toc">
  <header data-role="header" data-theme="e">
    <h1>WKFD Recipes</h1>
  </header>

  <article data-role="content">

    <ul data-role="listview">
```

```
        <li><a href="#recipe1">Lemonade<img src="http://www.webkitfordummies.com/
              MobileCookbook/images/lemonade.jpg" /></a></li>
        <li><a href="#recipe2">Soup<img src=" http://www.webkitfordummies.com/
              MobileCookbook/images/soup.jpg" /></a></li>

        <li><a href="#recipe3">Tortillas<img src=" http://www.webkitfordummies.
              com/MobileCookbook/images/tortilla.jpg" /></a></li>
    </ul>

  </article>

  <footer data-role="footer" data-theme="e">
    <a href="conversions.html" data-rel="dialog" data-transition="pop" data-
              icon="info">Conversions</a>
  </footer>

</section>
```

Figure 4-10 shows that this app is starting to look pretty delicious! Notice that even though these images are all different sizes, jQuery Mobile resizes your images to fit the buttons.

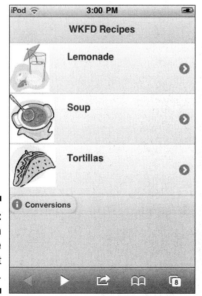

**Figure 4-10:**
Images on buttons are resized to fit the buttons.

## Adding forms with jQuery Mobile

jQuery Mobile has a set of touch-optimized form widgets that you can use to get user input. By default, jQuery Mobile will just do its thing and enhance any `form` elements it finds in your app. All you need to do is to write standard HTML code for a form.

To add a simple feedback form to the cookbook app:

1. **Create a new file in your project and save it as** feedback.html.

2. **Paste in your standard jQuery Mobile boilerplate and give the page the title `"Send Us Feedback"` in both the `title` element and the `h1` header:**

```
<!DOCTYPE html>
<html>
<head>
<meta charset="utf-8">
<meta name="viewport" content="width=device-width, minimum-scale=1,
        maximum-scale=1">
<title>Send Us Feedback</title>
<link href="http://code.jquery.com/mobile/latest/jquery.mobile.min.css"
        rel="stylesheet" type="text/css" />
<script src="http://code.jquery.com/jquery-1.6.1.min.js"></script>
<script src="http://code.jquery.com/mobile/latest/jquery.mobile.min.js">
        </script>
</head>
<body>
<div data-role="page">
<div data-role="header">
<h1>Send Us Feedback</h1>
</div>
<div data-role="content">

</div>
</div>
</body>
</html>
```

3. **Add in a standard HTML form by entering the following code inside the content area of the page.**

```
<div data-role="content" data-theme="e">

    <p>How do you like our Cook Book? Do you have suggestions for
            improvements to the app or to the recipes? Send them to us!</p>

<form action="form.php" method="post">
```

```
<label for="yourname">Your Name</label>

<input type="text" name="yourname" />
<label for="email">Your Email</label>
<input type="text" name="youremail" />


<label for="comments">Comments</label>

<textarea name="comments"></textarea>

<input type="submit" name="submit" value="Submit" data-theme="e" />

</form>


</div>
```

**4. Save your app and preview it in WebKit.**

The finished form is shown in Figure 4-11. This form won't actually do anything just yet because it hasn't been hooked up to a server-side script yet.

**Figure 4-11:** The CookBook App feedback form, which doesn't actually send feedback to anyone yet.

**5. Finally, put a link to the feedback form onto the TOC page by putting the following right after the Conversions dialog box in the `footer`.**

```
<a href="feedback.html" data-icon="star">Feedback</a>
```

# Chapter 5

# Testing and Debugging

· · · · · · · · · · · · · · · · · · · · · · · · · · · · · · · · · · · · · · · · · · · · · · · · · · ·

· · · · · · · · · · · · · · · · · · · · · · · · · · · · · · · · · · · · · · · · · · · · · · · · · · ·

*I*t's pretty much impossible to write perfect code. Numerous (and I mean *numerous*) systems and methodologies have been created over the years to attempt to make the extremely complex practice of writing computer code as predictable as the internal workings of the computers that run the code.

Good luck with that. Really. I mean that. Meanwhile, . . .

Despite progress in software development systems and theories, testing and debugging are still — and will always be — key elements of any software project.

# Testing Mobile Web Apps

Standardization on the WebKit browser engine with most mobile devices reduces the complexity of mobile app testing quite a bit. But, as is the case with any type of software, a lot can go wrong. Good testing can help you detect and find the causes of problems. It can also help you to find ways to optimize and improve your web app.

Some of the many variables in web-app development that need to be tested are

✔ **Functionality:** Is the app working as you expect it to?

✔ **Appearance:** Does the app look the way it's supposed to?

✔ **Performance:** Is the app responsive? Do pages load quickly? Are there any places where it seems to "hang" or where there may be delays while it's processing data?

✔ **User experience:** Is the app easy to use and intuitive? Does it work in a way that's consistent with how users would expect it to work? Are touch-enabled buttons large enough to be individually pressed by users with large fingers?

✔ **Accessibility:** Is the app usable on devices for the hearing or sight-impaired or with other physical limitations?

✔ **Compliance with standards:** Does the app conform to the standards?

Web browsers are forgiving when it comes to errors, but it still may impact performance, accessibility, and how your app renders if you have syntax errors or if you use nonstandard code.

✔ **File size optimization:** Are images used by the app compressed enough to load quickly, while not being so compressed that they don't look good?

✔ **Security:** Are there security holes in your app that could allow someone with malicious intent to do anything with the app that it isn't designed for? Can the app be hacked and modified?

✔ **Privacy:** Does the app properly secure any personal or financial information that it uses (such as names, addresses, e-mail addresses, credit card numbers, and so forth)?

✔ **Grammar and spelling of content:** Are your menu items spelled correctly? Does your app use proper punctuation and grammar in explanatory text and help files?

✔ **Documentation:** Is the app documented in a way that can be understood by the intended users?

This chapter will lay out the most popular tools and techniques that you can use to find and fix problems in many of these areas.

## *The best way to test an app*

The best way to test Mobile Web apps is to get your hands on every possible version of every possible device and operating system that will be used to access the app and to test every feature and every possible combination of features in your app using each of those devices. Then, run these tests under every possible combination of environmental factors (including different Internet connection speeds, different lighting, different users with different levels of experience and knowledge, and so forth).

So, there you go. Now you know everything you need to know about how to test web apps.

But, back to reality. Even the largest software companies don't have the resources to do this type of testing.

In the olden days, testing was something you did when development was finished. It was typically done by a separate team of people, called "testers," who compared what was developed with the specifications and made sure that everything worked correctly. These days, because of the fast pace of the Web and the need for more flexibility, testing is increasingly becoming an integrated part of the development process.

## Testing early and often

Web apps lend themselves to frequent testing and changing because the HTML5, JavaScript, and CSS code you write is the same code that runs in the browser. In other words, there's not an intermediate step required between creating your web-app files and opening them in a browser. Languages such as these are known as *interpreted* languages.

Native apps, on the other hand, must first be translated into machine code (that is, *compiled)* before they can be run. Compiled languages (such as Java or C) need to be written with a greater attention to detail, because they won't compile if they contain errors.

Because they don't require compilation, and because browsers are so forgiving of mistakes, it's very common to find errors in web apps. These errors may be harmless — as in the case of a simple syntax error that will be ignored or corrected automatically by the browser. Or, an error may have a significant impact on the performance, design, functionality, or security of your app.

Because of the increased potential for mistakes, you should test Mobile Web apps as early in the development process as you can, and as often during the development process as possible — preferably with input from the client or whoever will be the user of the app.

When I say to test "as early as possible," I mean it. An increasingly popular method of testing apps is to design tests *before* you write any actual code. After you design a test, you then write code to meet the requirements of the test. For example, you may design a test that says something like this:

*The words "Mobile Cookbook" should be displayed at the top of the page, and there should be three links under it which link to the three recipes.*

If you test your app before you write any code, your test will fail (of course). After it does, you should quickly write just enough code to make the test pass, then design a new test. As you write more tests and code, you should be constantly going back and improving the prior code that you wrote.

This methodology is known as *test-driven development.*

There is nothing more to testing than what I just described. First, you determine what the app should do. Then, you determine whether the app does that. In the rest of this chapter, I describe tools and techniques that can help you with different aspects of the testing process.

## Testing in WebKit

The easiest way to test the functionality and look of Mobile Web apps is by opening them in a WebKit browser. If you've read this book to this point, you've already been doing this type of testing with the applications in Chapters 3 and 4. The benefits of testing in a desktop browser are

- ✔ The tools provided by Web Inspector can help you track down any logic or display error messages in your code.

- ✔ You can make changes and test again very quickly.

- ✔ You can use the User Agent feature (under the Develop menu) to make your browser pose as a mobile device to a web server.

- ✔ To simulate the experience of viewing your app on a mobile screen, you can resize your browser window to the same dimensions as different mobile device screens.

  For example, to see an approximation of what your app will look like on an iPhone and many other devices with the same size screen as the iPhone, you can resize your browser window to 320 pixels x 480 pixels (for testing portrait mode) or 480 pixels x 320 pixels (for testing landscape mode).

Several Safari extensions are available that will resize your browser window to a specified size. One such extension is Resizer, which can be downloaded from `http://sixfoot1.com/safari-extensions/resizer/`. Resizer doesn't currently work in Windows. Another option (which is not free, but is low-cost), is available from `http://resizesafari.com`.

Figure 5-1 shows the Mobile Cookbook app in a desktop Safari browser that has been resized to the 320 pixels x 480 pixels.

**Figure 5-1:**
Resizing a desktop browser window to mobile-device screen sizes can test your app's interface — a little.

Testing Mobile Web apps in a desktop browser is convenient, but it should only be done as a first test. What you see on an actual mobile device will be significantly different.

## Testing with emulators

Where you don't have access to the actual devices and operating systems, emulators can provide the next-best thing. *Emulators* are software packages that run on a desktop computer and are designed to look and work just like a physical mobile device. Emulators are available for most smartphones and mobile operating systems. Although using an emulator is never the same as using the actual hardware, it is far better than simply using a desktop browser, and an emulator can give you a good idea of where you should focus your energy.

Because of the size of each of their markets, the iPhone Simulator and the Android Emulator are the most important tools to have at hand — especially if you don't have access to actual physical devices running iOS and Android.

Because emulators are running an operating system within an operating system, you're going to find that they're usually slower than using the actual devices. Make sure to run them on the fastest computer you have access to, and close as many other programs on your computer as you can before you start an emulator.

### iPhone Simulator

The iPhone Simulator comes with the iOS Software Development Kit (SDK) and Apple's integrated development environment (IDE), Xcode.

There are a couple of caveats, however:

- ✔ Xcode runs only on Mac OS X.
- ✔ To download the latest version of these tools, you have to sign up for one of Apple developer programs and pay the $99-per-year fee.

However, you can still obtain an older version of Xcode (Xcode 3), which includes the iPhone Simulator.

To get the free version of Xcode 3, follow these steps:

1. **Go to** `http://developer.apple.com/programs/register` **to sign up (for free) as an Apple Developer.**

2. **After you're signed up and logged in, go to** `http://developer.apple.com/xcode/index.php`**.**

   You'll see various links and text about signing up for Apple Developer Programs. Look toward the bottom of the page, tucked away in a corner, for the link to download Xcode 3.

3. **Download and install Xcode 3.**

   After it's installed (which takes a while), you'll find the iPhone Simulator app at the following location on your Mac:

   ```
   /Developer/Platforms/iPhoneSimulator.platform/Developer/Applications/iPhone
           Simulator.app
   ```

4. **Start the iPhone simulator by double-clicking it.**

A simulated iPhone will appear on your screen, as shown in Figure 5-2. You can then start Mobile Safari in the iPhone simulator and use it to see how your Mobile Web apps will look on the iPhone.

**Figure 5-2:**
The iPhone
Simulator
can be
obtained for
free with
Xcode 3.

The iPhone Simulator can also be used to see how your app will look on the iPad. In the main menu, choose either iPhone or iPad under Hardware ⇨ Device to switch between devices.

## Android Emulator

The Android Emulator is included with the Android Software Development Kit (SDK). It runs as a Java applet and will run on most operating systems.

To install the Android SDK, follow these steps:

1. **Browse to** `http://developer.android.com/sdk/index.html`.

You'll see a list of downloads for different operating systems.

**2. Select the download for your computer.**

**3. When the download is complete, double-click the file to begin installing (on Windows) or to unzip the files (on Mac and Linux).**

**4. Open the Tools folder inside the Android SDK folder and launch the app called android.**

The Android SDK and AVD Manager will appear, as shown in Figure 5-3.

**Figure 5-3:**
The Android
SDK and
AVD
Manager
is where
you install
the Android
platform.

**5. Click Available Packages from the left pane and expand the Android Repository collapsible list.**

You need to download at least one platform in order to create a virtual device, which will enable you to use the emulator.

**6. Select at least one platform from the available packages.**

For example, you may select the item named SDK Platform Android 3.2.

**7. Click Install Selected to begin the download and installation of the platform.**

**8. Click Virtual Devices.**

You'll see the same blank screen shown in Figure 5-3.

**9. Click New to start creating a new virtual device.**

The Create New Android Virtual Device (AVD) pop-up window appears.

**10. Type a name for your AVD and select a Target, as shown in Figure 5-4.**

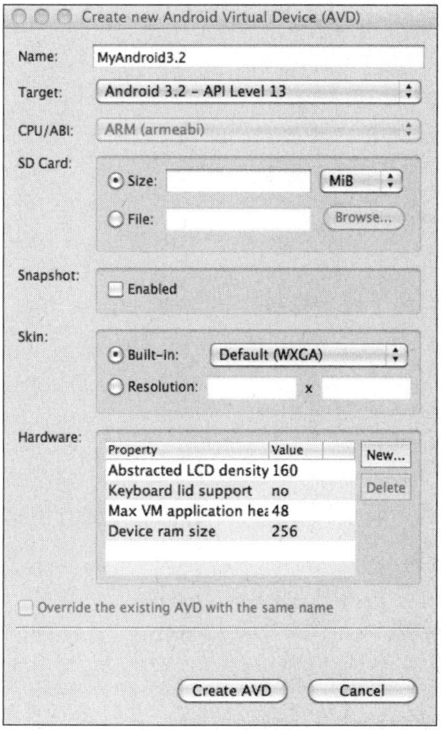

**Figure 5-4:**
You must
create
a new
Android
Virtual
Device to
run the
emulator.

11. **Select the AVG you just created; then click Start on the right side of the SDK and click AVG Manager to start the emulator.**

    The emulator may take a while to start. Be patient. When it loads, you'll see a screen similar to Figure 5-5 (if you created your AVD using the Android 3.2 platform).

12. **Drag the lock icon to the side with your mouse.**

    The Android home screen appears, after which you can use the virtual device just like a regular Android device.

13. **To test the Android browser, click Apps in the upper-right corner.**

    A screen showing all apps installed on the virtual device appears.

14. **Select Browser from the list of apps.**

    The Android Browser starts.

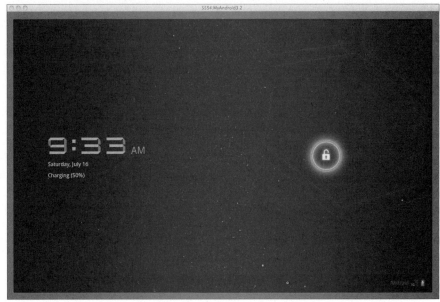

**Figure 5-5:**
You can use
the Android
Emulator
to test your
web apps
in the
Android OS.

## Release early and often

Google is famous for releasing new software in *Beta mode* (the latest version that's not quite ready for release yet) and keeping it like that for a long time while gathering data from users about how the software is being used and about bugs that users find.

Although you may not have the resources of a company like Google, you can release your Mobile Web app as soon as you like in order to start gathering input from real users. In this way, you can have access to a much larger team of testers than you would normally have.

# Debugging Mobile Web Apps

*Debugging* is a part of testing that has to do with finding and fixing errors. WebKit includes plenty of tools to help you, but sometimes the peskiest bugs can be squashed only by having the experience to know where and how to look for them. In this section, I show you how to use some of these tools to detect problems and then I show you some techniques for figuring out what to do about them.

# Debugging with the Web Inspector

The Web Inspector tools can be very helpful for solving problems with your app and for finding ways to improve your app. The Web Inspector tools that you use will depend on several factors:

- ✓ **The technologies used by your app:** If your app uses JavaScript, you'll likely have a need for the Error Console and the JavaScript debugger, for example.

- ✓ **The specific issues that you're trying to solve:** If you're trying to figure out why a piece of text isn't styled like you expect, you can use the elements and styles panes to track down the problem and test solutions.

- ✓ **The stage of development you're in:** The audits pane, for example, generally isn't used until you have something that's fully functional.

# Enabling the Debug Console on iOS

Mobile Safari features a subset of the WebKit Web Inspector functionality. This can be useful for seeing errors generated by your web app. To enable debugging on iOS devices, follow these steps:

1. **Open the Settings app on your iPhone, iPod touch, or iPad.**

   You'll see a list of different device settings that you can adjust (such as Network and Notifications settings), followed by App settings.

2. **Touch the Safari settings.**

   You'll see another list of options, such as the default search engine, auto-fill, and pop-up blocking.

3. **At the very bottom of the Safari preferences, touch the Developer link.**

   The developer settings will appear.

4. **Enable the Debug Console and then close the settings.**

The next time you open up Safari, the Debug Console will appear just under the address bar and will report whether the current page has any errors.

# Learning from my mistakes

The following is a true story of how I found and fixed an error that I had made while developing the Mobile Cookbook app I use in Chapter 4.

Figure 5-6 shows what happened in the Debug Console when I loaded my Mobile Cookbook app in Mobile Safari for the first time.

**Figure 5-6:**
This can't be true. How can my perfect cookbook app have errors?

I clicked the Error Message window to get details about each of the errors that the Debug Console has reported, as shown in Figure 5-7.

**Figure 5-7:**
Mobile Debugger is reporting errors in my app.

My first reaction was to remember that error messages don't necessarily mean that there's a problem that needs to be fixed. Clearly this must have been a case where the Error Console just doesn't understand some of the super-advanced technologies I'm using, or perhaps there's a bug with jQuery Mobile.

Still, it's important to track down and solve any errors that can be solved. So, I dug in. "What are these errors, and are they something that I need to worry about?" I asked myself.

Here's my quick checklist to go through when a mysterious error is reported with a Mobile Web app. Depending on the answers to the first couple questions, I may go through all or any combination of these steps when I'm trying to track down the cause of an error.

1. Does the web app have a problem that can be explained by this error?

   In this case, the answer is no. The supposed "extra HTML tag" isn't causing the page to not render properly or causing the app to not function.

2. Does this error happen when the page is viewed using a different web browser?

   Sometimes an error can be explained by the specific quirks of a certain browser, or even the debugging tool itself. Figure 5-8 shows what happens in the Error Console on the desktop version of Safari when I load this same page — absolutely nothing.

**Figure 5-8:**
Desktop
Safari
doesn't
think we
have a
problem.

3. View the source code of the page.

   If the error message gives you a specific line number where a problem was detected, look carefully at that line. However, be aware that the actual error may reside somewhere else in the file and it may just be the symptom that the Error Console is detecting at the line it reports, rather than the cause.

   Figure 5-9 shows the source code of the Mobile Cookbook app. The lines that the Error Console flagged are highlighted for you. Comparing these lines, I see only one `<html>` tag, and the `<head>` is clearly inside the `<html>` tags.

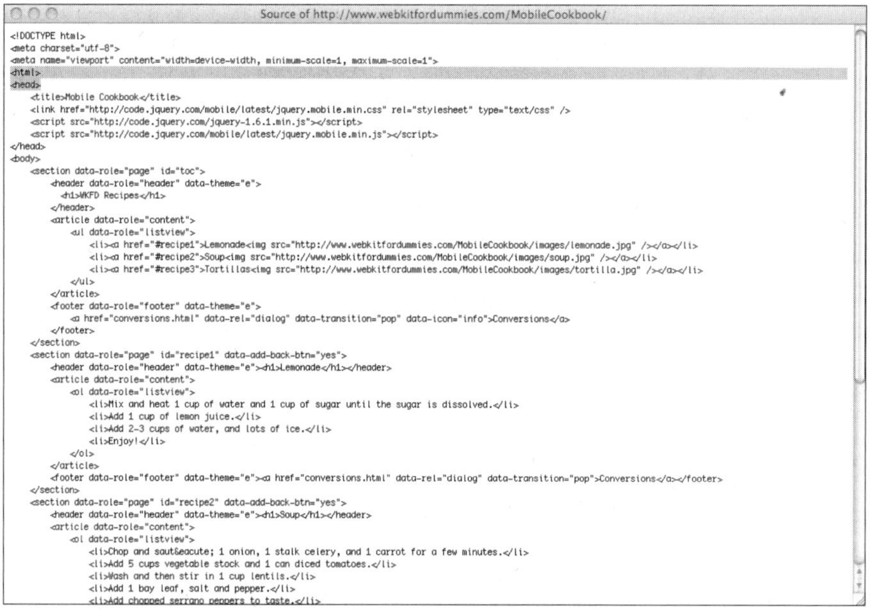

```
Source of http://www.webkitfordummies.com/MobileCookbook/
<!DOCTYPE html>
<meta charset="utf-8">
<meta name="viewport" content="width=device-width, minimum-scale=1, maximum-scale=1">
<html>
<head>
    <title>Mobile Cookbook</title>
    <link href="http://code.jquery.com/mobile/latest/jquery.mobile.min.css" rel="stylesheet" type="text/css" />
    <script src="http://code.jquery.com/jquery-1.6.1.min.js"></script>
    <script src="http://code.jquery.com/mobile/latest/jquery.mobile.min.js"></script>
</head>
<body>
    <section data-role="page" id="toc">
        <header data-role="header" data-theme="e">
          <h1>WKFD Recipes</h1>
        </header>
        <article data-role="content">
            <ul data-role="listview">
                <li><a href="#recipe1">Lemonade<img src="http://www.webkitfordummies.com/MobileCookbook/images/lemonade.jpg" /></a></li>
                <li><a href="#recipe2">Soup<img src="http://www.webkitfordummies.com/MobileCookbook/images/soup.jpg" /></a></li>
                <li><a href="#recipe3">Tortillas<img src="http://www.webkitfordummies.com/MobileCookbook/images/tortilla.jpg" /></a></li>
            </ul>
        </article>
        <footer data-role="footer" data-theme="e">
            <a href="conversions.html" data-rel="dialog" data-transition="pop" data-icon="info">Conversions</a>
        </footer>
    </section>
    <section data-role="page" id="recipe1" data-add-back-btn="yes">
        <header data-role="header" data-theme="e"><h1>Lemonade</h1></header>
        <article data-role="content">
            <ol data-role="listview">
                <li>Mix and heat 1 cup of water and 1 cup of sugar until the sugar is dissolved.</li>
                <li>Add 1 cup of lemon juice.</li>
                <li>Add 2-3 cups of water, and lots of ice.</li>
                <li>Enjoy!</li>
            </ol>
        </article>
        <footer data-role="footer" data-theme="e"><a href="conversions.html" data-rel="dialog" data-transition="pop">Conversions</a></footer>
    </section>
    <section data-role="page" id="recipe2" data-add-back-btn="yes">
        <header data-role="header" data-theme="e"><h1>Soup</h1></header>
        <article data-role="content">
            <ol data-role="listview">
                <li>Chop and saut&eacute; 1 onion, 1 stalk celery, and 1 carrot for a few minutes.</li>
                <li>Add 5 cups vegetable stock and 1 can diced tomatoes.</li>
                <li>Wash and then stir in 1 cup lentils.</li>
                <li>Add 1 bay leaf, salt and pepper.</li>
                <li>Add chopped serrano peppers to taste.</li>
```

**Figure 5-9:** Compare the source code with the messages from the Error Console. Do you see a problem?

4. Try a different, but similar, app. Does it give the same error message?

   This app is a very straight-forward HTML5 page, but with one big difference — it uses jQuery Mobile. Not only is it using jQuery Mobile, but it's using the nightly build of jQuery Mobile. If I were a betting man (who am I kidding? I love betting!), my money would be on a bug with jQuery Mobile at this point.

   Testing to see whether another jQuery Mobile app generates the same error messages is probably a good idea in this case. To test my theory, I wrote the page shown in Listing 5-1, containing nothing but the bare bones of a jQuery Mobile page.

**Listing 5-1:    A Bare-bones jQuery Mobile Test Page**

```
<!DOCTYPE html>
<html>

<head>
  <meta charset="UTF-8">

  <meta name="viewport" content="width=device-width, minimum-scale=1, maximum-
             scale=1">


  <title>Test Page</title>
  <link href="http://code.jquery.com/mobile/latest/jquery.mobile.min.css"
             rel="stylesheet" type="text/css" />
  <script src="http://code.jquery.com/jquery-1.6.1.min.js"></script>
  <script src="http://code.jquery.com/mobile/latest/jquery.mobile.min.js">
  </script>
</head>
<body>

                   This is a test.

</body>
</html>
```

When I checked out my test page with Mobile Safari, I saw the result shown in Figure 5-10.

**Figure 5-10:**
No errors.
The plot
thickens.

If a test of another jQuery Mobile app had produced the same error message, my theory that the problem was with jQuery Mobile would have some supporting evidence, and I could proceed down that path — perhaps by searching or posting on the jQuery Mobile support forum. But, because a simplified app worked with no errors, I have to look elsewhere.

5. Try a different debugging tool.

Here's a little trick I learned from dealing with medical and dental issues: If you don't like the results you're getting from a certain test, try testing a different way.

Because both errors that were detected were HTML errors, I decided to test the page using an HTML validation tool. An *HTML validator* checks the syntax of your page against the rules of the HTML specification and tells you about any errors it finds.

Many HTML validators are available, both as downloadable and web applications. For my test, I decided to use the online HTML validator from the World Wide Web Consortium (W3C), located at `http://validator.w3.org`.

Figure 5-11 shows the result of that test. These are the same error messages that Mobile Safari gives. My conclusion is that there must be a problem that I'm not seeing.

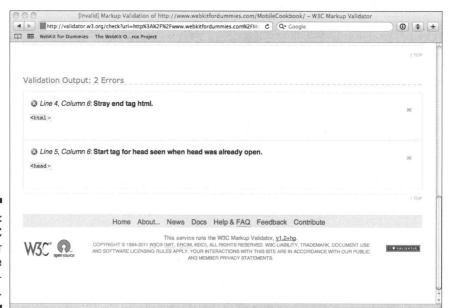

**Figure 5-11:**
The W3C validator says there are problems, too.

6. Google it.

Depending on your style of debugging, searching the web for the error message that you received may either be a last or first resort. Find the part of your error message that isn't specific to your domain or code, put it in quotes, and search. For this error message, I searched for

*"extra <html> encountered. Migrating attributes back to the original <html> element"*

What I found is that there weren't a lot of results, and none of them mentioned jQuery Mobile. That trail had gone cold. It wasn't until I switched my focus from assuming there was a bug with someone else's code to considering the thought that there might be something wrong with *my* code that I finally found the error message.

### Finding and understanding the problem

Most of the results for this search mentioned either typos in the code, or development tools that inserted text into the document that caused the browser to think that the `html` tag was an "extra" `html` tag.

Then it hit me: I looked again at my code and noticed, for the first time, that my `<meta>` elements came before the `<html>`. Look again at Figure 5-9. It was such a rookie mistake that I never even saw it, no matter how many times I looked at the code.

Here's the problem: In HTML, the `<html>` element is what's called the *root* element: All the markup in the document (except for the Document Type Declaration) has to be between its tags — namely, `<html>` and `</html>`. Furthermore, `<meta>` tags are always required to be inside the `<head>` of the document.

Although not technically required by HTML5, it's a good practice to be consistent how you capitalize tags. I use all lower-case letters. I find lower-case letters to be more readable (call me e.e. cummings), and lower-case tags are generally the most widely agreed-upon convention. browsers won't complain if you use all uppercase letters, or even if you use mixed cases. However, most computer languages do care — a lot — about whether things are upper- or lower-case. So, pick something that works for you and stick to it.

However, browsers are forgiving. Even though it's completely invalid for there to be `<meta>` tags before the `<html>` tag, the browser will try to help you out by assuming that you meant to put an `<html>` and `<head>` tag at the beginning of the document, which creates an interesting sequence of events. Looking at the process of rendering the web page as a give-and-take dialog between my code and the browser, I see something like the following:

> index.html: `<!DOCTYPE html>`
>
> *Mobile Safari: "Okay, no problem, chief. You're an HTML5 document."*
>
> index.html: `<meta charset="utf-8">`
>
> *Mobile Safari: "Interesting. I'm going to pretend you said "`<html>`" and then "`<head>`", which would have been the appropriate thing to say before you started in with the `<meta>`. Let me fix that for you. So, now I know that you're an HTML5 document and that you're using the utf-8 character set.*
>
> index.html: `"<meta name="viewport" content="width= device-width, minimum-scale=1, maximum-scale=1">"`
>
> *Mobile Safari: "I know what to do with that. I'm going to render this page full-size in the browser."*
>
> index.html: `"<html>"`
>
> *Mobile Safari: "I already put a `<html>` in your document and now you're giving me another one? You can't put two `<html>` tags in the same document. I'll fix this problem again . . . and this time I'll just completely ignore what you said. But this is just wrong, and I'm going to tell you about it."*
>
> index.html: `"<head>"`
>
> *Mobile Safari: "Not so fast, there, bud. I already put a `<head>` in your document, so this `<head>` is invalid. Jeez, some people!*

As you can see from this example, often the simplest errors are the hardest to track down and resolve. An almost sure-fire way that I could have found and fixed this problem much more quickly would have been to simply have someone else look at my code. Even better would have been to have someone else watching as I was actually writing the code. (This practice of having one developer observe while the other writes code is known as *pair programming*.)

Although at first glance, having two programmers working at one computer would seem to lower productivity, it's actually been shown to *improve* both code quality and coder productivity. There's something about being observed that makes us do better. Plus, programmers working in pairs get the benefit of learning from each other's experience.

### Fixing the error

To fix this error, I opened index.html in Komodo Edit and put the two meta tags inside the `<head>` element, and uploaded my file to the server. Figure 5-12 shows the result when I tested again in Mobile Safari.

**Figure 5-12:** Huzzah! We're error-free!

# Improving Your App with Audits

After you do have a functioning and error-free app, the audits panel is great for finding ways to improve it.

To test the Mobile Cookbook app with the Audits panel, follow these steps:

1. **In WebKit, go to your version of the Mobile Cookbook (if you've deployed it to your own web hosting account), or visit** `www.dummies.com/go/webkit` **to test mine.**

2. **Click the Web Inspector icon in your browser toolbar.**

   The Web Inspector opens at the bottom of your browser window.

3. **Click the Audits tab in the Web Inspector to open the Audits panel.**

4. **Click the Reload Page and Audit on Load buttons.**

5. **Click Run.**

   The current page will reload. When the page finishes reloading, you'll see the results of the Audit, which should look something like Figure 5-13.

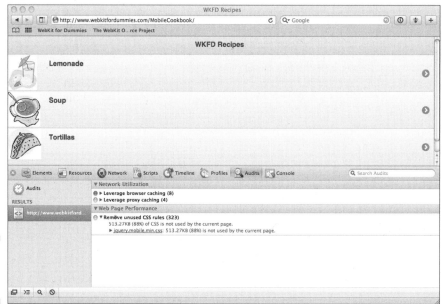

**Figure 5-13:**
The results
of the audit.

6. **Expand each audit result to see what recommendations the Audit tool has made for your app.**

   This audit reveals that in just a few areas, the Audit tool can recommend to improve the performance and network utilization of the MobileCookbook.

   - *Browser caching:* It's possible to tell web browsers how long to cache certain parts of your app by using HTTP `Expires` headers. For example, if you don't expect graphics or JavaScript files on your site to be changed very often, you can specify that web browsers should hold on to a file for a longer time before downloading the latest version.

     Setting expire headers is done on the web server. If you use the Apache web server, you can set Expires headers in the Apache configuration server configuration file (`httpd.conf`), or in a file with the `.htaccess` extension, located at the root of your website.

     Expire headers are set via "directives". These can be written as simple, easily readable statements. For example:

     ```
     ExpiresByType  image/gif "access plus 1 month"
     ```

     This statement instructs a web browser to hold on to `.gif` images downloaded from this server for a month after accessing them.

Doing so helps you reduce to a minimum the resources that must be downloaded the next time a user visits your site.

Mark Nottingham has a very good tutorial on caching on his website at `www.mnot.net/cache_docs/`.

- *Proxy caching:* The second recommendation in the list suggests that you set cache-control to public for certain resources. This is another setting that can be controlled in `.htaccess`. The command for setting cache-control to public for `.gif`, `.jpg`, and `.png` images looks like this:

```
<FilesMatch "\.(gif|jpe?g|png)$">
Header set Cache-Control "public"
</FilesMatch>
```

Setting `Cache-Control` to `public` instructs any devices that cache content before it gets to your browser to cache this content. For example, many business networks have proxy servers that cache frequently-used content on the local network.

- *Remove unused CSS rules:* The audit tool's third recommendation deals with the jQuery Mobile CSS file, which is required to render the nice-looking buttons and effects that jQuery Mobile provides. Because jQuery Mobile is a standardized framework, it contains a lot of code that may or may not be used by any single Mobile Web app. In the case of the Mobile CookBook, a full 88 percent of the jQuery Mobile CSS isn't used.

You can use the audit tool to identify and then remove unused CSS rules from your copy of the jQuery Mobile stylesheet, and thereby save some bandwidth. Or you can optimize caching instead and just accept that browsers are going to have to download a large CSS file the first time they visit the app.

To minimize problems later on when you want to upgrade to the latest version of jQuery Mobile — and to save yourself from having to slog through the stylesheet line by line — it's best to just focus on optimizing caching in this case.

# Chapter 6

# Flying Solo

*U*ntil recently, there was really no real way to make use of web content without an Internet connection — short of printing it out. Every modern web browser now supports new HTML5 standards for making use of data in offline mode. Thanks to WebKit, this capability is also available on mobile devices.

In this chapter, I'll show you some techniques that will make it possible for users to view and use your Mobile Web apps even when they're in airplanes, vacationing in the mountains, sailing the high seas, or sitting in that one spot in their house that never gets reception.

## Making Offline Web Apps

The primary tool for making web apps available offline is the Application Cache (or AppCache). By using the AppCache, you can make your app available even when users click the refresh button or a link when a network connection isn't available. You can also increase the speed of your app while users are online. A single file, called the *manifest,* makes it all possible.

### Writing your manifest

A manifest is a simple text file that tells the web browser what files are needed to run the app.

Here's all you need to do to enable the AppCache:

1. **Create a file with the extension `.appcache`.**

   For example, you may call your file `default.appcache`, or `sample.appcache`, or `fordummies.appcache`.

2. **List the resources that should be cached in this file.**

   This includes HTML pages, JavaScript files, CSS, and multimedia elements. The resources must be listed according to a specific format, which I'll explain shortly.

3. **Link to the manifest file from every HTML page that you want to be available in offline mode.**

Every page that you want to be available offline must link to the cache manifest file. It's not enough to just link to the manifest file from the homepage of your app.

The Mobile Boilerplate — and therefore the WKFD Bookmarks app — uses a manifest file for offline browsing. To see an example of a manifest file, follow these steps:

1. **In Komodo Edit, open the WKFD Bookmarks project.**

2. **Double-click `index.html` in the projects sidebar to open it.**

   You'll see that one of the first lines is the html tag, which contains a 'manifest' attribute, which points to a file named `default.appcache`:

   ```
   <html class="no-js iem7" manifest="default.appcache?v=1">
   ```

3. **Open `default.appcache` in Komodo Edit by double-clicking it.**

   The default Mobile Boilerplate has the following text in the `default.appcache` file:

   ```
   CACHE MANIFEST

           # version 1

           img/l/apple-touch-icon.png

           img/l/apple-touch-icon-precomposed.png

           img/l/splash.png

           img/m/apple-touch-icon.png

           img/h/apple-touch-icon.png
   ```

```
    img/h/splash.png

    css/style.css

    js/libs/jquery-1.5.1.min.js

    js/libs/modernizr-custom.js

    js/libs/respond.min.js


NETWORK:

#http://example.com/api/


FALLBACK:
```

# Understanding the structure of a manifest

A cache manifest file is made up of three sections: the explicit section, the online whitelist section, and the fallback section.

## The explicit section

The *explicit section* begins with the text CACHE MANIFEST and lists the files that the web app requires in order to be available offline. This may include such items as HTML files, images, CSS files, videos, and audio files.

When a browser loads a cache manifest file, the browser immediately downloads all the files in the explicit section. After the download is complete, you can go offline (turn off your Internet connection or climb Mt. Everest), and your web browser will use the cached versions of these files rather than trying to download them.

Cache manifest files don't keep track of whether cached files have changed. This can lead to a situation where you may modify a file that's included in the cache manifest but the browser continues to display the old version of the file because the cache manifest file hasn't changed.

This is where the line immediately after CACHE MANIFEST comes in:

```
# version 1
```

This line starts with a #, or hash symbol, which indicates that it's a comment and is meant to be read by humans, not by web browsers. One of the main reasons for including this line in your manifest, however, is actually what it makes a web browser do.

You need only change a single character in a cache manifest file to trigger a complete reload of all the files in the explicit section. So, by using a version number and updating it every time you want the pages in the app to be refreshed, you gain control over what version of a file is seen by offline users of your app.

If you look at default.appcache in the WKFD Bookmarks app, you'll see that it references each of the files that are linked from the default index. html that comes with the Mobile Boilerplate.

You can check to see whether files are being cached in the AppCache by using the Resources pane of the Web Inspector. Figure 6-1 shows the AppCache window in the Resources pane after loading the WKFD Bookmarks app from www.dummies.com/go/webkit.

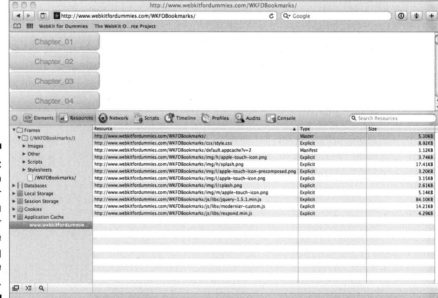

**Figure 6-1:**
The Web Inspector shows you whether files are being saved in the AppCache.

### The online whitelist section

The *online whitelist section* begins with the word NETWORK. In this section, you can define resources that shouldn't be cached. The purpose of this section is to eliminate resources that are network-dependant from your offline cache.

In the case of the WKFD Bookmarks app, the URL to the Google Feeds API shouldn't be cached, because it requires an Internet connection to function.

Currently, the WKFD Bookmarks app, as in its state in Chapter 3, won't function in offline mode. It depends on the Google API and the Delicious API to grab the most up-to-date list of tags from Delicious and to display them. It wouldn't be difficult to modify the app to grab the latest links and store them in a local database, but at the end of all that, you'd still have a list of links — all of which require an Internet connection to view. So, until you have enough bandwidth and storage to download an offline cache of the whole World Wide Web, you're stuck with this app being available online only.

Even in cases such as this where the app is dependent upon the web to operate correctly, using an AppCache still has benefits because it's much faster for an app to access cached local files than to download them.

### The fallback section

The *fallback section* begins with the word FALLBACK. It allows you to specify substitutions for pages that can't be cached or that weren't cached successfully.

Here's an example of a line that you may have in the fallback section:

```
photos/mypicture.jpg   photo/offline.jpg
```

This code simply tells the browser to display the image called `offline.jpg` (located in the photo directory) if the image named `mypicture.jpg` isn't available for some reason.

## Configuring your server for offline Apps

Although manifest files are supported by WebKit browsers, support for them isn't yet built in to most web servers. To support cache manifest files, you must modify how your web server serves files with the extension you use for manifest files. In our case, that's `.appcache`, but you can use other extensions as long as you tell the web server what you're using. For example, you'll sometimes see people use the extension `.manifest`.

If you use the Apache web server, you can simply add the following line to the `.htaccess` file in the root directory of your web app:

```
AddType text/cache-manifest .appcache
```

# Using Offline Databases

The lack of a good way to store data on a user's computer has long been one of the things holding back web applications. Thanks to HTML5, this is changing.

## Web storage

In the past, the only reliable method for storing key/value pairs (or any data at all, really) on a user's computer was with cookies. Cookies have a number of limitations, however, which seriously limit what can be done with them:

- ✔ **Cookies are transmitted to the server with each HTTP request.** If an application stores a significant amount of data in cookies, the additional bandwidth they require can have an impact on performance.

- ✔ **Cookies have a number of security vulnerabilities.** Although cookies are restricted to being accessed by the same site that set them, there are ways that a user's cookies can be compromised by third-party sites. Also, the data in cookies is sent unencrypted, so anyone who gets access to them can read their contents.

- ✔ **Cookies can't store much data.** The amount of data that can be stored in a cookie is very small.

Because of these limitations, HTTP cookies are mostly useful only for storing some sort of unique identifying information (such as a user ID) in a user's browser that links them to a more detailed profile stored on the server.

Web Storage, also known as Local Storage or DOM Storage, is a new API that allows websites to store *key/value pairs* (for example: `myname=Chris`) in a user's browser.

Web Storage is a part of HTML5 and is supported by WebKit and the latest versions of all the major browsers. The major advantages of Web Storage over cookies are

✔ It allows you to store up to 5MB of data in a user's browser.

✔ The data isn't transmitted to the server.

Web Storage allows web apps to store real data on a user's computer the same way that native apps can. Here are some possible uses of Web Storage:

✔ Give your web app a Save button that works offline.

✔ Store sensitive data on a user's local computer, rather than on the server.

✔ Store and remember where a user was in an app when they closed it so that they can be taken there again when they reopen your web app.

✔ Improve performance of your web app by storing frequently used data.

Web Storage actually gives you two different ways to store data:

✔ You use the `localStorage` object when you want to store data without any expiration date. For example, an e-commerce app may store user profile data, or a word-processing app would store user preferences.

✔ The `sessionStorage` object stores data just for the current browser session and erases it when the browser is closed. If you wanted to keep track of where a user is in the checkout process, or keep a user logged in until she closes her browser, `sessionStorage` is the way to go.

Using Web Storage is pretty easy, but you do need to know a bit of JavaScript. Listing 6-1 shows a simple example of how to store a few name/value pairs on a user's computer and then print them out.

### Listing 6-1:   Using Web Storage to Store Some Facts

```
<script type="text/javascript">
  localStorage.firstname="Sparky";
  localStorage.lastname="Minnick";
  localStorage.genus="Felis";
  localStorage.species="catus";
  document.write("Hello, " + localStorage.firstname + " "
  + localStorage.lastname);
            </script>
```

To really see Web Storage in action, you can run the code in Listing 6-1, and then remove the commands that store the data and just run the part that prints out values. Listing 6-2 is a sample web app to run after you run the code in Listing 6-1.

### Listing 6-2:    Run This Code by Itself After Storing the Values

```
<script type="text/javascript">
  document.write("Hello, " + localStorage.firstname + " "
  + localStorage.lastname);
</script>
```

You can use the JavaScript console in WebKit to run the scripts in both Listing 6-1 and Listing 6-2. Simply remove the `<script>` tags from the beginning and carefully type each line into the console, one at a time, completing each line by pressing Enter.

Figure 6-2 shows the results of running these scripts in WebKit. The values are written to the console window when you press Enter, and the `document.write` command writes text to the currently active browser window.

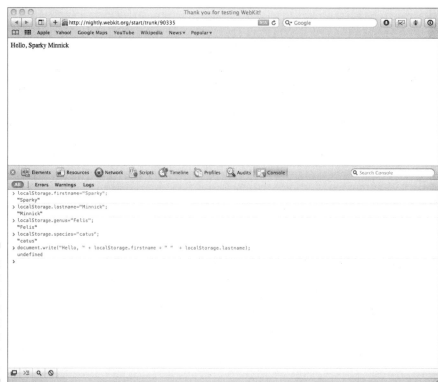

**Figure 6-2:**
Web Storage can be tested using the Web Inspector Console.

To verify that `localStorage` really saves data permanently, follow these steps after you run the commands in Listing 6-1:

1. **Close WebKit.**

2. **Start WebKit again.**

3. **Open the Web Inspector console.**

4. **Type the following code into the console, followed by pressing Enter.**

```
document.write("Genus: " + localStorage.genus + "<br>Species: " +
        localStorage.species);
```

If you typed everything correctly, you should see the `genus` and `species` values printed out in the browser window, along with label text before them.

You can use the Resources pane in the Web Inspector to view all the values stored in your browser. To check, and even modify, values stored using Web Storage, follow these steps:

1. **With the Web Inspector open, click the Resources tab.**

2. **Expanding the Local Storage list in the left column.**

   You should see at least one item — the URL of the site your browser was pointed to when you stored values using the console.

3. **Click the url under Local Storage.**

   A list of key/value pairs will appear in the right column. Notice that you can click any of these values and modify them.

## *Browser support*

WebKit supports Web Storage now, and it's safe to use for Mobile Web apps on most modern devices. As with all HTML5 APIs, it's a good practice to provide a backup plan in case someone with a browser that doesn't support it visits your web app.

Modernizr is a JavaScript library that detects support for HTML5 features.

You may have noticed that Modernizr is included in the Mobile Boilerplate, as I discuss in Chapter 3. To make use of it, all you really need do is download a version of Modernizr and then include it in your web app by using a standard HTML script element, such as the following:

```
<script src="js/libs/modernizr-custom.js"></script>
```

To simply detect whether the current browser supports `localStorage`, you can use the following code:

```
if (Modernizr.localstorage) {
  // do something with local storage
} else {
  //this browser doesn't support local storage
  //try something else
}
```

In JavaScript, two slashes indicate the beginning of a comment, or text that's meant for people to read rather than for the JavaScript engine to read. The JavaScript engine ignores everything from after the second slash to the end of the line.

Beyond simply enabling easy detection of browser support, Modernizr also supports loading alternate methods of supporting those HTML5 elements for which native browser support is lacking. These alternate scripts are called *polyfills,* and they currently exist for almost every HTML5 element.

To detect support for `localStorage` — and then load and use an alternate method if support is lacking — you can use code similar to Listing 6-3. Note that you would change the names of the actual files that you load to reflect the JavaScript files that are actually used in your app. The cute `yep` and `nope` commands are actually the correct code for using Modernizr.load.

### Listing 6-3:   Code for Detecting localStorage Support with Modernizr and Using a Polyfill If It's Lacking

```
Modernizr.load({
  test: Modernizr.localstorage,
  yep : 'storeLocal.js',
  nope: 'storeLocal-polyfill.js'
});
```

Fully covering all features of Modrenizr — and how to use polyfills — is beyond the scope of this book, but it's such a cool and important tool that I would be remiss if I didn't give you a taste of what's possible with it. Visit www.modernizr.com to read the fully documentation, download the script, and learn more.

# Part III
# Mobile Web Fundamentals

The 5th Wave                    By Rich Tennant

"This should unstick the keys a little."

## In this part . . .

Congratulations! You're a mobile Web app developer and you don't have to worry about that anymore. In this part, I show you some of the latest and greatest ideas and technologies that make the mobile Web so exciting.

The mobile Web is going places very fast. With each new advance in Web technology, mobile hardware, and browser engines we get a giant leap closer toward a future where we developers are free to do what we like to do (develop) and where Mobile apps finally get hip to this thing we call the World Wide Web.

On the technical side of things, I'll take you on a guided tour of the core languages that WebKit speaks and understand and that are already powering the next generation of mobile apps.

# Chapter 7

# Web versus Native

*W*hen most people think of smartphone or tablet "apps," they imagine programs (downloaded from an app store) that are tightly integrated with the operating system, such as iOS or Android. These are known as *native* apps.

On desktop computers and mobile devices, however, the differences in capabilities between apps written specifically for one platform and the web-based apps that run inside a browser are becoming smaller. There are some things, in fact, that the web is already much better at than native apps.

There are people on both "sides" of the native and web-app debate who have strong feelings, which can sometimes make it seem like there's some sort of epic struggle going on among mobile developers. This is further complicated by authors who like to write articles and chapters with names like "Web versus Native." (Oops). If HTML5 and WebKit make it possible for better cross-platform apps to be written less expensively, and if the creators of those apps can find a way to monetize them that doesn't involve giving control of your software and a large percentage of sales over to an app store, HTML5 is a natural choice for writing mobile apps.

As to the question of which will "win," I don't believe there needs to be a winner — but as the web standards advocate and CSS expert Eric A. Meyer said, "Betting against the web is the sure losing bet of technology."

It wasn't too long ago that no one could have imagined that the web would ever replace our e-mail programs, home finance software, office productivity suite, and DVD players. Today, it's doing just that. Mobile is the next frontier, and you're at the forefront of the transition. In a couple years, I hope and expect that everyone will look back and wonder why I found it necessary to write this chapter at all. For now, however, I need to dispel some of the myths about Mobile Web apps and put them in the larger context.

# Understanding How Mobile Web Apps Evolved

Not too long ago, Mobile Web apps were fairly limited in their capabilities, and creating them required knowledge of some sort of mobile markup language, such as Wireless Markup Language or XHTML Mobile Profile. Today, these languages are rapidly becoming extinct because of HTML5 and WebKit.

## How Apple invigorated the Mobile Web

Ironically, Apple enabled the sophisticated Mobile Web apps that are possible today. Apple did this by including a full-featured and standards-compliant web browser, Mobile Safari, with the iPhone.

In fact, the iPhone originally didn't have a Software Development Kit (SDK) for developing native apps, and all third-party iPhone apps were web apps. Thanks to Apple, we have WebKit in its present form — and that it's become so ubiquitous on mobile devices.

## WebKit takes off

After Apple introduced the iPhone, other smartphone manufacturers jumped on the bandwagon with enabling full-featured web apps using standard web technologies.

### webOS

When the people at Palm released webOS in 2009, they created an innovative hybrid of web apps and native apps that allows native apps to be created using web technologies. The webOS browser, oh-so-creatively named *web,* is based on WebKit.

Today, Palm and webOS (with the slightly modified capitalization) are owned by HP, although they discontinued the production of webOS devices in October 2011.

### Android

Google's Android operating system also comes with a full-featured WebKit-based browser. Android also has a WebView feature, which allows native applications to embed web content. Many native Android apps simply use WebView to give users access to a web app — which further shows that the line between native and web apps is growing increasingly fuzzy (if not absent altogether).

### Other platforms

Following Apple, Palm, and Google's lead, other smartphone devices now come with a WebKit browser, including these:

- ✔ BlackBerry version 6.0+
- ✔ Nokia Series 40+
- ✔ Polaris 7 series

# Thinking Differently about Apps

Vendors of operating systems and mobile devices have a stake in having the apps written for their devices look as good as possible. The apps are how users interact with their devices — so (naturally) if the apps are shoddy, people will have a negative impression of the device.

Native apps give developers a great deal of power to interact with the device hardware and operating system. This arrangement can be potentially damaging to the overall user experience of the device.

That's one reason why Apple strictly controls distribution and sales of iOS apps through the Apple App Store.

More cynical people may say that another reason Apple tightly controls the distribution of native apps is so it can make a (very sizable) profit on every app sold.

## Benefits of native apps

Despite my belief that native apps are just a temporary solution, they have certain benefits over web apps:

✔ Your app gets listed in a directory that's prominently linked to and from every device that ships for that OS (whether it's Android, Palm, iOS, Blackberry, or another).

✔ Potential users — that is, customers — feel safer using your app because they know it has passed some level of testing in order to get listed.

✔ Positive reviews in a trusted forum, such as an app store, may influence people to download or purchase your app.

✔ An app store makes it easy for people to purchase your app, and you, as the app creator, don't need to worry about implementing the e-commerce and security mechanisms needed for people to buy your app.

✔ Native apps can access the hardware more directly and can thereby integrate with cameras, accelerometers, GPS systems, and other systems that may not be currently accessible to browser-based apps.

✔ Mobile operating systems, such as iOS and Android, have graphical elements, animations, functionality, and standard responses to user actions built in to them — and app developers can use these to give their apps a certain "native" look and feel.

Most of these benefits are business-related, not functionality-related — and web apps are well on the way to replicating them.

## Benefits of web apps

Web apps have the following benefits over native apps:

✔ **Mobile Web apps all use the same core web technologies: HTML, CSS, and JavaScript.** Any device that supports these can run any Mobile Web app. If the device has a WebKit-based browser (which, as you've seen, most do), the developer can expect a fairly consistent user experience across devices.

✔ **Mobile Web apps are "installed" by just going to the URL of the app.** Developers of web apps don't need to get approval from an app store to distribute their apps, and they don't have to pay a fee to an app store when they make money from the app.

- ✔ You don't need to pay an annual fee or subscribe to a vendor's developer program to be a developer of Mobile Web apps.

- ✔ You can fix bugs and release new versions of a web app instantly, without getting approval from the app store.

- ✔ Web apps can be built much faster and at a lower cost than native apps.

- ✔ You don't have to worry about web apps consuming large amounts of valuable storage space on a smartphone. Fewer installed apps means more space for photos, video, and mp3s.

- ✔ Web apps allow you to access your data anywhere. A web-based grocery-list app, for example, would allow you to add items to your list while using your phone and then review your list on your desktop computer (or anywhere else you have access to a web browser). Native apps are often *silos* of data — that is, they store data on your device, and you must connect to a desktop computer or otherwise take some action to get that data off the device.

# Debunking the Myths

"But Chris," I hear you saying, "Aren't web apps slower? Don't they require you to be connected to the Internet to use them? What about games? You can't possibly be saying that all apps can be web apps, are you?"

Okay, calm down — I deal with your questions one by one.

## Myth #1: Web apps are slower

Although some web apps are slower than some native apps, it's also true that some native apps are slower than some web apps. It's fully possible to create a Mobile Web app that is just as fast and responsive as a native app — and, more importantly, an app that *feels* faster and more responsive to the user.

JavaScript performance has become many times faster even just in the last few months. Today, the JavaScript engines used by WebKit browsers actually transform the code into native code prior to running it, which gives HTML5 apps the potential to run every bit as fast as native ones.

## Myth #2: Web apps require you to be connected to the Internet

This is simply not true. HTML5 and WebKit offer a variety of offline storage options, and Mobile Web apps can be developed to be fully functional in offline mode, as I discuss in Chapter 6.

## Myth #3: Some kinds of apps need to be native

This one is partially true, but not to the extent that most people believe. The most common reason people state for mobile apps to be native is usually that the app needs access to device features and hardware, such as the camera, accelerometer, and GPS. Presently, native apps have better access to more of a device's hardware. But the walls are coming down as I write (as you see in later chapters).

## Myth #4: Web apps can never look as good as native

This myth confuses looking "the same" with "as good."

If you read as many peoples' objections to Mobile Web apps as I do, you see that a common feeling is native apps work better or are more responsive. You also see that a lot of Mobile Web apps attempt to emulate the look and feel of native apps exactly (especially the look and feel of iOS native apps). I believe that the attempts to exactly emulate the iOS with web apps are part of the problem.

Web apps and native apps are different creatures. What works for native doesn't always work for web.

Furthermore, when you try to imitate native interactions and features too closely, you risk triggering a negative reaction in the user — in effect, the *uncanny valley* phenomenon — as was suggested by programming guru Martin Fowler in a blog post about cross-platform mobile frameworks (http://martinfowler.com/bliki/CrossPlatformMobile.html).

The phrase originated in the field of robotics: If a robot looks very similar to a human being but is just a little off, the resemblance provokes strong feelings of revulsion. ("Uncanny valley" must have sounded cooler than "Ewww, that thing creeps me out.")

A web app that has all the buttons just right, gets the animations right, and has all the multi-touch navigation aspects of a native app, but that pauses while loading in a different way than a user would expect from a native app risks being perceived as far inferior to a native app because of this one difference.

For web apps, a better approach is often to embrace the parts of the native look and feel that work for your purposes, but also to not be shy about embracing the characteristics and common user interface elements of the web and of the browser that make it such a great platform.

Figure 7-1 shows the iOS version of YouTube, and Figure 7-2 shows the web-app version. The native app has the standard blue iOS header and custom navigation buttons at the bottom. The app is easy to figure out because it uses standard iOS user interface components and standards. The web-app version has a customized header and the Mobile Safari navigation bar at the bottom.

**Figure 7-1:** YouTube's native app for iOS looks very familiar.

Although the standard iOS header color and font are easily duplicated with HTML and CSS, YouTube decided (in this case) to customize the header with the YouTube logo — and to put a link to a custom navigation screen and a search icon in the header — rather than try to make the mobile app look native. The resulting app is, in my opinion, brighter and more exciting than native.

**Figure 7-2:**
YouTube's web app looks great, but not necessarily native.

# Exploring Some Great Mobile Web Apps

The biggest players on the web are getting hip to the potential of Mobile Web apps. Google, obviously, is a huge fan. Just that endorsement alone should be enough to convince even the most die-hard skeptics that the time for Mobile Web apps has come.

Google has created Mobile Web apps for many of its most popular services, including Google Search, Gmail, Google Reader, Google Talk, Google News, and YouTube.

Here are a few more Mobile Web apps to whet your appetite and demonstrate the capabilities of WebKit.

Apple has directory of Mobile Web apps at `www.apple.com/webapps`, although it seems to have abandoned it. A couple other good directories are at `www.makeuseof.com/dir` and `www.zeewe.com`. In addition, `http://openappmkt.com` features plenty of web apps.

## Twitter

The Twitter web app is one of the best I've seen. To try it, simply go to `http://m.twitter.com` with a smartphone. After you log in, you see a screen similar to Figure 7-3. Some of the details to pay attention to are the way you can drag the screen down to refresh and get the latest tweets, the simplicity of the interface, and the nice animated icon that displays while pages load.

**Figure 7-3:**
The Twitter
Mobile Web
app parties
hard on iOS
(left) and
Android
(right).

## Financial Times

In June 2011, The Financial Times (FT) rolled out its Mobile Web app at
`http://app.ft.com`. Figure 7-4 shows FT's web app on the iPad.

**Figure 7-4:**
FT's web
app proves
that great
newspaper
apps don't
need to be
native.

FT's app has allowed them to bypass the App Store while simultaneously providing a better user experience. The app stores data locally so it can be read offline, updates automatically, has more content, and is faster than the old native app.

## TripiT

TripiT.com is a travel planning site that provides a very simple interface to help you organize all the details of trips — including flights, lodging, activities, meals, and so forth.

Figure 7-5 shows TripiT.com's Mobile Web app (www.tripit.com), which has the same functionality as the native app.

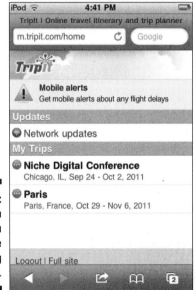

**Figure 7-5:**
Tripit.com helps you organize upcoming trips.

## ESPN.com

ESPN's Mobile Web app at http://espn.go.com/mobile, shown in Figure 7-6, features home page videos that can be scrolled through with swipe motions and live play-by-play updates.

**Figure 7-6:**
ESPN.com has impressive video capabilities, dynamic play-by-play animations, and live updates.

# Chapter 8

# Mobile Web App Design

● ● ● ● ● ● ● ● ● ● ● ● ● ● ● ● ● ● ● ● ● ● ● ● ● ● ● ● ● ● ● ● ● ● ● ● ● ● ● ● ● ● ● ● ● ● ● ● ●

## In This Chapter

▶ Designing for usability

▶ Understanding progressive enhancement

▶ Implementing the W3C Mobile Web Application Best Practices

● ● ● ● ● ● ● ● ● ● ● ● ● ● ● ● ● ● ● ● ● ● ● ● ● ● ● ● ● ● ● ● ● ● ● ● ● ● ● ● ● ● ● ● ● ● ● ● ●

*E*ven if you limit our focus to just browsers that use WebKit, designing apps for these devices still presents a number of unique challenges. In addition to normal design considerations (such as which fonts and colors to use), you also have to consider that your users have wildly different screen sizes, bandwidth limitations, and base operating systems.

This chapter takes a look at some of the latest theories and best practices related to the design of Mobile Web apps. Then I show you some examples and concrete techniques for how to implement them.

Whether you're a Web designer who's making the transition to mobile, or primarily a user of desktop and laptop computers who wants to get into creating Mobile Web apps, you have an adventure ahead. It's important to keep an open mind — not only to the similarities between desktop app design and mobile design, but also to the (very big) differences.

Users of mobile apps are mobile. They aren't seated in one place, and your app most likely doesn't have their full attention. Many of the tips and rules I talk about in this chapter stem from this single fact.

## Design for Many Devices

WebKit and HTML5 have reduced the complexity and cost of entry for cross-platform app development. They have not eliminated those factors, however.

Even if you live in a magic land where you know for certain that all your users will be using iOS, you still have to make adjustments for several different platforms. Older iPods and iPhones don't have the high-resolution Retina display; iPhones and iPods have different capabilities and slightly different screens; older iPhones and iPods are limited in what versions of iOS they can run; there's portrait and landscape modes to consider on each device — and designing for the iPad is completely different. (Yikes.)

If you add Android devices (see Figure 8-1), suddenly you're dealing with much more variability in such things as screen sizes, processor speeds, Internet-access speeds, and device capabilities.

So say you get your app working well on every single iOS and Android device. Good job! But you're not done — not by a mile.

Next, you have to adjust for HP/Palm webOS devices, Blackberry, Windows Mobile, and Opera. Developing true cross-platform Mobile Web apps is not easy. Or quick.

**Figure 8-1:**
The world of WebKit mobile browsers contains multitudes.

So where do you start? My opinion is that it's best to start by understanding the people who will use the app.

# Designing for People

When designing software, it's a common practice to create profiles of your users. These profiles are meant to give you a clear picture of who your users will be. They can be a very helpful tool in helping to define the functionality and user interface of your app.

## Developing user profiles with User Stories

You can record user goals and needs using a technique known as User Stories. Typically, User Stories are very short statements that describe one very specific goal. They follow a format similar to the following:

"As a [*role*], I want [*goal/desire*]."

You can create user stories based on conversations with actual users or based on your knowledge of the users (or potential users). The initial creation of user stories should be a quick-fire process of just recording everything that comes up. Editing and deciding which stories to act on should come later.

After you start developing your app, you'll quickly realize that some of the user stories you wrote are much too complicated to be contained in just a single story. At this point, you should break them up into much smaller chunks. You'll also realize that there are some user stories that don't really fit into your app, or that would make the app too complicated to be used. These user stories should be discarded or filed somewhere where you'll never look at them again.

Here are a few possible user profiles for the Mobile Cookbook app used as a running example in this book. When you're imagining these users of your app, put yourself in their shoes. What would John, Margaret, or Stephanie want to accomplish with the Mobile Cookbook app?

### User Profile #1: Margaret

Margaret is a technically savvy professional woman. She's married with no children, works a full-time job, takes adult-education classes, goes to the gym, and eats out frequently. She cooks meals at home occasionally, but usually just sticks with a few basic dishes that she can prepare quickly from memory and without a lot of complicated steps.

Margaret downloaded the Mobile Cookbook app to her iPad so that she could find something she could make for dinner with the ingredients she has in the refrigerator and that wouldn't take very long.

If you're in Margaret's shoes, a few of your User Stories may be along these lines:

"As a user, I want to search for recipes by how long they take to prepare."

"As a user, I want to search for recipes that use ingredients in my refrigerator."

"As a user, I want to read the recipe while I cook."

### User Profile #2: John

John is a college-educated professional in a high-stress job. On weekends, he enjoys unwinding by cooking and drinking fine wine. He often plans elaborate dinners and dinner parties well in advance. He downloaded the app so he could get ideas and start to plan his Sunday dinner party while riding the train to and from work.

John's User Stories may look like this:

"As a user, I want to create a shopping list of the ingredients involved in recipes."

"As a user, I want to choose and organize recipes to create a meal."

"As a user, I want to make notes on recipes while I'm on the train and then edit them when I get home to my desktop computer."

### User Profile #3: Stephanie

Stephanie is a self-published cookbook author and a mother. She has her own blog where she talks about cooking and food and promotes her book. She downloaded the app in order to get her recipes published in it and get more users to visit her blog and hopefully buy her cookbook.

Stephanie's User Stories may include

"As an author, I want to submit recipes for possible publication in the Mobile Cookbook."

Then, if we assume that Stephanie's recipe was good enough to be published, she may say the following:

"As an author, I want to give readers the opportunity to buy my cookbook."

## Designing for simplicity

In real life, your users probably don't have both of their hands free, and your app probably doesn't have their full attention. They may be grocery shopping, trying to catch a bus, running a marathon, or any one of the millions of things that people do each day. The goal of your app is to help them in some way with some little piece of their day.

Although it's tempting to want to include everything you can imagine in your app, this often will result in clutter and a less usable app. Your goal in designing for mobile devices should be to do a limited number of things very well and with a user interface that's easy to use on the target screen size by someone who is doing something else.

# Progressive Enhancement

*Progressive enhancement* is a "bottoms-up" philosophy and methodology for web development. Its basic idea is to start with something that works everywhere, and then add on features for specific devices and browsers that support them. It's a different approach from "Degrading gracefully" (see the accompanying sidebar for details).

---

## Degrading gracefully

Before many people gave much thought to the Mobile Web, the prevailing strategy for cross-platform web development was *graceful degradation*. This methodology says to build your app with all the gee-whiz features you want, but make sure to do it in such a way that less-capable browsers will still be able to render it and the users of those browsers will still be able to use it.

Graceful degradation meant, for example, that it was okay to use fancy JavaScript drop-down menus and Flash splash screens that don't work on some browsers as long as

✔ You provide text-based alternatives.

✔ The site has some sort of coherence without those fancy drop-down menus.

Graceful degradation has a major flaw, however, that becomes apparent when large (and growing) numbers of mobile device users are using sites built to degrade gracefully, as shown in this image: All these mobile devices are downloading, or attempting to download, a lot of stuff that they can't display. That's a waste of bandwidth and time, and slows down web apps unnecessarily.

*(continued)*

*(continued)*

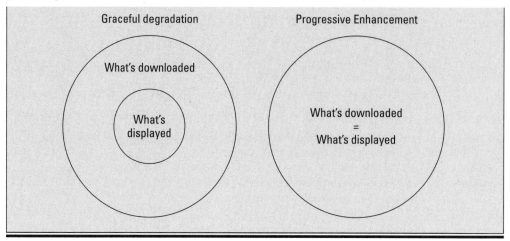

Progressive enhancement is a strategy where web developers start with very basic, but meaningful, HTML that can be read by the most basic web browsers. A good example of a starting point for progressive enhancement would be our Mobile Cookbook app.

Listing 8-1 shows the app in its most basic form, before any JavaScript, CSS, or special jQuery Mobile attributes were added. The code is completely readable and understandable by a person with basic HTML knowledge, and it's simple enough to be understood by any device that can read HTML. In fact, this is basically how the page will be read by a very primitive web browser.

### Listing 8-1:    The Most Basic Form of the Mobile Cookbook App HTML

```
<!DOCTYPE html>
<html>
<head>
  <meta charset="utf-8">
  <title>Mobile Cookbook</title>

</head>

<body>

  <section>

    <header>

      <h1>WKFD Recipes</h1>

    </header>

    <article>
```

```
    <ul>

      <li><a href="#recipe1">Lemonade<img src="http://www.webkitfordummies.
          com/MobileCookbook/images/lemonade.jpg" alt="Lemonade" /></a></li>

      <li><a href="#recipe2">Soup<img src="http://www.webkitfordummies.com/
          MobileCookbook/images/soup.jpg" alt="Soup" /></a></li>

      <li><a href="#recipe3">Tortillas<img src="http://www.webkitfordummies.
          com/MobileCookbook/images/tortilla.jpg" alt="Tortillas" /></a>
          </li>

    </ul>

  </article>

  <footer>

    <a href="conversions.html" data-icon="info">Conversions</a>

  </footer>

</section>

<section>

  <header><h1>Lemonade</h1></header>

  <article>

    <ol>

      <li>Mix and heat 1 cup of water and 1 cup of sugar until the sugar is
          dissolved.</li>

      <li>Add 1 cup of lemon juice.</li>

      <li>Add 2-3 cups of water, and lots of ice.</li>

      <li>Enjoy!</li>

    </ol>

  </article>

  <footer>
    <a href="conversions.html">Conversions</a>
  </footer>

</section>
...
</body>
</html>
```

The structure and meaning of this HTML page is apparent. Furthermore, this page contains all the same functionality as the jQuery Mobile-ized version of the app. Figure 8-2 shows what the basic version of the app looks like in a text-based web browser, Lynx.

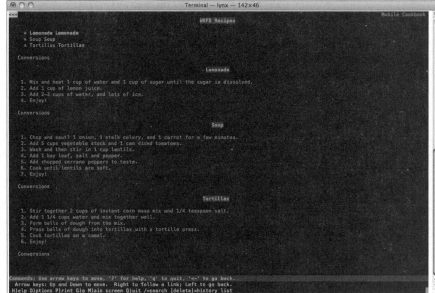

**Figure 8-2:**
The Mobile Cookbook works just fine on this text-based Web browser, Lynx.

If you take out the content and all but the most structural elements of the document, you're left with the very clear and simple document shown in Listing 8-2.

### Listing 8-2:    Reducing the Mobile Cookbook to an Outline

```
<html>
  <head></head>
  <body>
    <section>
      <header></header>
      <article></article>
      <footer></footer>
    </section>
    <section>
      <header></header>
      <article></article>
      <footer></footer>
    </section>
    <section>
      <header></header>
      <article></article>
```

```
        <footer></footer>
    </section>
    <section>
        <header></header>
        <article></article>
        <footer></footer>
    </section>
  </body>
</html>
```

On top of this very basic document, you can then add layers. The way to add layers in progressive enhancement is to use external files. So, instead of including a lot of JavaScript and styling code in our beautiful HTML document, add links to external documents into the header.

Linking to JavaScript and CSS files rather than pasting their contents into the HTML document itself keeps the HTML file from becoming cluttered. It also reduces the amount of code that a browser must download in order to render a page that makes some sort of sense.

Keeping the file size as small as possible is very important for cross-platform Mobile Web app development.

# Mobile First

A further evolution of the idea of progressive enhancement was suggested by Bryan Rieger in his very popular presentation, Rethinking the Mobile Web (www.slideshare.net/bryanrieger/rethinking-the-mobile-web-by-yiibu).

Bryan pointed out that

- ✔ Most mobile users don't have iPhones
- ✔ Most mobile devices don't support a CSS technique (called *@media queries*) that is typically used by Web apps to test for certain capabilities and then to progressively enhance Web apps based on those tests.

Here's an example of an @media query:

```
@media only screen and (max-device-width: 480px)
```

This code allows you to test the maximum screen width. If the device's maximum width is 480 pixels (as is the case for the iPhone, for example), you can include special CSS code for that device.

When a device that doesn't support @media queries encounters an @media query, it simply ignores it, which can lead to unexpected results and a bad user experience.

Listing 8-3 demonstrates one way to use @media queries in a CSS stylesheet. Don't worry if you don't fully understand this code — I cover CSS in Chapter 10.

What's important to see here is that this stylesheet contains two definitions of the section tag:

- ✔ A definition used by default
- ✔ A definition used by devices with a maximum device width of 480px

One big problem with this strategy for supporting mobile devices is that it uses more code (and therefore a larger download) than simply creating a mobile-only version of the stylesheet. This is completely backward: Mobile versions should be smaller because the bandwidth on mobile devices is likely to be more limited than it is on desktop computers.

**Listing 8-3:  Using a Media Query to Create a Mobile Version from a Desktop Version**

```
section {
  width:1000px;
  font-size:148px;
  border:medium solid #000;
}
@media only screen and (max-device-width: 480px) {
  section {
    width:480px;
    font-size:12px;
    border:thin solid #000;
  }
}
```

Bryan suggested that the best way to create truly cross-platform web apps was to write simple HTML code and then test first for the *absence of support* for @media queries before progressively enhancing your page.

This Mobile First strategy assumes that everyone has a very basic mobile phone. If it turns out that they don't, they can download code that will take advantage of their more advanced web browser or larger screen — and this arrangement covers devices all the way up to a desktop computer.

# W3C Best Practices

One good guide to the nitty-gritty of how to design Mobile Web apps is the Recommendation published by the W3C titled "Mobile Web Application Best Practices." The full Recommendation contains 35 things that developers of Mobile Web apps can do to provide the best possible user experience on mobile devices. You can read the whole document at `www.w3.org/standards/web design/mobilweb`. These are the most useful elements you'll find therein:

✔ **Use cookies sparingly.** The W3C discourages the heavy use of cookies in Mobile Web apps. The most important reason for this practice is that cookies are sent to the server with every single HTTP request a browser makes; they can really waste bandwidth if overused.

✔ **Enable automatic sign-in.** Imagine if you had to type a username and password every time you started your word-processing program. Or if every program on your computer had a different login. It's important for apps to secure your personal information, but you should always offer your users the option to be automatically signed in the next time they visit.

✔ **Minimize application and data size.** Besides the obvious meaning of this best practice — that you should limit the amount of data that must be sent to a mobile device — it also refers to *minification,* the (often automated) process of stripping out extra whitespace, comments, and other code from your apps before deployment.

✔ **Avoid redirects.** Redirecting users between pages in a web app takes time and slows down your app. Avoid it if you can.

✔ **Optimize for application startup time.** How long a web app takes to start is often the biggest factor influencing whether users perceive it as on a par with a native app. Use technologies such as AppCache to store files locally and make your app open right up when it's launched.

✔ **Minimize perceived latency.** After startup time, delays while using a web app are the next biggest complaint I hear about them. Although it may not be possible to completely avoid delays while data is being processed or transferred, you can avoid having a negative impact on the user experience by keeping the user informed of what's going on (with progress bars or "spinners" for example) and by doing as much as *possible in the background.*

✔ **Make telephone numbers "click-to-call".** This one is easy. If your users are viewing your app on a phone, they should be able to dial phone numbers in your app by clicking them. Here's how you do this handy trick with a simple HTML link:

*(continued)*

*(continued)*

```
<a href="tel:[PHONE-
NUMBER]">[PHONE-NUMBER]
</a>
```

✔ **Ensure paragraph text flows.** Your app may be seen on screen sizes ranging from very small, feature phone screens to large tablets. If you use fixed widths for paragraphs of text, or try to make your paragraph lines break in certain places, you're going to run into bad user experiences for many of your users.

✔ **Use the Meta Viewport element to identify desired screen size.** The Meta Viewport element can keep certain browsers from zooming out on content that has already been optimized for mobile devices. The standard Meta Viewport element looks like this:

```
<meta name="viewport" content="width=device-
width, initial-scale=1.0"/>
```

✔ **Offer users a choice of interfaces.** No matter how much you do to try to develop your app for every mobile device, there's always going to be something different or a user with different needs. If there is also a desktop version of your web app, you should make sure that all versions of your app automatically try to detect which version is best to show to any one use —, but you should also give users of any version the choice of switching to the other versions if they want.

# Chapter 9

# HTML5

*H*TML5 is the next version of the HyperText Markup Language, which gives structure to the Web. In this chapter, I'll quickly run though how we got to HTML5, talk about what makes it so great, and then jump in to some actual code examples so you can see some pretty cool new technologies that are possible with HTML5 in many of today's desktop and mobile browsers (including, of course, WebKit browsers).

# Understanding How We Got to 5

On WebKit browsers — therefore, on most mobile devices — HTML5 is ready to use right now. In fact, if you've followed this book along to this point from the beginning, you've already used it quite a bit in this book.

HTML5 isn't just one thing. It's actually a bunch of different languages and standards that you can pick and choose from as you develop your web applications. This is great news because it means that you can use parts of HTML5 today even though other parts aren't quite ready for prime time yet.

The road to this point has been long, and it hasn't always been smooth.

## The early years

This chapter isn't meant to be a complete guide to HTML5. I'm going to skip talking about an awful lot of technologies that led up to HTML, the people and organizations that made it possible, the debates and discussions, the early web browsers, the formation of standards organizations and the rest (plenty of other great books cover this stuff in detail), and focus on just a couple of key aspects of HTML and HTML5 to show you why I'm so jazzed about them.

### The little language that could

Back in the late '80s and early '90s, HTML was designed by some academic types to be a document markup language for scientific papers. HTML was used to "mark up" the different parts of documents and show their structure.

For example, a document has a header with a title inside it, a body with paragraphs in it, and so forth. These are shown using "tags" — simple codes inside of brackets. For example, the p tag in HTML stands for "paragraph."

To indicate that some text should be formatted as a paragraph, you simply put it inside a beginning tag (<p>) and an ending tag (</p>), as shown in Listing 9-1.

### Listing 9-1:    A Paragraph of Text

```
<p>The beginning tag, the text, and then the closing
       tag, when considered as a whole, are called an
       element. An HTML document may be made up of
       many individual elements nested together.</p>
```

The beginning tag, the text, and then the closing tag, when considered as a whole, are called an *element.* An HTML document may be made up of many individual elements nested together.

A web browser's job is to look for tags and follow a set of rules about what to do when it encounters them.

Figure 9-1 shows a diagram of a simple HTML page. Notice that every part of it has an equivalent in the pre-web paper world.

Really, there's not much to it — heck, HTML even borrowed most of its syntax almost exactly from a couple of really old languages that were developed in the late '60s and '70s.

So much for the *ML* part of HTML. It was those first two letters (HT) that got a lot of people excited and eventually changed the world — HyperText.

### Putting the hyper in HTML

Tim Berners-Lee, the inventor of the web, didn't invent hyperlinks. What he did invent was HyperText Transfer Protocol (HTTP), which makes it possible for HTML documents to be linked to each other — not just in the same computer or across the same network, but around the globe and between different operating systems and hardware platforms.

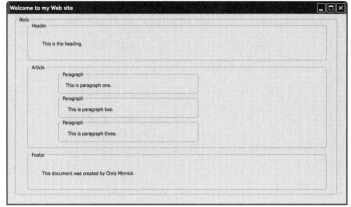

**Figure 9-1:**
Eureka!
HTML
documents
are just
like "real"
documents!

When this beautifully simple markup language, HTML, was combined with this beautifully simple protocol, HTTP, it wasn't long before the World Wide Web was born.

### Lots of people added tags to HTML

As it became more popular, and more web browsers started popping up, the language started growing. The <img> tag was added for linking and displaying images. The <table> tag was added for displaying tabular data (and, later, became a favorite way for people to make all sorts of crazy layouts). The <font> tag was added as a way to change the typeface, size, and color of text. HTML became a do-it-all language.

At around the same time, the World Wide Web Consortium (W3C) was formed to try to bring some order and standardization to this whole thing.

## HTML 3.2 and 4

In 1995, the W3C wrote the first really widely accepted version of HTML, 3.2. It codified all these tweaks that people were making to HTML. In 1997, HTML 3.2 became a real and approved standard.

Less than one year later, HTML 4 was published — which, most significantly, provided support for stylesheets (in particular, Cascading Style Sheets; CSS) and scripting (with JavaScript).

## XHTML

Around 2000, the W3C decided that HTML was too easy to write. So they spent a lot of time reformulating it to make it much more difficult. Just kidding, but it felt that way.

The new language that grew out of this effort was XHTML. The XHTML specification laid out a bunch of rules for how "well-formed and valid" documents must be written. Furthermore, the W3C dictated that web browsers should refuse to display anything at all (except maybe a big red error message) if an XHTML page contained errors.

Needless to say, XHTML didn't exactly catch on as expected. It was a success in wasting a lot of time, however.

Author's note: I co-authored a book about XHTML way back in 2001. To be fair to XHTML, it had good intentions — they just turned out to not be very realistic.

## What's up with WHATWG?

In 2004, while the W3C was still tinkering around trying to develop the next version of XHTML, a group of web browser manufacturers started the Web Hypertext Applications Technology Working Group (WHAT Working Group; also known as WHATWG), and proceeded to get some really cool stuff done toward the goal of extending HTML to make it easier to develop web apps.

Along with the cool web-application technologies the WHATWG invented, it also contributed perhaps the most important mindset changes that took place with HTML5: Instead of focusing on how to make people write better code, it put a lot of effort into figuring out how the language (and browsers) could do a better job at handling errors.

After all, if history has taught us anything, it's that people will make mistakes. Web browsers have always recognized this fact and have done their best to work around it. The WHATWG put the workarounds in writing.

## Meanwhile, Back at the W3C . . .

At the W3C, they were still trying to finish XHTML 2, but web developers weren't paying attention because they hadn't yet figured out how to use XHTML 1.1.

## W3C gets some sense

In 2006, the W3C could no longer ignore what was going on with the WHATWG. Tim Berners-Lee announced that the W3C would work together with the WHATWG to evolve HTML. A couple of years later, the W3C formally abandoned XHTML in favor of HTML5.

# Browsing the spec

A popular trick among computer book authors is to reprint parts of a specification or an entire specification in order to bulk up a book. So, that's what I'm going to do right now! Just kidding — that's not the way *For Dummies* books work.

If I were to reprint the spec here, or if you were to visit it online at `http://dev.w3.org/html5/spec/Overview.html`, you would discover that it's a pretty long and dry document. The HTML5 Specification, although not yet final, comes in at around 130,000 words, by my count (and, yes, I counted each one while I was reading the whole thing).

It's not without its hilarious moments, however, such as this gem near the beginning:

```
1.7.1 How to read this specification
This specification should be
            read like all other
            specifications. First, it
            should be read cover-to-
            cover, multiple times.
            Then, it should be read
            backwards at least once.
            Then it should be read by
            picking random sections
            from the contents list and
            following all the cross-
            references.
```

You'll also find a lot of real-world code snippets in the spec, such as this one, from one of my favorite parts, the cleverly named section 4.4.11.1:

```
<body>
  <nav>
   <p><a href="/">Home</a></p>
  </nav>
   <p>Hello world.</p>
  <aside>
   <p>My cat is cute.</p>
  </aside>
</body>
```

For the most part, however, the HTML5 specification, like most markup language specifications, is not meant to be read by anyone who wants to get real work done (unless his work involves writing about the spec or writing a browser, that is . . . and maybe the first group only really needs to skim it).

In the next part of this chapter, I'm going to get you up to speed with HTML5 with just 1 percent of the page count, and at least 110 percent of the laughs (or at least chuckles?) of the W3C's specification.

### *Now it's serious: We've got a logo*

In early 2011, the W3C unveiled the official HTML5 logo, shown in Figure 9-2. If having a cool logo is how you judge a technical standard these days, HTML5 has arrived. But seriously, I think it's a pretty cool logo.

**Figure 9-2:**
This is probably the best (or maybe only?) markup language logo I've seen.

## *What's the Big Deal with HTML5?*

So, why not just stick with HTML 4 with a sprinkle of XHTML like we've been doing all this time anyway?

Well, to tell you the truth, you're totally free to do that if you want. Realistically speaking, HTML 4 will continue to be supported by browsers well into the future, and your pages will continue to work as browsers become more HTML5-compliant. There are some really compelling reasons to start using HTML5 right now, especially on mobile devices, however.

### *Using Multimedia without plug-ins*

Perhaps the coolest parts, and also the easiest parts to use (in terms of bang for your buck), are HTML5's new built-in video and audio support.

Before I show you just how cool HTML5 audio and video are, I feel that it's important that I set something straight from the get-go. A lot of people are talking about HTML5 video right now, and its potential for eliminating the need for plug-ins.

While it's true that one goal of HTML5 is to reduce or eliminate the need for plug-ins, I get the feeling that there's a big misunderstanding about exactly what HTML5's role is. Just to be crystal-clear: HTML5 does *not* play video in the same way that the QuickTime video player does or the Adobe Flash Player does. HTML5 simply tells the browser to embed the video in a way that is compliant with the HTML5 specification. The web browser does the actual loading and playing of the video.

### HTML5 video

Listing 9-2 shows the code necessary to embed a video in an HTML5 document.

**Listing 9-2:   Code for Video in HTML5**

```
<video src="myvideo.ogg" width="550" height="400">
  <p>Insert text to display for old browsers here</p>
</video>
```

That's all there is to it. The video will be embedded in the page where this element appears. No plug-in is required. If a browser doesn't understand the video element, it will *degrade gracefully* (in effect, not-play what it can't play — see Chapter 8), and it will just display whatever is in between the beginning and ending tags. For example, if you were to open a page containing this code in a browser that doesn't support HTML5 video, it would just display the text `Insert text to display for old browsers here`.

Figure 9-3 shows a video running in WebKit using the `<video>` element. This demo can be found at `www.html5rocks.com/en/features/multimedia`, and it uses some cool effects — a "glow" around the video, as well as picture-in-picture so you can switch between two different videos!

The HTML5 video element isn't magic. What it does, however, is to make use of the same technique described in Chapter 4 with jQuery — abstraction — to make something very complicated appear to be very simple.

The video tag has several options that you can specify, such as whether it will display controls and whether audio will start muted. But, even with every option that you can customize, it remains beautifully simple.

**Figure 9-3:**
A video,
embedded
with the
<video>
element,
running in
WebKit.

The best things about the HTML5 specification defining how browsers should play video, and about HTML5 having a brand new `<video>` tag, are

✔ **It greatly simplifies the process of embedding video.** It takes only one very simple line of code to embed video in an HTML5 page.

✔ **It makes more aspects of the video controllable by the web page.** This makes it possible for HTML5 code to start and stop the video, move the video around the browser window, resize the video, and much more.

✔ **It makes properties of the video accessible to the web page.** This is really handy if you want to display information such as the length of the video or the current play position of the video.

Compare the video tag with what was previously the simplest way to embed video in an HTML page, shown in Listing 9-3. Keep in mind that in order to use this code, you still need to create the `.swf` file that actually plays the video (using Adobe's Flash Professional software), and the users must have the appropriate plug-in (in this case, the Flash Player plug-in) installed on their browsers.

**Listing 9-3:   Simple Code for Embedding Flash Video in an HTML Page**

```
<object classid="clsid:d27cdb6e-ae6d-11cf-96b8-444553540000" width="550"
          height="400" id="movie_name" align="middle">
    <param name="movie" value="myvideo.swf" />
    <!--[if !IE]>-->
```

```
        <object type="application/x-shockwave-flash" data="myvideo.swf" width="550"
              height="400">
          <param name="movie" value="myvideo.swf" />
    <!--<![endif]-->
          <a href="http://www.adobe.com/go/getflash">
              <img src="http://www.adobe.com/images/shared/download_buttons/get_
              flash_player.gif" alt="Get Adobe Flash player" />
          </a>
    <!--[if !IE]>-->
      </object>
    <!--<![endif]-->
  </object>
```

When it was first introduced and became popular, Flash Video greatly simplified the process of posting and viewing video on the Web. Two main factors that allowed it to do so:

✔ **Availability:** Flash Player is almost universally installed in web browsers.

✔ **Simplicity:** Adobe simplified the process of creating and embedding video in HTML.

It's for these same two reasons that HTML5 video is now poised to replace Flash Video: It's even simpler to embed, and all it requires is a browser that supports it (which all new major browsers do).

### HTML5 audio

Embedding audio in a web page with HTML5 is just as simple as video, as demonstrated in Listing 9-4.

### Listing 9-4:   Embedding Audio in an HTML5 Document

```
<audio src="song.ogg" controls="controls">
<p>Your browser does not support the audio element.</p>
</audio>
```

Figure 9-4 shows a demo that can be found at `www.apple.com/html5/showcase/audio`. This demo uses the `<audio>` element to embed an audio clip.

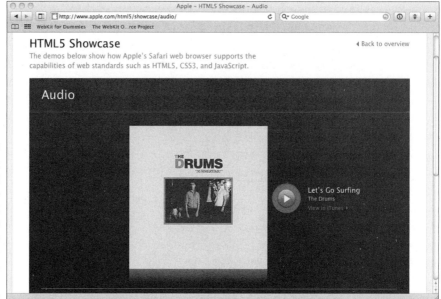

**HTML5 Showcase**
The demos below show how Apple's Safari web browser supports the
capabilities of web standards such as HTML5, CSS3, and JavaScript.

◀ Back to overview

Audio

THE **DRUMS**
*"SUMMERTIME"*

Let's Go Surfing
The Drums
View in iTunes ▸

**Figure 9-4:**
The HTML5
<audio>
element
simplifies
the process
of embed-
ding audio
in HTML.

Both the video and audio files in the previous HTML5 examples use the `.ogg`
extension. This is the extension for the free Ogg container format, which is
used to encapsulate video files that have been encoded using the (also free)
Theora format (for video) and Vorbis format (for audio). You don't need to
use `.ogg` files with HTML5 video and audio, and other formats are supported
by browsers that support `.ogg` files. Internet Explorer doesn't support `.ogg`
files but does have support for `.mpeg` video. To create cross-platform video
with the `<video>` element, you need to make at least two different formats
available. The web browser will decide (automatically) which format to use.

## Simplified syntax

HTML5 has reduced the complexity of certain parts of writing HTML, and it's
positively relaxed when compared to XHTML. Right from the way you begin
documents, HTML5 demonstrates that it's serious about reducing clutter.

Listing 9-5 shows one version (there are actually around nine possible varia-
tions) of the recommended code that must be at the beginning of every
XHTML document.

### Listing 9-5: The Right Way to Start an XHTML Document

```
<?xml version="1.0" encoding="UTF-8"?>

<!DOCTYPE html PUBLIC
  "-//W3C//DTD XHTML 1.1//EN"
  "http://www.w3.org/TR/xhtml11/DTD/xhtml11.dtd">
<html lang="ar" dir="rtl" xmlns="http://www.w3.org/1999/xhtml">
```

Just try to memorize that one. Listing 9-6 shows the correct way to start an HTML5 document.

### Listing 9-6: The Right Way to Start an HTML5 Document

```
<!doctype html>
<html>
```

HTML5, unlike HTML 4, is no longer tied to SGML. SGML is the Standard Generalized Markup Language, developed at IBM in the 1970s and standardized in the 1980s as an ISO standard. It is the granddaddy of most modern markup languages, including HTML, XHTML, and even XML. Although this is unlikely to have any effect on anything you do, it does represent a significant break from the past. The W3C seems to be asking, "Why should we hold ourselves back by trying to maintain compatibility with a markup language that's much less widely used than HTML?" Suddenly HTML is its own language, free to develop in a way that works best *for HTML.*

## Improved interoperability between browsers

For the first time, the HTML5 specification details how browsers should react when they encounter incorrect syntax, rather than simply specifying what is incorrect and leaving it up to browser makers to decide what to do in the case of errors.

This represents a huge change in the thinking behind HTML parsing. Whereas browser manufacturers have long recognized that people sometimes write bad code — and have always tried to make pages render okay in spite of it — the goal with HTML5 is for every browser to handle bad code in the same way.

Additionally, the HTML5 spec was designed in such a way that older browsers will ignore new HTML5 elements. Any HTML5 web pages that you create today will render, in some form or another, on previous versions of web browsers.

Using CSS, you can adapt HTML5 pages to work just fine, and even to look good, on older browsers.

### Cross-platform mobile development

Although not specifically written into the spec, one extremely big benefit that has come out of the development of HTML5 is that the Mobile Web now has a solid language for cross-platform development. It couldn't have happened at a better time, either.

The big players in mobile (Apple, Google, Microsoft, Palm, RIM, and Adobe) have pretty much all rejected each other's favorite native-app solutions, but everyone is excited about HTML5 — and nearly everyone has a web browser based on WebKit.

## Markup Changes

The markup changes in HTML5 can fill a large book (and several are available). Rather than trying to be comprehensive, I'm going to just focus on the changes that will make the biggest different to you right now. For a complete rundown on everything that's new with HTML5, check out "HTML5 differences from HTML4" from the W3C at www.w3.org/TR/html5-diff.

### Out with the old

HTML5 continues the cleanup efforts that began with HTML 4. Several elements and attributes that serve functions that are better done with style sheets or new HTML5 markup have been outdated (or, to put it in W3C language, *deprecated*).

However, the spec recognizes that outdated markup will continue to be, and needs to be, supported by browsers — otherwise millions of web pages would simply break. Accordingly, the spec clearly distinguishes between conformance requirements that apply to content creators and web page designers (the people who build web pages) and user agents (the programs that scan or display those pages, including your web browser).

For example, authors can't consider their documents to be valid HTML5 if they use <font> elements. On the other hand, browser makers can't consider their browsers to conform to the HTML5 spec if they don't render the <font> element.

Some of these elements and attributes were deprecated because they don't really fit in with the big idea of markup language: to describe the structure of a document. For example, elements like <font> and <big> describe how text should be displayed (form), rather than the role the text plays in the document (function). Many of these deprecated elements are from the pre-CSS days of HTML, when they served functions that are better handled today using CSS.

Many of the deprecated elements and attributes were originally deprecated in the HTML4 specification (such as font, applet, and center). In a few cases, attributes were un-deprecated.

The deprecated elements are

| | |
|---|---|
| acronym | applet |
| basefont | big |
| center | dir |
| font | frame |
| frameset | isindex |
| noframes | strike |
| tt | u |

## In with the new

HTML5 defines a bunch of new teams of tags, too. Here are a few of my favorites. All new tags listed here currently work in the latest versions of the major browsers (Internet Explorer, Firefox, Opera, Chrome, and Safari):

- ✔ article is for representing self-contained compositions, such as a blog post, or news story, or forum post.

- ✔ aside is for representing content that is tangentially connected to the content around it.

- ✔ audio is for embedding audio.

- ✔ bdo stands for *bidirectional override*. This element can be used to specify the direction of text. For example, the following markup specifies that the text inside the element should be written from right-to-left:

```
<bdo dir="rtl">
Hebrew and Arabic languages are written from right-to-left.
</bdo>
```

Figure 9-5 shows an example of how the <bdo> element can be used to reverse the direction of text.

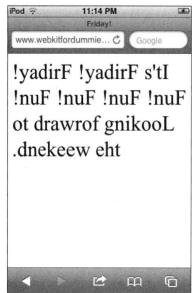

**Figure 9-5:**
Hold it up
to a mirror
to reveal a
secret
message.

- ✔ canvas creates a scriptable and drawable region in the HTML document.

- ✔ figcaption encloses a caption for a figure.

- ✔ figure specifies self-contained flow content that is related the main content of the page, but doesn't change the flow of the document if it's removed. Examples of figure content may include drawings, photos, code, or diagrams. Figure 9-6 shows an example of a document containing a figure.

   The term *flow content* is used to refer to what was previously known as *block* content: the chunks (okay, blocks) of content — such as sections, articles, and paragraphs — that make up the hierarchical structure of the content on your page.

- ✔ footer designates the footer of a document or section.

- ✔ header designates the header of a document or section.

- ✔ hgroup is for grouping together headers within a document. For example, it's common in magazine articles to have a head and a subhead. With hgroup, you can indicate that the two elements belong together. Here's an example:

```
<hgroup>
  <h1>Mama Tried<h1>
  <h2>The Story of Merle Haggard</h2>
</hgroup>
```

- ✔ mark designates text that should be highlighted.

- ✔ nav identifies navigation links.

✔ `section` defines a section of a document.

✔ `source` defines media resources for media elements, such as `<audio>` and `<video>`. Here's an example:

```
<audio>
    <source src="swingingdoors.ogg" type="audio/ogg" />
    <source src="swingingdoors.mp3" type="audio/mp3" />
</audio>
```

✔ `video` defines a video.

**Figure 9-6:**
Figures inserted into the main body content don't affect the flow if they're removed.

# Checking Out HTML5's New APIs

Besides containing new ways to define data, HTML5 also contains a bunch of new application programming interfaces (APIs) that enable some incredible (and incredibly useful) new functionality in the latest bunch of browsers. I detail some of these in later chapters; meanwhile, here's a brief taste of what's possible with a few of them. . . .

## Contacts API

The Contacts API (`www.w3.org/TR/contacts-api`) allows web apps to access a user's address book. This one is particularly handy for mobile devices.

# Media Capture API

The Media Capture API (www.w3.org/TR/media-capture-api) provides access to the audio-, image-, and video-capture capabilities of the device.

# Calendar API

The Calendar API (www.w3.org/TR/calendar-api) defines a mechanism for web apps to access the user's calendar.

# HTML5 Web Messaging

When AJAX techniques were invented, a major stumbling block was that browsers prevent web pages from different sites that are being displayed in the same window (usually with iFrames) from talking to each other. This restriction was in place because of very legitimate privacy and security concerns.

The result of this restriction, however, was that web developers had to create strange mechanisms in order to let different websites share data.

HTML5's Web Messaging API (www.w3.org/TR/webmessaging) resolves this problem — and thereby enables more secure use and combination of various Web-based services.

# Geolocation

The Geolocation API (www.w3.org/TR/geolocation-API) provides access to information about the physical location of the device.

# Offline storage

The Web Storage API (www.w3.org/TR/webstorage) gives you the ability to store key/value pairs on a user's computer (as you saw in Chapter 5).

The Indexed Database API (www.w3.org/TR/IndexedDB) gives web apps access to more sophisticated database technologies, which can be optimized for searching and sorting.

# Chapter 10

# CSS3

Cascading Style Sheets (CSS) is the language that's used to tell a browser (or other user agents) how to format an HTML document. CSS makes it possible for you to create web pages and web apps that keep style and content separate — which makes them much more flexible and easier to maintain, as you'll see in this chapter.

# The Elements of Style

To use CSS, you write rules that point to — *select* — elements within your HTML document. After you identify the element or elements that you want affected by the CSS rule, you can set properties of that element to cause the browser to display it in a different way.

Listing 10-1 shows a basic HTML document. Notice that all the markup simply describes the purpose of the content.

**Listing 10-1:  A Simple but Logical HTML5 Document**

```
<!DOCTYPE html>
<html>
<head>
  <meta charset="utf-8">
  <meta name="viewport" content="width=device-width, minimum-scale=1, maximum-
              scale=1">
  <title>Testing CSS</title>
</head>
<body>
  <header>Hi World!</header>
  <article>
    <p>It's time to learn some CSS!</p>
  </article>
<footer>with Chris Minnick</footer>
</body>
</html>
```

Figure 10-1 shows the code in Listing 10-1. This is a very plain-Jane document with no styles applied to it other than the default styles applied by the web browser.

Listing 10-2 shows a CSS file that can be used to style the HTML in Listing 10-1. Notice that it contains references to the elements in the HTML document, followed by code inside of curly brackets. These references to the HTML elements are *selectors*. I'll talk more about them in just a bit.

The purpose of CSS is to describe how the HTML element should be styled ("presentation semantics," if you like fancy words) rather than what they mean or the role they play in the logical structure of the document.

**Figure 10-1:**
An unstyled HTML document uses the default browser styles.

## Listing 10-2:  A CSS File, style.css

```
@import url(http://fonts.googleapis.com/css?family=Luckiest+Guy&v2);
body {
  font-family: 'Luckiest Guy';
  }
header {
  font-size: 36px;
  -webkit-animation-duration: 3s;
  -webkit-animation-name: slidein;
}
@-webkit-keyframes slidein {
  from {
```

*(continued)*

**Listing 10-2** *(continued)*

```
    margin-left: 100%;
    width: 300%
    }
    to {
    margin-left: 0%;
    width: 100%;
    }
}
article {
    -webkit-border-radius: 15px;
    background: -webkit-gradient(linear, left top, left bottom, from(#999),
              to(#ccc));
    height: 200px;
    padding: 10px;
    border-style: solid;
    border-width: thin;
    border-color: #000;
}
p {
    font-size: 18px;
}
footer {
    float: right;
    margin-top: 2px;
}
```

To style this document by using the rules in `styles.css`, you just need to reference those rules by linking to them inside the `head` element of the document with the following code:

```
<link rel="stylesheet" type="text/css" href="style.css" />
```

Figure 10-2 shows the code in Listing 10-1 when the code in Listing 10-2 is applied to it.

**Figure 10-2:**
Adding style
can make a
page much
more
exciting.

If you're trying this code at home and in your WebKit browser, you'll get a special surprise: the Hi World! header will fly in from the right of the screen when the page loads.

# Using Selectors to Choose Elements

CSS style rules are applied to elements based on selectors. *Selectors* are patterns that match the element in HTML documents based on a variety of aspects of the element.

## Resetting browser default styles

Every web browser has a set of default styles built in to it that it uses as a backup when you don't explicitly define a style for an element used in the document. For example, this code tells a browser to display the text between the tags as a first-level header.

```
<h1>This is a header</h1>
```

In WebKit browsers, the default way to display a first-level header is with a font size of 2em, bold, and with a .67em top and bottom margin.

Other browsers may display elements differently by default. This can lead to inconsistent display of your web app in different browsers or on different platforms.

You can view the default WebKit stylesheet at

```
http://trac.webkit.org/browser/trunk/Source/WebCore/css/html.
    css
```

You can view the default Mozilla stylesheet by typing the following into your browser address bar while using a Mozilla browser, such as Firefox:

```
resource://gre/res/html.css
```

The solution to inconsistencies between browser default styles is to use a "reset" stylesheet. Perhaps the most complete reset stylesheet is the one created by Eric Meyer, which is available from his website at `http://meyerweb.com/eric/tools/css/reset/`.

A reset stylesheet resets all default element styles and gives you a baseline set of styles that will be nearly consistent on any browser. The result is that styling cross-platform web apps is more predictable.

## Getting to know your first selectors

The two most basic selectors are element type selectors and the universal selector. *Element type selectors* are used to redefine the style of an element, such as p, img, or div. Listing 10-2 uses a number of element type selectors. For example, take a look at the following:

```
p {

  font-size: 18px;

}
```

This rule says that every p element should have a font size of 18 pixels (px) applied to it.

Element type selectors are formed by simply putting curly brackets after the element name and putting CSS rules inside the brackets.

The universal selector, *, can be used to change the style for every element. For example, to quickly make sure that no elements in a document have borders, you can use the following code:

```
* {
  border: none;
  }
```

## Using more advanced selectors

Element selectors and the universal selector are like the dynamite of CSS — they make it easy to do a lot of work very quickly, but with not much precision. When you need to get down to fine details, CSS lets you be much more precise.

Other selectors include

- ✔ **Class selectors:** Applied based on the value of a class attribute in an element. They're meant to be used to apply to a group of similar content. For example, you may have a class called warning that you use throughout your app. In the HTML, you'd need to add class="warning" to every element that should be styled using the warning class selector.

  ```
  <p class="warning">You can never add too much water to a nuclear reactor.
          </p>
  ```

  Class selectors start with a period, as in the following example.

  ```
  .warning {
    font-color: red;
    font-weight: bold;
    }
  ```

- ✔ **ID selectors:** Used to apply a style to a particular element in a document. In the HTML, each element can have a unique id, like this:

  ```
  <div id="footer_logo"></div>
  ```

  ID selectors start with a # symbol:

  ```
  #footer_logo {
    background-image:url('fordummies.gif');
    }
  ```

✔ **Attribute selectors:** Select elements based on the value of any attribute. For example, the following selector will apply the CSS rule if the value of the type attribute is password.

```
[type="password"] {

}
```

✔ **Pseudo-classes:** Act the same as a regular class, but they aren't explicitly written into the document. A pseudo-class is defined by a colon (:) in the CSS.

HTML links, for example, have pseudo-classes for link, visited, and active. Pseudo-classes are referenced in style sheets by using the colon symbol.

```
:hover {
  font-weight: bold;
  }
```

## Chaining selectors together

Selectors can be chained together in any combination. By chaining selectors together, you can do things like the following:

```
.warning a:hover {
  font-color: blue;
  }
```

This rule will cause links inside an element that belongs to the warning class to turn blue when you hover your mouse over them.

# Navigating the C in CSS

At this point, you may be asking yourself what happens if multiple style rules apply to the same element. For example, consider this HTML:

```
<p class="normaltext">Here is some text</p>
```

If a stylesheet attached to the document containing this HTML contained the following two style rules, how would this paragraph be styled?

```
p {
  font-size: 18px;
  }

.normaltext {
  font-size: 12px;
  }
```

The answer to this question is determined by *cascading,* which refers to the rules that browsers use to determine which style to apply to a given element. The browser assigns importance, or weight, to different style rules based on the cascade order defined in the CSS specification.

You can picture elements in an HTML document falling down a series of steps on their way to the user's eyes. At each step, the elements pick up style rules, such as size, color, border, and so forth. Style rules with higher weights are placed on lower steps and override any conflicting rules that may have been applied earlier in the cascade.

Because the .normaltext selector follows the style rule associated with the HTML p element in the preceding CSS, the HTML that references the normaltext class will be rendered in a font that's 12px in size.

## Defining selector importance

Three main factors determine the importance of a rule — ownership, specificity, and order.

### Ownership

CSS rules can be created (and therefore "owned") by the browser, the author, or the user. The most important of these, all other things being equal, are the rules specified by the author.

After author rules, the user rules are considered. User rules are styles specified in a user style sheet. It's not generally well known, but every browser has a way for users to specify styles that should be applied to the sites they visit.

In WebKit, you can specify a user style sheet by choosing Preferences⇨ Advanced and then choosing Other from the Style sheet drop-down menu. You can then select a stylesheet on your hard drive. After restarting Safari, the new styles will be applied to web pages (in accordance with the cascading rules, of course).

Although author styles typically override user rules in the event of a conflict, users who want or need to make sure that their style rules are always followed can add ! important to the end of a style rule to make sure that the browser uses it.

For example, the following style rule will cause text within p elements to always be displayed 50-percent larger than otherwise displayed.

```
p { font-size: 150%;!important }
```

Last in the order of importance for ownership are style rules set by the browser.

### Specificity

CSS rules can be applied to many elements or to a single element. Selectors that are used for styling many elements are lower in importance than selectors that apply to only one element.

For example, your stylesheet may make the following declaration:

```
p {font-size: 24px;}
```

Another rule in the same stylesheet may say the following:

```
p.first {font-size: 36px;}
```

This rule identifies a group, or class, of p elements as "first," and then specifies that they should have a special, larger font size. Paragraphs that don't use the first class will continue to have text size of 24px.

### Order

Finally, browsers consider the order in which rules were defined in making a decision. As a simple example, imagine that your stylesheet contains this line:

```
p {font-size: 12px;}
```

and then later in the document, it has this one:

```
p {font-size: 10px;}
```

The font-size for p elements in this document — unless it's overruled somewhere else — is 10px because that's what the last rule of two identical selectors said.

## Studying the browser's logic

The Style pane in WebKit's Web Inspector, when used in combination with the Elements tool, can give you valuable insight into why an element looks the way it does in a browser.

To see how a browser arrives at a particular style for an element, do the following:

1. **Start WebKit and go to** www.webkit.org/.

   Or, if you're tired of looking at that site, choose another site and change my directions accordingly.

2. **Click the Web Inspector icon to launch the Web Inspector.**

   The Web Inspector window opens at the bottom of your browser.

3. **Open the Elements tab and then select the Inspector tool (the magnifying glass).**

   The tool turns blue, and selected parts of the web page are highlighted as you hover over them.

4. **Click an h2 element in the web page.**

   You can find an h2 by moving the Inspector tool around the window.

   Figure 10-3 shows what happens when you click the words `Getting Involved`. Clicking an h2 element displays the code in the Elements window; the style rules applied to it appear in the Styles pane.

**Figure 10-3:**
Click an h2
element.

There's a lot of information here, but the first thing you should notice is that some of the style rules in the Styles pane are crossed out. If you look closely at which ones these are, you'll see that one of them is inside the h2 element that is defined by the User Agent Stylesheet. As mentioned earlier, this is the stylesheet that defines the default style for elements.

What the WebKit.org site has done is override the User Agent Stylesheet definition of the h2 font size (1.5em) with a different font size (16px). As you probably figured out, this was done because the author's stylesheet is considered more important than the browser's stylesheet.

# Learning CSS3 Modules

CSS version 3 has been in the works since 1999. Rather than being defined by one huge document (as the previous versions were), the CSS3 specification is divided into parts called *modules*. Today, there are more than 40 CSS3 modules: some of them in a very stable, or complete, form, and others that are still in earlier phases of development.

In this section, I take you through some of the great new CSS3 capabilities that you can use right now in WebKit browsers.

## Understanding browser prefixes

Because the CSS3 spec is still a work in progress, different browser engines have implemented different ways of doing things. Because their versions of new CSS rules may be nonstandard, browser makers have added prefixes to their implementations of the rules to identify them as the browser's version of the rule, rather than a standard CSS implementation.

For example, the CSS3 `border-radius` can be used to create rounded corners. However, if you want to use `border-radius` with WebKit browsers, you currently need to use `-webkit-border-radius`. Likewise, if you want to use it with Mozilla-based browsers, use `-moz-border-radius`; and for Opera, use `-o-border-radius`.

For now, the safest bet when developing web apps is to use multiple browser prefixes for each CSS3 rule. And because this is a book about WebKit, I'm just going to use the WebKit prefix. If you want to use the markup you see here in this book on your own website, you should identify your target browsers and include proper prefixes to match them.

## Media queries

*Media queries* provide web page authors with a way to test browsers for certain characteristics and use different stylesheets depending on the results. Media queries are logical expressions that produce a `true` or `false` result. They can be placed in a media attribute of the HTML `link` element or in an `@import` rule in the CSS, or they can be written with an `@media` rule in the CSS.

Here's an example media query that resolves to `true` when the device displaying the page is a screen (as opposed to a projector, or a printer, for example) with a maximum width of 480px.

```
@media screen and (max-width:480px) { ... }
```

Between the curly brackets, you can place CSS rules that should be used only if the media query is `true`.

Here are a few more examples of media queries:

```
@media all and (orientation:portrait) { ... }
@media all and (orientation:landscape) { ... }
@media all and (min-width:300px) { ... }
```

Here's an example of how to use a media query in an HTML `link` element to tell a browser to load the stylesheet if the page is viewed on a color screen:

```
<link rel="stylesheet" media="screen and (color)" href="color.css">
```

## CSS multicolumn layout

The multicolumn layout module defines two ways to flow text in columns: specifying the width of each column or specifying the number of columns.

To use the column-idth method, you can use the `column-width` rule:

```
-webkit-column-width: 14em;
-webkit-column-gap: 1em;
```

To create a multicolumn layout by defining the number of columns, use `column-count`, like this:

```
-webkit-column-count: 3;
-webkit-column-gap: 1em;
```

## Borders

CSS3 has some cool new things you can do with borders.

### border-color

Create multicolored borders for elements.

This is currently supported only in Mozilla.

### border-image

Use an image for a border.

```
.starbox {

  border:30px;

  -webkit-border-image: url(star.jpg) 30 30 30 30 round round;
}
```

### border-radius

Create rounded corners.

```
-webkit-border-radius: 1em;
```

### box-shadow

Create super-cool drop shadows on boxes. You can specify the color of the drop shadow, size, blur, and offset.

```
-webkit-box-shadow: 5px 5px #dadada;
```

## Text effects

New CSS3 properties can make your text look much better by applying effects to them without requiring you to convert them to images, as was previously the only way to do fancy things with text. Here are a few of the better-supported text effects.

### text-shadow

Create a shadow behind text. It takes four parameters (in this order): x-axis, y-axis, cast-length/feathering, and color.

```
text-shadow: 3px 3px 3px #000;
```

### *word-wrap*

Allow long words to be broken and wrap to the next line. It has two possible values: `normal` or `break-word`.

```
word-wrap: break-word;
```

If this property is set to `normal`, a long text element (a ULR, for example) will push the boundaries of an element. If it's set to `break-word`, though, long text elements are broken up and wrapped to the next line.

# Chapter 11

# Scripting with JavaScript

*J*avaScript is a *scripting language* — a type of programming language that is generally easier to learn than full-blown programming languages and is used for smaller tasks. At least that used to be the idea behind the distinction.

Today there are so many powerful and capable scripting languages that are used for so many tasks (not all small) that the line between scripting and programming really has become meaningless. JavaScript has become quite a powerful language for enabling interactive web applications on just about any web browser.

In earlier chapters of this book, you can see how HTML gives your Mobile Web apps structure, and how CSS gives them style. In this chapter, you get a look at how JavaScript makes your apps actually do things. Also, you can see some JavaScript in action in earlier chapters, working with Google's APIs and jQuery. Now I'm going to take a step back and show you how JavaScript works at a lower level.

My goal with this chapter isn't to make you into a JavaScript ninja, but give you a practical understanding of what JavaScript does and to make you comfortable with how you can use it to make your Mobile Web apps more dynamic.

# Understanding the Role of JavaScript

JavaScript is typically either linked from HTML pages or embedded in the page directly using the `<script>` element. WebKit translates the JavaScript you write into a language it can understand (through the process known as *compilation)* and then runs it.

JavaScript is what is known as a *client-side* scripting language. To understand what that means, you need to have an understanding of client-server computing.

## Client-server computing

Your experience of the web is made possible by two main components: a server and a client. The *server* is a piece of software whose job it is to listen for requests and send data (such as web pages and images) in response. A *client* is software whose job is to request and process that data.

In the case of the web, your web browser is the client, and a web server program is the server. The interaction and division of tasks between the client and the server is *client-server computing.*

## Running scripts on the server

Web servers usually run on computers that are designed and optimized for serving files as quickly as possible. Such computers are also called servers. So yes, you can have a server running on a server. (Yeah, I know — confusing. It's been that way for years.)

Programs that run on the same computer as the web server are referred to as *server side.* Programming languages such as Perl, PHP, Java, Python, C, and Ruby are typically used for server-side processing of data. Web browsers, on the other hand, typically run on computers that are doing a lot of other things (such as playing MP3s, running word processors and spreadsheets, sending IMs and e-mails, and so forth).

In the old days of client-server computing, clients were considered "dumb": Their only job was to just display what came down from the server. The web browser was originally an extension of this model. Most of the heavy lifting on the web was traditionally done on the server, which is what made those tasks "server side."

## *Running scripts on the client*

The days of the dumb client are gone (well, not entirely, but that's a story for my secret blog). Today, user's computers are very capable of doing sophisticated data processing. Most often, when web apps are involved, this client-side processing is done with JavaScript.

As client computers become more powerful and JavaScript engines become more highly optimized, great app speed and functionality benefits can be achieved by shifting more of the work of the web to the browser. The benefit to the user comes from familiarity: The closer to the user the action happens, the more responsive — and the more like a "native" app — a web app will feel.

For example, in the old "dumb-client" web, a web page required an entirely new page to be downloaded from the server each time something needed to change on the user's screen. Modern web apps use techniques such as AJAX to modify only the parts of the screen (or onscreen data) that must be updated. Much faster.

# *Writing JavaScript Code*

Listing 11-1 shows a very simple JavaScript program that will display a list of numbers. To try this code, just create a new HTML document in your code editor and enter it anywhere inside the <head> or <body> of the document.

Figure 11-1 shows the result of running this program in your web browser. Notice that the program is only a few lines long yet prints 10,000 numbers. This very simplistic example demonstrates the power of programming to do things that would otherwise be tedious or impossible.

**Listing 11-1:    Printing a List of Numbers with JavaScript**

```
<script>
  var i;
  for (i=1; i<=10000; i++) {
    document.write (i + " ");
  }
</script>
```

The WebKey Web Inspector Timeline is open in Figure 11-1. I recorded the loading of this page to show that the actual counting took the browser about one second on my computer (with several browsers, a word processor, iTunes, and much more running at the same time).

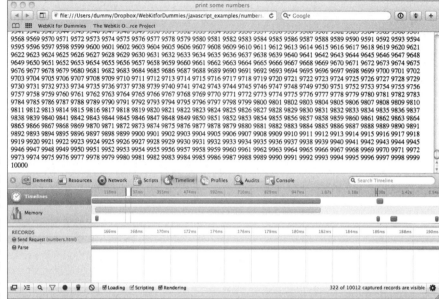

**Figure 11-1:**
JavaScript is great for automating tasks that would otherwise be very dull.

This example demonstrates a number of important principals of JavaScript programming, so I'll go through it line by line. After that, I show you a JavaScript program that does something that's a bit more useful.

## Creating an HTML5 script block

First, the `<script>` element is used to enclose the JavaScript code. Previous versions of HTML required you to specify what scripting language you were using by including a "language" attribute in the script element. HTML5 is smart enough to just assume that you're using JavaScript (and it will be correct almost all the time).

## Holding data in variables

The second line of this mini-program creates a new variable, using `var`. Variables in programming are like boxes for data. They can contain numbers, letters, words, and more. The contents of the variable are its `value`. They're called variables because the value of a variable can be changed, as you see happening in this example.

Within certain rules, variables can be named anything you want. For the sake of brevity, I called this variable `i`, but I just as easily could have written it with a variable name of `bunnies`:

```
var bunnies;
```

Variables' names function like labels stuck on boxes; they refer to data they contain.

## Looping with a for statement

Line 3 of Figure 11-1 is a `for` loop statement. Loops in programming are used when you want a line, or multiple lines, of code to run repeatedly.

```
for (i=1; i<=10000; i++){
```

The `for` statement has three parts:

- ✔ **Initialization:** Initialization (`i=1`, or `bunnies=1` if you decided to change the variable name) is where the initial value of the variable is set. No matter how many times the for loop loops, the initialization command is executed only once — prior to the first run-through.

- ✔ **Condition:** The condition (`i<=10000`) is evaluated to determine whether to run the next part and to continue with the loop.

- ✔ **Modification:** The last part of the `for` statement tells how the variable will be modified with each loop. In this case, I'm using a special shortcut (`++`) to increment the variable by one. Another longer way to write the same thing is `i++` is `i=i+1`.

    In other words, just increment 1 to the value of `i` every time you loop.

Notice that this line ends with an opening curly bracket (`{`). This bracket is used to indicate the beginning of the code that should be run with each loop.

## Writing to the document

The next line in the program is this:

```
document.write (i + " ");
```

This line uses the ability of JavaScript to write text into the HTML document (`document.write`). The part of the statement in between parentheses specifies what should be written. In this case, I'm telling JavaScript to write the value of `i` and to combine (`+`) that with a blank space (`" "`). The semicolon at the end of the line simply indicates that the statement is complete.

On the next line, the closing curly bracket (`}`) tells the JavaScript interpreter that I'm at the end of the `for` loop and that it should return to the beginning of the `for` loop statement and check whether the condition is still true before proceeding with the modification and then the code between the curly brackets again.

Finally, the ending tag of the script element (`</script>`) indicates to the browser that it should stop interpreting the text as JavaScript code.

# Speaking Precisely

HTML coders and designers working with JavaScript often find the most difficult aspect to be the precision that it requires. JavaScript is actually more forgiving than most other programming languages, but it certainly won't let you get away with the kind of questionable (or bad) coding practices that HTML5 interpreters will let slide.

JavaScript has a few strict rules that must be obeyed in order for a program to run without errors. In programming, the rules about how code must be written are the *syntax*. Errors that result from violations of these rules are *syntax errors*. If you find that you can't seem to get a JavaScript program to run correctly, it may be simply that you violated one of the rules.

In my experience, when a simple JavaScript program fails to run, it's almost always the result of one of a few syntax errors. Computers are great at noticing typos and tiny misspellings. People, not so much.

## Pay attention to your capitalization

JavaScript is case sensitive. If you name a variable `tiger` in one place and then use `Tiger` (with a capital T) in a different place, these are not the same variable. The same goes for JavaScript commands. If you write a `for` loop but spell it `For` (with a capital F), JavaScript interpreters will refuse to run your code.

## Separate your statements correctly

Each statement in a JavaScript program should either be on a separate line or should have a semicolon at the end of it. To be safe, it's always best to end a statement with a semicolon.

## Put strings in quotes

Characters that are meant to be treated as textual data (as opposed to numbers, for example) are *strings* and must be enclosed in either single or double quotes. For example, to give a variable named `color` a value of `blue`, use the following statement:

```
var color="blue";
```

The following statement would also be valid:

```
var color='blue';
```

This one, however, would result in an error:

```
var color='blue";
```

And this one would cause an error or unexpected results:

```
var color=blue;
```

A JavaScript interpreter would see the previous statement, without quotes around the word `blue` and think that you're trying to set the value of the `color` variable equal to the value of a variable named `blue`. If this variable doesn't exist, JavaScript will set the value of color to `undefined`.

That's enough about the rules for now. Time to get back to the fun stuff.

# Validating Form Data with JavaScript

Interactive web apps almost all have some sort of user input that must be gathered by using HTML forms. For example, you may have a sign-up form that asks users to enter a username, password, and other data, such as addresses and phone numbers.

Users can, and will, enter all sorts of data into these forms. If a user submits the form with invalid data (for example, if he doesn't enter the area code in a phone number field), it wastes server processing time to determine that a problem exists, and it wastes the end user's time if he has to wait for a response to come back from the server telling him that his data is invalid.

A better way to deal with validating user-entered data is to use JavaScript to prevent the users from submitting the form in the first place unless their data passes a series of tests. The code in Listing 11-2 demonstrates a JavaScript program for checking a user-entered phone number to make sure that it contains exactly 10 numbers (a three-digit area code and a seven-digit phone number).

Doing some sort of JavaScript validation on the client-side can dramatically improve the quality of data that you collect from users of your web app. This phone number validation script is useful for phone numbers that are expected to conform to the standard 10-digit dialing format used in the United States and Canada.

**Listing 11-2: Validating Phone Numbers with JavaScript**

```html
<html>
  <head>
  <script>
    function validate(f) {
    var phone = f.phone.value;
   var error = '';
    var stripped = phone.replace(/[\(\)\.\-\ ]/g, '');

    if (stripped.length !== 10) {
      error = "The phone number is the wrong length. Make sure you included an
              area code.\n";
    }

    if (error !== "") {
      alert (error);
      return false;
    }
    return true;
    }
  </script>
  </head>
  <body>
    <form method="get" id="myform" action="process.php" onSubmit="return
              validate(this)">
    <label for="phone">Enter Your Phone Number</label><input type="text"
              name="phone" id="phone">
    <input type="submit" value="Submit">
    </form>
  </body>
</html>
```

The JavaScript in Listing 11-2 does the following things:

1. Accepts input from the user and strips punctuation marks that are commonly put into phone numbers (such as periods, dashes, and parentheses).

2. Checks that the resulting number is 10 digits long.

3. Reports an error if it's less than 10 digits.

Figure 11-2 shows the script in action. The great thing about this type of validation is that it gives nearly instant feedback to the user.

I believe in keeping client-side validation of data as simple as possible. I could have checked the phone number to make sure that all of the entered characters actually were numbers, but that may have frustrated someone who is used to entering her phone number as 555-GET-ACAR.

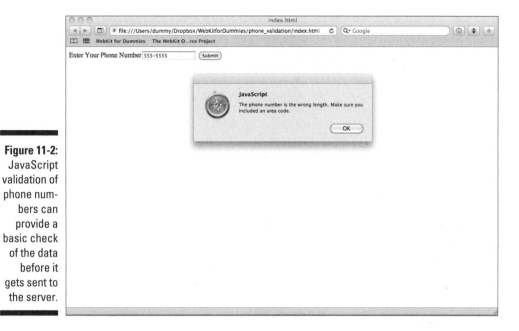

**Figure 11-2:**
JavaScript
validation of
phone num-
bers can
provide a
basic check
of the data
before it
gets sent to
the server.

In my time as a web developer, I've seen many overly clever, e-mail validation scripts that checked to make sure that an e-mail address ended with a period followed by three characters (such as .com). The result of this script was that users from much of the world outside the United States, whose e-mail addresses often end with something like co.uk, for example, were kept out.

Validate important data on the server side as well because someone can bypass JavaScript validation (by turning off JavaScript in his browser, for example).

Don't freak out if some things in this code seem completely unintelligible. It's actually all pretty simple, but there are just a few things I need to explain first.

## Sending data to JavaScript

The first thing I want to show you is how the phone number gets into the validation script in the first place. Here's how this validation script works:

```
<form method="get" id="myform" action="process.php" onSubmit="return
        validate(this)">
    <label for="phone">Enter Your Phone Number</label><input type="text"
        name="phone" id="phone">
    <input type="submit" value="Submit">
</form>
```

This is a simple HTML form, but with one special attribute in the `<form>` element. The `onSubmit` attribute is an *event handler,* which tells the browser to perform some action when the Submit button is clicked.

In this case, the action is `return validate(this)`. What this says is that the browser should run the validation code (`validate`) using the data entered into this form (`this`) and then return the result of running the code (`return`) to the `form` element. So, when you click the Submit button, all the values from the form are sent to the browser's JavaScript processor to be used by a piece of JavaScript (a function) that I named `validate`.

## Grouping statements with functions

*Functions* are a way to create reusable chunks of programming code. In JavaScript, functions are created by using the following format:

```
function functionName (input values) {
}
```

Inside the curly brackets, you can put any code that you want to be run when this function is run. Take a look at the first line of this validation function:

```
function validate(f) {
```

This line defines a function (piece of code) named `validate` and says that it will accept one input value. The `f` indicates what the variable created from this input value should be called.

## Extracting form data

In the second line of the `validate` function, the `f` variable (which, if you recall, was created from the values submitted with the form) is used to extract the value submitted from the phone input field.

```
var phone = f.phone.value;
```

This line (and many lines in programming) should be read backward: "Get the `value` of the `phone` input field from the form called `f` and assign that value to a new variable named `phone`."

Then, create a variable named `error` that you can use to hold any validation messages later in the function:

```
var error = '';
```

## Stripping extra characters

The next line does some fancy footwork to create yet another variable from the phone number input value.

```
var stripped = phone.replace(/[\(\)\.\-\ ]/g, '');
```

In this line of code, the replace command searches through the phone variable for certain characters and replaces them with ' ' — that is, nothing. The basic format of the replace function is

```
string.replace(/search/,replace);
```

The characters inside the search part of the replace command look like a messed-up jumble. The key to understanding what's going on here is that the backslash character (\) is an "escape" character. It just tells the JavaScript processor to treat the next character as that character, rather than as JavaScript code. The escape character needs to be used with certain characters (including a period, a slash, parentheses, and dashes) that have special meaning in JavaScript.

The square brackets in this command indicate that the JavaScript processor should look for any of the characters indicated inside them. The g stands for "global." It says, "Don't stop with just one; I want to find every occurrence of these characters."

The replace value portion of this command has two quotes right next to each other — in other words, nothing.

So what this line does is to look for parentheses, periods, and dashes in the user input and to replace them with nothing — or, in other words, remove them.

The result from this statement is then stored in the new variable called stripped.

## Getting logical with if

The next line of code uses a statement called if to determine whether something is logically true or false.

```
if  (stripped.length !== 10) {
```

In this case, it uses the "not identical" comparison operator (!==) to compare the length of the stripped variable wotj the number 10.

So, essentially what this line of code is saying is, "If the length of the value of `stripped` is not equal to `10`, proceed with running the code between the curly brackets."

Inside the curly brackets is the following statement, which assigns a value to the `error` variable that I created earlier.

```
error = "The phone number is the wrong length. Make sure
         you included an area code.\n";
}
```

Simply having a variable named `error` doesn't do much at all, however, which is where the next `if` statement comes in:

```
if (error !== "") {
```

If you apply what you gleaned from the previous `if` statement, you can probably figure out that this is saying the following: "If the value of `error` is not equal to nothing, proceed with the code between the curly brackets."

To put it in plain English: If there's an error, do the following.

```
alert (error);
return false;
```

The `alert` statement is what pops up the window shown in Figure 11-2. Putting the error variable in the parentheses tells the `alert` command to pop up the text in that variable.

The next line, the `return` statement, halts the execution of the script and answers the request that was made when I first called this function back in the `onSubmit` attribute. It sends a value of `false`, which tells the browser that it's not okay to continue with sending the form data to the server.

Finally, if there was no error, the code inside the previous two `if` statements would not have been run. The validation of the data was successful, and it should let the form know that everything is fine to continue with submitting the form. The way to do that is with the following statement:

```
return true;
```

At the very end of the function, just put in one last curly bracket to indicate the end of the function:

```
}
```

# Understanding the HTML DOM

WebKit and other web browsers parse HTML documents by converting them into a sort of map, called a Document Object Model (DOM).

The purpose of the DOM is to provide a way for you to identify and manipulate the parts of an HTML page using a programming language such as JavaScript. Using the DOM to access and manipulate HTML elements programmatically is the basis for all the great things people are doing with JavaScript today.

## Representin' with objects

The "object" part of Document Object Model refers to abstract representations of the different parts of HTML that are defined by the DOM. Like physical objects, objects in the DOM have things that can be done *with* them and things that they *are*. To put it more accurately, they have (respectively) *behaviors* and *properties*.

An HTML document and its parts have properties. Examples of properties of the <p> element, for example, include `border size`, `line spacing`, `font-face`, `font-size`, and many others. The parts of an HTML document have behaviors as well. For example, links and buttons have `click` behaviors. Other elements, such as `form` elements, have a behavior called `focus`, which makes them "active."

A towel is a physical *object,* but its *properties* may be that it's red, dry, and large. There may be other properties, such as wet, that this particular towel can have. And there may be other properties that other towels can have, such as blue or small.

A towel can do several things, or, perhaps, there are several things that you can do with a towel — for example, you can use it to dry things, you can roll it up and use it like a pillow, or you can snap it to fend off monsters.

And a towel may be enclosed within a larger object. For example, it may be one component of a stack of towels, or it may be contained within the contents of a closet or dresser object.

Here's some JavaScript that may be used to represent a towel in a program:

```
towel.color = 'red';
towel.material = 'cotton';
towel.size = 'large';

towel.snap();
towel.wipe();
```

Behaviors in object oriented language are *methods*.

## Climbing the DOM tree

The objects in the DOM are organized in a hierarchical way, referred to as the "DOM tree."

Figure 11-3 shows a DOM tree for a basic HTML document. Instead of showing the document as a series of nested tags, a DOM tree organizes the content according to how it maps to the object model.

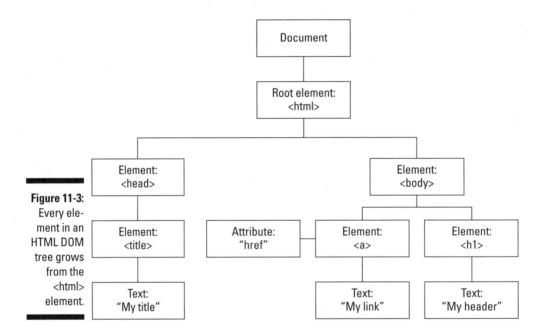

**Figure 11-3:** Every element in an HTML DOM tree grows from the <html> element.

### The document object

The most basic object in the DOM is the document object. It represents your document as a whole, and contains all the other objects. The DOM specifies what characteristics (or "properties") a document object has — things such as the title, the date it was last modified, and the URL.

It also specifies the behaviors (methods) of the document. The `document` object's methods include common things you may do with a document; such as `close`, `open`, and `write`. The `document` object also has a couple of methods for finding elements inside the document:

```
getElementById()

getElementsByName()

getElementsByTagName()
```

These methods of the `document` object are useful when you want to find or modify a property of a certain element in your document. For example, take a look at Listing 11-3. This is a very simple HTML document, but at the end of it is a script block that uses `getElementById` to change the contents of the `div`.

### Listing 11-3:   How Document Methods Make It Possible to Change the Contents of an HTML5 Page Dynamically

```
<html>
  <head>
    <title>What's My Name?</title>
  </head>
  <body>
    <div id="author">Chris Minnick</div>
  <script>
  document.getElementById("author").innerHTML="Superman";
  </script>
  </body>
</html>
```

If you load this document in a browser and watch very closely, you may see my name come up and then change very quickly to `Superman`. This same technique (but just with a lot more supporting code) is how sophisticated web apps, such as Gmail, are able to change HTML pages without refreshing the whole page.

### HTML element objects

After the `document` object, the first HTML element object is always the root element. The root element in a markup language is always the name of the markup language itself. In this case, that's HTML. Under the root element is every other HTML tag in your document. Each of these HTML element objects has properties and methods.

The most commonly used element properties include values that can be set in attributes — things like `height`, `width`, `title`, `id`. Element objects also have properties that represent their positions in the document. For example, the following code locates an element's parent element — in other words, the element that contains the element in question.

```
document.getElementByID("copy_warning").parent();
```

If this code is run on the following HTML document, it will return the `<footer>` element.

```
<html>
  <body>
    <footer>
      <p>Thank you for visiting my site.</p>
      <p id="copy_warning">Unauthorized reproduction of
          this content is wrong.</p>
    </footer>
  </body>
</html>
```

If this all seems a little cerebral right now, don't worry. It will all become much more clear as you work with this stuff.

## Using dot notation with the DOM

The most common way that JavaScript programmers work with objects in the DOM is by using a system called "dot notation." You can see dot notation in action in various other places in this book, such as in stylesheets.

Here's an example of dot notation being used to change the background color of a HTML page:

```
document.body.bgColor="black"
```

You can try this right now by typing it into the console in WebKit. The result is shown in Figure 11-4.

In this simple example, each dot separates a different DOM object. The `window` refers to the browser window. The `document` refers to all the HTML code being displayed in the window. The `body` refers to the HTML body element within the document.

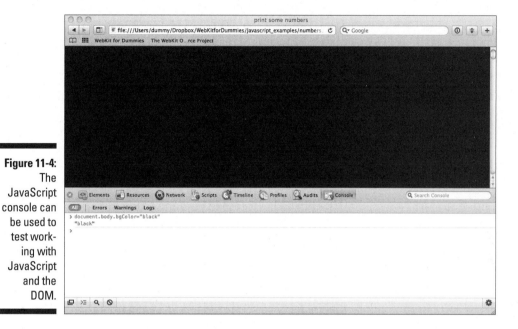

**Figure 11-4:**
The JavaScript console can be used to test working with JavaScript and the DOM.

Think of this bit of code as a street address. For example, if you were to write a street address using dot notation, it may look something like this:

```
USA.California.Mockingbird Heights.1313 Mockingbird Lane.Herman Munster
```

The items (or "objects") in dot notation are specified with the most general object on the left, and then increasingly more-specific items to the right of it, separated by periods ("dots").

## Identifying nodes and relations

There are many ways to identify, or address, the different parts of an HTML document. For example, here's a simple HTML document:

```
<html>
  <head>
    <title>Hi there</title>
  </head>
  <body>
    <h1>How are you?</h1>
    <h2>I'm great!</h2>
  </body>
</html>
```

If you wanted to use the DOM to address and maybe manipulate the value of the <h1> element in this document, either of the following would work:

```
document.body.h1
```

or

```
document.body.firstChild
```

Both methods of addressing the <h1> have flaws, however. In the first example, there may be more than one <h1> in the document body. If you wanted to point to only one particular <h1>, this code wouldn't work.

If your goal is just to identify and do something with this <h1>, this is *not* the way to go. If your goal is to identify and do something with the first child of the <body> element, regardless of what it may be, this *is* the way to go.

# Using JavaScript for Much More Than Eye Candy

Now that you have a basic understanding of what JavaScript is and how it works in conjunction with the HTML DOM, look at some advanced examples of what these two can do together on mobile devices.

## NextBus

NextBus, shown in Figure 11-5, is a Mobile Web app that uses GPS data to give users real-time predictions of when a bus will arrive. When you first visit NextBus.com with your smartphone, it asks for permission to use your current location. It then uses that location to tell you when the next bus will arrive at your location.

NextBus uses a technique called *mash-up* to display a live Google map of where the nearest buses are. The bus locations are updated as you watch the map.

 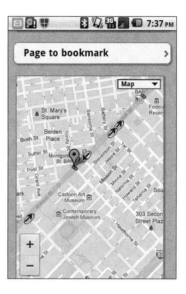

**Figure 11-5:**
NextBus uses GPS and a mash-up to display real-time bus locations.

## Chalk

Chalk, shown in Figure 11-6, is a free browser-based iPad app from 37signals (the creators of the Basecamp project management application). Chalk simulates drawing and erasing on a chalkboard. It uses JavaScript and the HTML5 `Canvas` element to create a very smooth and fun quick-sketching app.

## Fiddling with JavaScript

jsFiddle (`http://jsfiddle.net/`) is a web-based testing tool for JavaScript. It allows you to enter HTML, CSS, and JavaScript code, and then run them to instantly see the results. Figure 11-7 shows a sample app.

**Figure 11-6:**
Chalk uses JavaScript to manipulate the Canvas element in response to the user drawing on the screen.

This example application uses the jQuery library to retrieve data from Twitter. It then displays this data in an HTML list that's styled using CSS.

All the code for the app is available to edit in one place. This makes it a great tool for experimenting with JavaScript, which is really the best way to learn any new language (hint, hint).

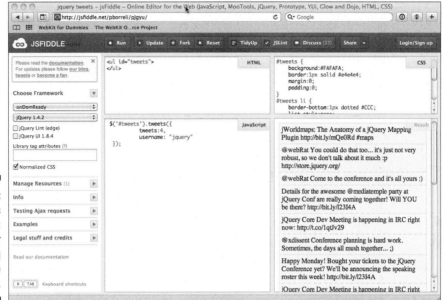

**Figure 11-7:**
jsFiddle is
a fantastic
tool for
learning
to use
JavaScript.

# Part IV
# Optimizing Your Apps

## The 5th Wave

By Rich Tennant

"Run Nigel! It's the mummy's cursor!"

# In this part . . .

**H**ow do you get into the elite ranks of mobile Web app developers? Optimize, optimize, optimize!

While the browser engine may be the same (or at least similar) on the majority of mobile platforms, each mobile operating system has its own quirks and specializations. In this part, I'm going to tell you about some of the things to watch out for with several different mobile platforms. In the process, you'll get a much better understanding of the terminology and unique problems of developing for mobile devices.

After I've shown you the different platforms and mobile browsers, I'll dive into a discussion of performance. You'll learn about some of the tools that are available for making your apps faster, lighter, and more responsive.

This part ends with a chapter about going all the way and actually making your Web app into a native app—it's actually much easier than you would think.

# Chapter 12

# Optimizing for iOS

Apple's iOS was made for web apps. As I discuss in earlier chapters, you can be well on your way to making your web apps feel at home on the iPhone, iPod touch, and iPad just by adding a few meta tags to your HTML.

In this chapter, I show you how to take full advantage of all the tools that Apple has provided — and a few tricks that web developers have come up with on their own — to take your Mobile Web apps to the next level on iOS.

## Configuring Your Web App for iOS

To really make your web apps shine on iOS, you must have a good understanding of what the viewport is and how to control it. For this reason, I'll spend most of this chapter talking about the viewport.

### Understanding the viewport

The first thing you should do to make any Mobile Web app look better on iOS is to set the viewport width correctly. Doing so helps ensure that your app is correctly sized for any mobile device.

The *viewport* is the rectangular area of a website viewable onscreen. It determines how content is laid out and where lines of text wrap. If a web page is larger than the viewport, the browser will allow you to scroll to view other parts of the page — or to bring them into the viewport.

To illustrate a viewport, it's helpful to see what it's not. Specifically, the viewport is *not* the same as the screen size or the entire visible area of the website.

### Screen size

The screen size in pixels (also known as the *screen resolution)* of the iPhone 4 and newer is 960 x 640 pixels. Prior to the iPhone 4, iOS devices had a resolution of 480 x 320.

These two dimensions may be either the height or width, depending on whether you're looking at the device in *portrait orientation* (height greater than width) or *landscape orientation* (width greater than height).

Pixel dimension numbers are constant. Your iPhone will always have the exact same number of pixels and the same pixel dimensions, no matter what you do. Well, I suppose you could take a saw to it to reduce the pixel dimensions that way if you really wanted to. (Warning: This would void the warranty; I don't recommend trying it at home or anywhere else.)

Be sure you're using the correct measurements:

- **pixels:** The size of a screen is usually measured in pixels. These are the actual tiny dots of light that make up the words and pictures that you see on the screen.

- **points:** Viewport size is measured in points, which may be larger or smaller than pixels, depending on the size of the viewport and the screen density (which you can read about in the next chapter . . . I'm giving you enough confusing terms already for this chapter).

### Visible area

The actual usable space (the *visible area*) in mobile Safari is important to know for when you're designing page layouts and graphics. Because of the various tools, bars, and buttons that surround an actual web app, the visible area isn't the same as the screen size.

Figure 12-1 shows that by the time the status bar, the address bar, and the bottom button bar have had their way with your screen real estate, you're left with considerably less space to work with in your browser display area.

The *visible area,* like the screen size, is measured in pixels. For example, the visible area of Mobile Safari, when you account for all the different panels on the screen is actually 712 x 640 (in portrait view), rather than 960 x 640.

### Desktop browser viewports

In desktop browsers, the visible area actually is the same as the viewport. This is because you can adjust the width and height of the browser window in desktop browsers — and you generally zoom in on a desktop browser. In effect, you change the size of the desktop browser viewport by changing the size of the browser.

Figure 12-2 shows how the size of the viewport can be changed by the user in desktop WebKit.

When you change the browser size (viewport size) in a desktop browser, the text on the site will reflow to the new browser size, unless the designer of the page has chosen to not allow the text to re-flow (as is the case in Figure 12-2).

In mobile Safari, though, users can't change the window size or the viewport size. By using different finger gestures, you can zoom in on the viewport or use a flicking motion to view more of the viewport — but the viewport size remains the same.

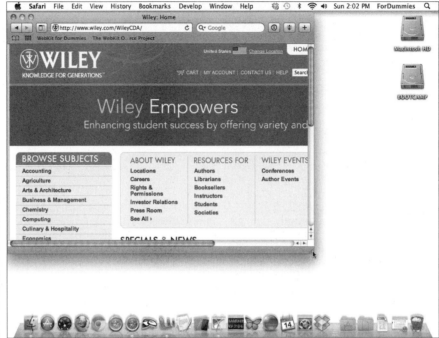

**Figure 12-2:**
Users of
desktop
browsers
can adjust
the viewport
size
themselves.

To understand what's going on here, you need to understand the difference between device pixels and viewport pixels, which is what I tell you about next!

## Understanding device pixels and viewport pixels

Until the iPhone 4, a pixel was a pixel. That is, if you displayed a 320px-wide image on the screen in portrait orientation, it would take up the width of the device screen. With iPhone 4, Apple introduced the Retina display, which increased the number of pixels on the screen to 960 x 640.

Rather than breaking every app in existence up until that time, Apple created a distinction between points and pixels:

- ✔ A *pixel* is the physical dot of light on the device screen.

- ✔ A *point* is a device-independent pixel. Because the viewport always has to fit the entire size of the device, a point will be larger on the screen if the viewport is smaller.

## Controlling the viewport size

As a Mobile Web developer, you are in control over how large the viewport is.

✔ If you don't take control and specify your viewport size, mobile Safari will use a default value, and your viewport will be 980 points wide, in either landscape or portrait mode. In landscape mode, the page will be zoomed in a bit to take advantage of the larger visible area, but the viewport size will remain the same.

This default behavior is great *if* the content of your web app happens to be designed for a 980-*point*-wide screen and has large fonts to make it readable on a small device. It's more often the case that a 980-*pixel*-wide design will be completely illegible on a small screen, as shown in Figure 12-3.

✔ If you design your web app to be 320 pixels wide in portrait mode but use the default viewport width, your app will take up only about one-third of the viewable width, as shown in Figure 12-4.

**Figure 12-3:**
The default viewport width usually requires users to zoom.

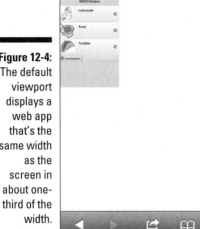

**Figure 12-4:**
The default
viewport
displays a
web app
that's the
same width
as the
screen in
about one-
third of the
width.

If you want to display your app as large as possible on the iPhone, you need to set the viewport equal to the width of the device. Mobile Safari lets you use a simple HTML <meta> tag for just this purpose.

Here's the easiest way to make your Mobile Web app look a lot better on iOS:

```
<meta name="viewport" content="width=device-width, initial-scale=1.0">
```

This code sets the width of your viewport to the width of the device, rather than 980 points, and will set the initial scaling of your viewport to 1 — meaning that it won't be zoomed in.

Figure 12-5 shows the same page that's displayed in Figure 12-4 but with this meta tag in the page.

In addition to width and initial scale, the viewport has a several other properties that can be set using a meta tag:

- ✔ height specifies the height of the viewport. You don't usually need to worry about this one, as it probably won't do anything.

- ✔ minimum-scale is the minimum amount the user can zoom out to. On mobile Safari, it has a default value of .25, meaning that users can view content at one-quarter the actual size.

✔ `maximum-scale` is the maximum amount the user can zoom in. The default on mobile Safari is 1.6.

✔ `user-scalable` is a property with a value of `yes` or `no`. If it's set to `no`, the user won't be allowed to zoom.

**Figure 12-5:**
Setting the viewport width equal to the device width will make your web apps fit on the screen.

## Making your app full-screen

You can make your app display in full-screen mode when launched from the home screen by using the following meta tag:

```
<meta name="apple-mobile-web-app-capable" content="yes">
```

Figure 12-6 shows what the Mobile Cookbook looks like in full-screen mode. Notice that all toolbars are hidden from the app.

**Figure 12-6:**
Full-screen
mode makes
your web-
app display
area equal
to the full
screen.

When you design for full-screen mode, be aware of the following potential got-chas and restrictions:

✔ There's no way to force the user to open the app in full-screen mode. The only way that can happen is if the user adds your page to his home screen. So, don't count on having those extra pixels available for your app to use. Design as if the address and button bars are still there.

✔ Full-screen mode doesn't have any of the standard browser features (such as the Back and Forward buttons and the address bar). Make sure that your app contains good and fully usable internal navigation buttons.

## Using Apple-specific tags

The following sections introduce a variety of Apple-specific HTML5 tags that you may find useful for building your Mobile Web site, especially if you expect a lot of iOS users to make themselves at home on your pages.

### *Home-screen icon*

When users add your app to their home screens, iOS creates an icon for the web app, using a miniature view of your app. If you want to control what shows up (and maybe use a logo or custom icon), you can specify either `apple-touch-icon` or `apple-touch-icon-precomposed` by using an HTML `link` tag.

Here's how you specify the home icon for iPhones with the Retina display:

```
<link rel="apple-touch-icon-precomposed" sizes="114x114" href="img/h/apple-
          touch-icon.png">
```

Here's how you specify the home icon for first-generation iPads:

```
<link rel="apple-touch-icon-precomposed" sizes="72x72" href="img/m/apple-touch-
          icon.png">
```

Here's how you specify it for older iPhones:

```
<link rel="apple-touch-icon-precomposed" href="img/l/apple-touch-icon-
          precomposed.png">
```

All these can be included in your app at the same time; then your app uses the most appropriate image for each device.

You may also use just `apple-touch-icon` instead of `apple-touch-icon-precomposed`. The difference is that if you use the regular `apple-touch-icon`, iOS adds a glassy button-like effect to your image, as shown in Figure 12-7. By adding `-precomposed`, you maintain control over how your icon appears.

**Figure 12-7:**
iOS adds
a glossy
effect
to home
screen
buttons
unless
they're
marked as
precom-
posed.

## Making a splash

You can specify an image to use as a startup screen (also called a *splash screen)* that appears while your app is loading, just after being launched from the home screen. You do so by using an `apple-touch-startup-image` link.

```
<link rel="apple-touch-startup-image" href="img/l/splash.png">
```

The image you specify here must be 320 x 460 pixels for the iPhone and iPod touch.

## Hiding the status bar

Even in full-screen mode, the iOS status bar still occupies the top of the screen.

If you want to customize the look of this status bar, you can do so with the `apple-mobile-web-app-status-bar-style` meta tag, like this:

```
<meta name="apple-mobile-web-app-status-bar-style" content="black-translucent">
```

By setting the value of this meta tag to `black-translucent`, you give your app access to the whole screen, and make the status bar overlap it. Figure 12-8 demonstrates why this may not always be desirable.

Other possible values for this meta tag are default and black. Setting it to just black or default changes the color of the status bar, but will not cause it to overlap your content.

**Figure 12-8:** You can give your app access to the whole height of the device, but this may not always be a good idea.

# Getting in Touch with Touch Events

One of the key elements of modern smartphones is the touch screen. Many phones, such as the iPhone and Android, now support multi-touch screens, which uniquely identify multiple fingers and allow you to use complicated gestures and press multiple buttons on the screen simultaneously.

Apple released its touch events API with iOS 2.0, and iOS 4+ has very good support for touch events in the browser.

The four basic types of touch events are

- ✔ `touchstart`: Triggered when a finger touches the screen (or other touch-sensitive device).
- ✔ `touchmove`: Sent when a finger moves on the screen.
- ✔ `touchend`: Sent when your finger is lifted from the screen.

- ✔ `touchcancel`: Sent when the system cancels tracking the touch. This may happen, for example, if you're in the middle of a touch event when a notification comes in.

Because touch screens need to support multi-touch, each touch event tracks three lists:

- ✔ `touches`: A list of Touch objects representing all the touches involved in the current touch event.
- ✔ `targetTouches`: A list of fingers on the current element (as described by the document's DOM).
- ✔ `changedTouches`: A list of touches that changed during the current event. For example, if you have three fingers on the screen but you move only two, this list indicates which fingers moved.

Touch events are combined to form gesture events. For example, a swipe of two fingers on the screen is recognized as a touch event, but it may also represent a special gesture that performs a particular function in an app.

Gesture events make it possible for app developers to define special combinations of multi-touch events that are significant in an app and make the app pay attention to those.

Examples of common gestures include

- ✔ The multi-finger *pinch* gesture is used to shrink or expand elements on the screen.
- ✔ The *flick* gesture involves a rapid touch movement in one direction.
- ✔ The *tap* gesture is treated just like a mouse click.

Apple's iOS was the first of the current breed of mobile operating systems to have good support for touch events in the browser. However, the other operating systems are rapidly catching up (or are already caught up). Result: It's now possible to use some level of touch events in cross-platform Mobile Web apps.

In addition, libraries and frameworks such as Sencha Touch and jQuery Mobile have made using touch events much easier for the app developer.

I talk more about touch events, and how to use them it in cross-platform web apps, in Chapter 18.

# Chapter 13

# Optimizing for Android

- - - - - - - - - - - - - - - - - - - - - - - - - - - - - - - - -

## In This Chapter

▶ Developing for different screen sizes

▶ Understanding screen density

▶ Targeting screen density

▶ Testing for screen density

▶ Setting the home icon on Android

- - - - - - - - - - - - - - - - - - - - - - - - - - - - - - - - -

*A*ndroid is Google's mobile-device operating system. It's based on Linux, and, like Linux, it's free and open-source software.

Unlike Apple's iOS, any device manufacturer can create a device that uses Android. Google does play a role in authorizing the use of the Android logo, but as far as the actual hardware that its operating system runs on, it's basically a free-for-all.

The flexibility that device manufacturers have to use the OS has made Android devices so popular.

However, flexibility in screen sizes, hardware specs, and user interface have made developing Mobile Web apps for Android somewhat more challenging than developing for iOS.

## Sizing Your App

If you remember from Chapter 12, Apple created a distinction between a *point* and a *pixel* in iOS when the 960-pixel-wide Retina display was introduced with the iPhone 4.

Android has always had different devices with different screen sizes and numbers of pixels, and they used pretty much the same solution as Apple, but with slightly different terminology.

# Understanding Android "dips"

Android invented the idea of having a unit of measurement that can be used in the viewport on devices with different screens. Android calls this the *density-independent pixel,* or *dip* (also written *dp*).

The *dip* is the same idea as a *point* with iOS — it's an abstract unit of measurement that can be used between devices with different numbers of pixels on the screen.

*Point* and *dip* — and their abbreviations *pt* and *dp,* respectively — can be used interchangeably in most cases. It's also quite common to see people use the term *pixel* to refer to physical-device pixels as well as points and dips, but that's just incorrect and causes confusion.

If you just keep in mind that the viewport has points (or dips), and the physical screen has pixels, you'll understand everything.

# Setting the viewport to device width: It's the least you can do

The viewport of the Android browser is a minimum of 800 dp wide by default. This 800-dp-wide view is called *overview mode* on Android.

Chapter 12 mentions that the default viewport on iOS is 980 points. So if you just designed all your apps to be 980 points wide to fit the iOS screen perfectly, you'd better go back to the drawing board to get 'em to fit Android.

Fortunately, Android, like iOS, understands the `viewport` meta tag (for more information about the viewport meta tag, see Chapter 12). To resize the view port to fit your mobile app, you can put the same meta tag in the `<head>` element of your HTML document that you use on iOS:

```
<meta name="viewport" content="width=device-width,
          initial-scale=1.0">
```

If you wanted to make sure that the app always fits the viewport the same way, you can prevent the user from zooming by setting the `user-scalable` attribute to `"no"`. Here's an example:

```
<meta name="viewport" content="width=device-width,
          initial-scale=1.0" user-scalable="no">
```

# Picturing the viewport

The viewport on Android can get pretty complicated because of the variety of devices, different screen sizes, and different screen resolutions. The best way to understand it is to see some pictures.

Figure 13-1 shows a 320-pixel-wide image displayed in both portrait and landscape modes on an Android phone. Notice that the width of the viewport is the same (800 dp) in either mode. In landscape mode, the screen width is larger, so the 800-dp viewport is displayed at a larger size.

**Figure 13-1:**
The default viewport width is the same in portrait and landscape mode.

## Viewport smaller than content width

Figure 13-2 has the same image, but with the viewport set to less than the width of the image. Here's the meta tag being used:

```
<meta name="viewport" content="width=280">
```

What you may expect in this case is that the browser window would be made smaller. However, this image seems to fit perfectly with the `viewport` meta tag set to a smaller width.

**Figure 13-2:**
When the web app is wider than the viewport, the result isn't what you would expect at first.

What's happening here is that Android ignores viewport width settings of 320 dp or less — and assumes that you meant to set the width equal to the device width.

### Viewport the same as content width

Figure 13-3 shows what happens when the viewport is set to the same width as the content. As you would expect, the content fits perfectly, width-wise.

**Figure 13-3:**
Setting the viewport to the same width as the image results in a perfect fit. That's Mr. Jones. Isn't he handsome?

### Viewport larger than content width

When the viewport is set to a width that's larger than the content, it behaves like you would expect, as shown in Figure 13-4. The number of pixels to the right of the image, plus the width of the image (and any borders and margins, of course), is equal to the size of the viewport. In this case, I've set the viewport equal to 400 dp.

**Figure 13-4:** Setting the viewport to wider than the image results in white space to the right of the image.

Android uses the viewport and the idea of dips to scale and resize apps to fit different devices. To create a better user interface that gives users the impression that the app was designed for their particular devices, rather than stretched or shrunk to fit their devices, you need to know a bit more about screen density.

## Looking deeper into density

*Screen density* is the number of pixels, or dots, per inch (dpi). In addition to having different physical dimensions, Android devices also have different screen densities.

The density of a screen may range from 100 dpi (on the low end) to 300 dpi and up on the high end.

Screen density is important to understand because the higher the density of the screen, the smaller objects on it will display.

To keep things relatively simple, Android supports four screen-density categories:

✔ Low (ldpi)

✔ Medium (mdpi)

✔ High (hdpi)

✔ Extra-high (xhdpi)

The higher the density, the closer the pixels are together. When your pixels are closer together, the image they form takes up less space on the screen. Think of it as like squeezing a snowball or a piece of bread: Higher density means the same amount of stuff takes up less space.

By default, the Android browser will display everything as if the screen is medium density. If your screen is higher density, the content will be scaled up — which may produce adverse effects with images that weren't designed to *be* scaled.

To illustrate, Figure 13-5 shows how scaling an image reduces the quality. An image that looks crisp and smooth when displayed at medium resolution will look less than ideal if it's scaled on a high-density screen.

**Figure 13-5:**
Displaying an image at a lower density than the screen supports will result in scaling and a reduction in quality.

If you don't want the viewport to be scaled to medium density, you must specify a target density equal to the screen density of the phone, using the `viewport` meta tag. You should also set the width of the viewport equal to the device width to make the web page fit the screen.

```
<meta name="viewport" content="target-densitydpi=device-dpi, width=device-width"
    />
```

Figure 13-6 shows a 320-pixel-wide image displayed in the Android emulator on a medium-density screen (HVGA) with the `target-density-dpi` set to the `device-dpi`, and the same web page on a high-density screen (WVGA800). Both screens are the same height. Notice that the medium-density image takes up more space.

**Figure 13-6:**
An image takes less space on a high-density screen when the target density is set to the device density.

You don't have to adjust your web apps for screen density, but doing so will let you take better advantage of high-density screens to present users with high-resolution graphics, pictures, and video.

# Using Media Queries with Android

To make your apps look the best that they can on Android, you can create separate style sheets for low-, medium-, and high-density devices. Each of these style sheets can specify that different images and font sizes are used for each of the three supported densities.

To switch between these style sheets, use the `-webkit-device-pixel-ratio` media query. The `device-pixel-ratio` refers to the number of device pixels that make up a screen pixel.

Keeping in mind that the default Android viewport is 800 dp wide, if a device has 1200 actual pixels that make up that 800-dp-wide display, this equates to a device-pixel ratio of 1.5. If 800 physical (device) pixels make up a viewport with 800 density-independent pixels, this is a ratio of 1. If there are more screen pixels than dips, the screen is low density.

To target devices by device-pixel ratio, you can use the following media queries:

```
<link rel="stylesheet" media="screen and (-webkit-device-
        pixel-ratio: 1.5)" href="highdensity.css" />
<link rel="stylesheet" media="screen and (-webkit-device-
        pixel-ratio: 1.0)" href="mediumdensity.css" />
<link rel="stylesheet" media="screen and (-webkit-device-
        pixel-ratio: 0.75)" href="lowdensity.css" />
```

## Determining screen density with JavaScript

Another option for determining the screen density in Android is to use the `window.DevicePixelRatio` DOM property. This property is what the Android browser uses to determine how to scale your web app. This property will always have one of three values, depending on the device's screen density:

✔ If the value of `window.DevicePixelRatio` is 1.5, the device is considered high density, and pages are scaled up by a factor of 1.5 by default.

✔ If the value of `window.DevicePixelRatio` is 1, the device is considered medium density, and no scaling is done.

✔ If the value of `window.DevicePixelRatio` is .75, the device is considered low density, and the page is scaled down by default.

You can use JavaScript to find out the current value of `window.DevicePixelRatio`. When your JavaScript program knows that value, it can use the information to customize your app for different densities.

The script in Listing 13-1 displays the device-pixel ratio of the current screen viewing it.

### Listing 13-1:    A Simple Script for Displaying the Device-Pixel Ratio of the Current Device

```
<script>
if (window.devicePixelRatio == 1.5) {

  alert("You have a high-resolution display");

}

if (window.devicePixelRatio == 1) {

  alert("Yours is a medium-resolution display");
```

```
}

if (window.devicePixelRatio == .75) {

alert("Low Resolution Alert!");

}
</script>
```

Figure 13-7 shows the result of running this script in my emulated medium-resolution and high-resolution Android devices.

**Figure 13-7:**
The device-
PixelRatio
property
reports the
correct
device-pixel
ratio for my
emulated
browsers.

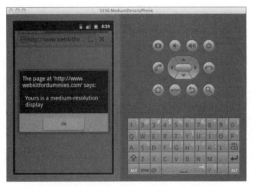 

**Figure 13-7:**
The device-PixelRatio property reports the correct device-pixel ratio for my emulated browsers.

# Setting the Home Screen Icon

Unlike mobile Safari on iOS, the Android browser doesn't have some of the cool capabilities to hide the browser functionality, use a start-up image for a web app, and so forth. It does support one of Apple's special tags, however.

The following element can be used to display a high-resolution icon on a user's home screen when he creates a shortcut to your web app:

```
<link rel="apple-touch-icon-precomposed" href="http://www.
        yoursite.com/custom_icon.png"/>
```

On some Android devices, the preceding tag works only if the link to the custom icon file is a full URL, rather than a relative one. If you're going to use this tag and you expect to have Android users, it's best to just link to it with the full URL.

Adding a web-app link to the home screen on Android is a bit more involved than the same process is with iOS. Here's what you do:

1. **View the web app in your browser and bookmark it.**

2. **Go to your home screen you want to add the link to.**

3. **Long-press a blank area on the screen.**

   The Add to Home Screen menu appears.

4. **Choose Shortcuts from the menu.**

   A new menu appears, showing the different types of shortcuts you can add.

5. **Select Bookmark.**

   A list of the sites you have bookmarked in the browser appears.

6. **Select the bookmark you want to add to your home screen.**

Figure 13-8 shows the result for Google.com, which contains a link to a desktop icon.

**Figure 13-8:**
Google.
com adds
a custom
icon to your
Android
home
screen
when you
add a
shortcut.

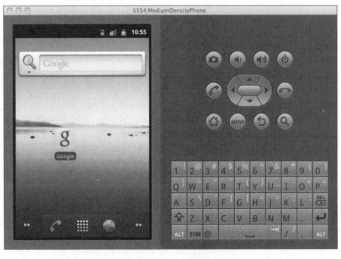

# Chapter 14

# Optimizing for BlackBerry

· · · · · · · · · · · · · · · · · · · · · · · · · · · · · · · · · · · · · · ·

· · · · · · · · · · · · · · · · · · · · · · · · · · · · · · · · · · · · · · ·

*R*esearch in Motion's BlackBerry operating system and devices have been the gold standard for mobile e-mail for more than a decade. Where BlackBerry was traditionally lacking (to put it mildly) was in web-browsing functionality.

Starting with version 6, however, BlackBerry jumped to the front of the pack with its WebKit-based browser called, appropriately enough, BlackBerry Browser. The BlackBerry Browser scores 100/100 on the Acid3 test, which is currently the most common test of browser compatibility with World Wide Web standards.

# Understanding the Types of BlackBerry Apps

You have three options for developing apps for BlackBerry: native apps, web apps, and WebWorks.

## Developing native apps

Native BlackBerry apps are built using the Java programming language and the BlackBerry Java SDK; they run in a Java virtual machine on BlackBerry devices. You can download and install native apps from the BlackBerry App World app store.

## Developing WebWorks apps

BlackBerry's WebWorks is a system that allows you to build your app as a web app — using HTML5, CSS, and JavaScript — and then package and distribute it as a native Java app.

WebWorks apps, previously known as Widgets, can use JavaScript functions and the WebWorks APIs to interact with the BlackBerry hardware as well as other native apps.

By using WebWorks, you can essentially turn your web apps into native apps for BlackBerry. If you're a web developer looking to create native BlackBerry apps, this is a great way to get started.

In this book, however, I stick to what can be done with cross-platform WebKit-based apps.

## Developing HTML5 apps

BlackBerry has a full WebKit browser, introduced with version 6 of BlackBerry OS. As with the other devices I talk about, any standard HTML5 app you write for WebKit will work on BlackBerry 6+.

Keep in mind, however, that BlackBerry does have a number of unique features and capabilities that you should be aware of; you may want to optimize your app for them.

# Optimizing Mobile Web Apps for BlackBerry

The same techniques that you use to optimize your web apps for Android and Mobile Safari apply to BlackBerry. Most important, of course, is the viewport.

Currently, roughly 14 BlackBerry devices can run version 6 or newer of the BlackBerry operating system. Although the variety of devices doesn't approach that of the Android devices, there's still quite a large range of screen sizes and screen densities to contend with.

## Optimizing for display sizes

Most BlackBerry smartphones have one of the following screen pixel sizes: 360 x 400, 320 x 240, and 360 x 480.

The BlackBerry Playbook tablet has a display size of 1024 x 600.

What matters to you, as a web-app developer, isn't the physical display size of a device. What matters is the screen density and viewport size.

## Optimizing the viewport

BlackBerry Browser 6+ supports the standard `viewport` meta tag. The default viewport for BlackBerry is 1024 pixels wide.

This is different from Android (where the default is 800 pixels) and iOS (where the default is 980 pixels).

What this means is that if the viewport width isn't set to `device-width` using the `viewport` meta tag, your web content will tend to appear smaller on a BlackBerry device with the same size screen as other smartphones.

## Optimizing for screen density

BlackBerry devices have screen densities in the range of 160-to-mid-200s pixels per inch (ppi). This places them in the medium- to high-resolution categories, as defined by Android's screen-density categories.

# Using the Web Inspector with BlackBerry

BlackBerry Browser, beginning with BlackBerry 7, is the first mobile WebKit browser to include the full set of Web Inspector debugging tools.

## Enabling Web Inspector on the Playbook

To enable the Web Inspector on the BlackBerry playbook:

1. **Select the Privacy and Security tab in the Browser options on the Playbook.**

2. **Switch Enable Web Inspector to On and then type your BlackBerry Playbook password.**

Figure 14-1 shows Web Inspector running on the Playbook. This is pretty much the same Web Inspector that you can make use of with your desktop WebKit browser.

**Figure 14-1:**
Web
Inspector
on the
BlackBerry
Playbook
enables
local debug-
ging of web
apps.

## Remote debugging

To make Web Inspector usable on small devices, BlackBerry uses a *remote debugging* technique to support viewing the Web Inspector. When you enable Web Inspector, your BlackBerry device is given a unique address on your computer network. You can then connect to that address using a browser on another computer, and the Web Inspector will be shown.

To use remote debugging, you need to have your BlackBerry connected to a Wi-Fi network. If you're using the BlackBerry simulator and the computer it's running on is connected to the Internet, this approach works with the network your computer is on.

To enable remote debugging on a BlackBerry smartphone, follow these steps:

1. **Go into the BlackBerry Options and enable the Developer Tools.**

2. **Open the BlackBerry Browser and go to the Browser Options.**

3. **Highlight the Developer Tools menu item.**

   A sub-menu appears, showing two options, as shown in Figure 14-2.

4. **Select Enable Web Inspector.**

   A pop-up window appears onscreen, as shown in Figure 14-3. This is the network address to use for remote debugging.

**Figure 14-2:**
The Developer Tools submenu is accessible in the BlackBerry Browser (on Black-Berry 7).

**Figure 14-3:**
After you
enable
remote
debug-
ging, the
BlackBerry
gives you
an address
to use for
debugging.

5. **Enter the address given to you by the BlackBerry device into a computer on the same local network.**

   The Web Inspector for the current page on the BlackBerry appears in your desktop browser, as shown in Figure 14-4.

As far as web developers are concerned, this is just about the coolest feature of any smartphone browser out there.

With remote debugging, you can load a web page on your BlackBerry, or even in the BlackBerry emulator, and see all the standard Web Inspector reports about that page (including the Timeline, Audit, Profiles, and Resources tabs) in a full desktop browser.

You can even make changes in the elements or CSS windows on the desktop computer and see them reflected instantly on the BlackBerry device.

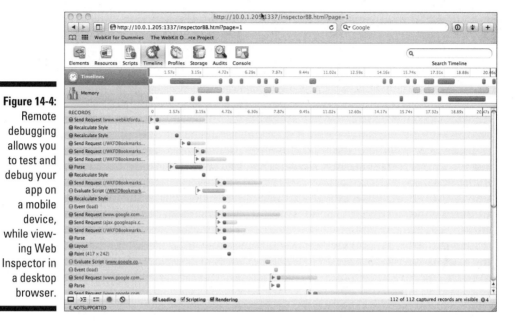

**Figure 14-4:**
Remote
debugging
allows you
to test and
debug your
app on
a mobile
device,
while view-
ing Web
Inspector in
a desktop
browser.

# Accessing Native Events

BlackBerry smartphones have a controller — the *trackpad* — that works like a laptop trackpad or a joystick. In addition to the trackpad, many Blackberry devices also have a touchscreen. By default, the BlackBerry browser interprets and handles touch- and trackpad events in a way designed to make browsing easier on small screens. These usability enhancements include the standard mobile-device interactions people have become familiar with — such as dou-ble-tapping on the screen to zoom, or swiping the screen to scroll.

In some cases, however, web developers may want to change the way these events are handled. BlackBerry browser supports two meta tags that can give you control over how the browser handles touch and trackpad events on the device: `cursor-event-mode` and `touch-event-mode`.

To set the value of either of these event modes, you use a standard HTML meta tag placed in the header of a web page. Here's an example:

```
<meta name="cursor-event-mode" content="native" >
```

## Cursor-event-mode meta tag

The `cursor-event-mode` meta tag specifies how the browser should handle trackpad events. It has two possible values:

✔ native: Setting the `cursor-event-mode` to `native` tells the browser to handle trackpad events the same as they would be handled in a desktop browser. In other words, mobile-only optimizations, such as zooming and showing the contextual menu when the user holds down a click on the trackpad, are disabled.

✔ processed: This is the default setting, in which trackpad events are interpreted by the browser.

### Touch-event-mode meta tag

The `touch-event-mode` meta tag specifies how the browser should handle touch events. It has three possible values:

✔ native: In the `native` mode, touch events are sent directly to the web page, rather than being processed by the browser. Using this mode allows web developers to write JavaScript code to handle events individually.

✔ pure-with-mouse-conversion: This is a hybrid type of mode that passes some touch events directly to the web page, and converts others into equivalent mouse events. For example, double taps and pinch-to-zoom will still work in this mode, and users can touch form fields to make them active, and scroll a page by swiping.

✔ processed: This value tells the browser to use default touch-event handling.

# Submitting Web Apps to BlackBerry App World

BlackBerry App World allows you to submit web apps to be included in the app catalog along with native apps. There is one catch, however: You must create a *web icon,* which is actually a native BlackBerry app whose only purpose is to launch the BlackBerry browser with a predefined address. Web icons serve the same purpose that the `apple-touch-icon` meta tag serves on iOS. Because they're actually native apps, web icons are a bit more complicated to create than the `apple-touch-icon`.

If you're brave and want to give it a try, you can go to `http://support forums.blackberry.com/t5/Web-and-WebWorks-Development/Web-Icon-From-Start-to-Finish/ta-p/447600` to watch a video about creating web icons.

When you have your web icon, you can register as an app vendor at `https://appworld.blackberry.com/isvportal/home/login.seam` and submit it to BlackBerry App World.

# Downloading and Installing the BlackBerry Simulator

If you don't have access to a BlackBerry device, the BlackBerry simulator, which currently runs only on Windows, is the next best thing.

Research in Motion provides separate simulators for each version of the BlackBerry OS. Here's how you can try one:

1. **Go to** `www.blackberry.com/developers/downloads/simulators` **in a web browser.**

2. **Click the Download a Device Simulator link.**

3. **Select one of the device simulators from the drop-down list and then click the Next button.**

   You see a list of downloads. Each of these corresponds to a different device.

4. **Choose one of the devices and click the Download link.**

   It doesn't really matter too much at this point which one you choose. You're informed that you must register or become a BlackBerry developer in order to download the software.

5. **Click the link labeled Not a BlackBerry Developer Zone Member?**

   You see a form that you need to fill out to download the software.

6. **Fill out the form and then click the Next link.**

   You're presented with a terms of use document.

7. **Read this document, select the Agree check box, click Next, and then click the Download button that appears to start your download.**

   The BlackBerry simulator downloads are large (a version 7 simulator is more than 170MB). Depending on your Internet connection, downloading may take a little while.

8. **When the download is complete, double-click the downloaded file to begin installation.**

9. **If the installer asks whether you want to install any required software, answer Yes.**

10. **Proceed through the installation by selecting all the default values when a dialog box pops up.**

    Eventually the installation is complete.

11. **Find the simulator in your Start menu or Program Files folder, and then launch it.**

12. **If a dialog box appears, asking whether you want to fit the simulator to your screen, answer Yes.**

The simulator appears on your screen, as shown in Figure 14-5. Because the simulator runs as a virtual device on your computer, the home screen may take a long time to appear. If you're patient enough, or if your computer is fast enough, before too long you can use the device, launch the web browser, and visit web pages.

**Figure 14-5:**
The BlackBerry Device Simulator can be used to test your web apps if you don't have access to every BlackBerry device.

# Chapter 15

# Optimizing for webOS

**H**P's webOS (formerly Palm's webOS) is the most WebKit-centric of the major mobile operating systems. Native apps in webOS are written using standard HTML5, JavaScript, and CSS. What this means for you is that you already have all the basic skills and tools you need to start building native apps for HP's tablets and phones.

# Understanding the Two Types of Web Apps on webOS

Native apps on webOS are web apps, but not all web apps are native webOS apps. Got it?

Although native apps on webOS are built with standard HTML5 languages and tools, there is still a significant difference between how native web apps and non-native web apps work, look, and behave on webOS.

## Developing browser-based web apps

Any web app you create using the techniques in this book is likely to run inside the browser on webOS in the same way that it runs on Android or BlackBerry. As long as you write good code, you shouldn't have to do too much more to get something functional.

As with the other mobile platforms I've talked about so far, your goal in creating cross-platform Mobile Web apps should be to first make your app look as good as possible in the WebKit browser on each device.

### Developing native web apps

With webOS, you may decide that you want to take the next step and create a native app that can be downloaded and installed from the HP App Catalog.

Native web apps on webOS are similar to installed web apps on iOS, in that they are launched and run outside of the web browser. Apps in webOS go beyond simply installing an icon, however — they're actually installed on your phone and can store data locally and interact with the device hardware.

# Optimizing Web Apps for webOS Devices

Only a limited number of mobile device models currently run webOS. The good news for developers: You have less variation in target platforms.

Each of these devices has a very different form factor:

- ✔ The Veer is a tiny phone with a 2.4-inch screen. Its pixel dimensions are 320 x 400.
- ✔ The Pre is a standard-size smartphone with a screen size of 480 x 800.
- ✔ The TouchPad has a 9.7-inch screen with a resolution of 1024 x 768.

In August 2011, HP announced that it would discontinue production of all webOS hardware devices, including the Pre, the Veer, and the TouchPad. It's unclear at this point what this means for the future of webOS.

### Designing for the web Web browser

That's not a typo. The name of the webOS web browser is *Web*. When optimizing for the webOS browser, there are a couple obstacles to be aware of.

The first is that the vertical size of the browser is not the same as the vertical size of the screen. This is nothing surprising, and is the case almost all the time with mobile browsers — the address bar, toolbar, and various other types of bars take up some of the space.

Figure 15-1 shows a webOS smartphone along with the measurements of the various operating-system and web-browser parts that take up some of the screen.

Notice that the amount of vertical space taken up can change as a result of the notification bar that pops up onscreen when you get a new message.

**Figure 15-1:** The vertical dimensions of the webOS browser can, and will, change.

Notice also that the browser applies rounded corners to the viewport. These eat up a few more pixels on the screen.

Perhaps the most important two things to keep in mind when optimizing for the webOS browser are that the locations of the Back and Refresh buttons on the screen. These two buttons effectively further reduce the space available for your app if you want it to be functional on webOS. If an important button in your web app happens to fall underneath one of those buttons, it's going to pose a usability problem.

## Designing for the webOS viewport

The webOS web browser has a default viewport size of 960 pixels. This is slightly smaller than the iPhone's default viewport (980).

Fortunately, the webOS browser supports modifying the viewport by using the `viewport` meta tag and all its properties.

The screen density of webOS devices varies based on the device. The original Pre has a density of 186 ppi, the new Pre3 has a density of 260 ppi, the Veer has a density of 197 ppi, and the Touchpad's density is 160.

Just set your viewport equal to the `device width` with the appropriate meta tag, and you should be good to go — or at least good to start testing.

# Running the Emulator

The webOS emulator is part of the webOS SDK. Before you can use the emulator, you need to install VirtualBox, which is free virtual-machine software available from Oracle.

You can download VirtualBox from `www.virtualbox.org`. Follow the instructions on that site to install it, and then proceed with these steps to get the webOS emulator running:

1. **Go to** `http://developer.palm.com` **with a desktop browser on your Windows, Mac OS X, or Ubuntu Linux computer.**

2. **Click the Download SDK link under the Resources navigation item.**

3. **Select your computer's operating system to jump to the download links and instructions.**

4. **Click the correct link to download the SDK for your operating system.**

   As is the case with every emulator you've seen in this book, the download for the webOS SDK is massive. Now is a good time to take a break or a short nap.

5. **When the download is complete, double-click the installer (Windows) or open the disk image and double-click the file that ends with `.mpkg` (Mac OS X).**

6. **Agree to the license agreement when you're prompted.**

   After the license agreement, you see the screen shown in Figure 15-2, if you're installing on Mac OS X. You can deselect the option to install the PDK.

**Figure 15-2:** There's no need to install the PDK. I just saved you half a gig of storage space! You're welcome.

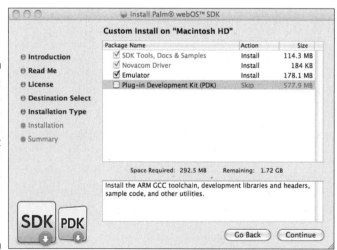

**7. When installation is complete, launch the emulator from inside your Applications folder (Mac OS X) or your Program Files (Windows).**

VirtualBox creates and launches a virtual machine.

Keep in mind that webOS is based on the open-source Linux operating system. When you start the emulator, you see a Linux bootup screen. Be patient and enjoy reading all the cryptic messages that fly by, as shown in Figure 15-3. The boot process will take some time, and you'll probably see a bunch of messages about errors, things being rejected, killed, and recovered. These sorts of messages are completely normal for Linux, and you can just ignore them.

The emulator eventually appears, as shown in Figure 15-4. By default, the emulator runs the latest version of webOS, which is currently version 3 — the version used by the TouchPad, so the emulator is sized to the dimensions of the TouchPad tablet.

**Figure 15-3:** webOS runs on Linux, and the emulator gives you a brief peek into what's going on behind the scenes as it's launching.

**Figure 15-4:**
The webOS
emulator
runs inside
VirtualBox.

If you want to see how your app looks on a webOS smartphone, you can download an older version of the SDK by scrolling to the bottom of the SDK download page.

After you download additional emulators and install them, you see multiple options when you launch the palm-emulator program. Figure 15-5 shows an emulated version of webOS 2.1 running in an emulator with a device size of 320 x 480 pixels.

On webOS devices, you use a "flicking" motion to close and switch between apps. In the emulator, you use mouse movements to simulate these motions. The Esc key is also extremely important in the emulator, because it returns you to the home screen from within an app.

**Figure 15-5:**
The emulated webOS 2.1 displays at the size of the Pre2's screen.

# Chapter 16

# Optimizing for Performance

As desktop computers and browsers have become more powerful, websites have become much larger and complicated. We've all had the experience of waiting a minute or longer to load a web page on a mobile device. With some knowledge of why this happens that can be gained from a couple easy-to-use tools, we can hopefully start to solve this problem.

Understanding how to optimize web apps for performance is especially important with the arrival of full-featured WebKit browsers on mobile devices. Today, any website can be viewed on mobile devices. As a result, every website is now a *mobile* website — whether it's ready or not (and most are not).

## Testing with Online Tools

Several great sites are available for testing and helping you to fix problems with Mobile Web apps. Many of these tools are free. In this section, I take a look at a few of them.

### Google Page Speed

Google Page Speed is similar to the Web Inspector Audits tool; it analyzes your web app and tells you what you can do to make it download faster and run faster. Three versions of Page Speed are available: a plug-in for Google's Chrome browser, a plug-in for the Firefox browser, and a web-based version.

The web-based version is the most relevant for our purposes because it has all the functionality of the plug-in version, but with an additional option that tells you how well your app is optimized for mobile devices. Additionally, it gives you some pointers on how to make it faster specifically for the Mobile Web.

To use Google Page Speed to test some mobile sites, follow these steps:

1. **Open your WebKit browser and go to** `http://code.google.com/speed/page-speed/`.

   You see the homepage of Page Speed, as shown in Figure 16-1.

2. **After you read about Page Speed and watch the videos, find the link to Page Speed Online, or type the address directly into the address bar.**

3. **Choose File⇨New Tab from the main menu of your WebKit browser.**

   A new browser tab opens.

4. **In the new tab, go to** `http://cantoni.mobi/`.

   This site is a categorized list of mobile websites. It will give you plenty of URLs to try while you experiment with Page Speed.

5. **Choose a category and find a site you'd like to test.**

   For example, I went to the technology category and chose Engadget.com at `www.engadget.com`.

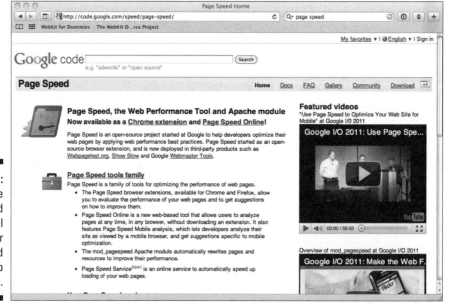

**Figure 16-1:** Google Page Speed has several offerings for testing and speeding up your apps.

6. **Right-click the name of the site and choose Copy Link Address from the contextual menu.**

   The URL of the site is saved to your Clipboard.

7. **Return to the tab where you have Page Speed open and paste the URL into the form.**

8. **Click the Analyze button.**

   After a moment, the results screen appears, as shown in Figure 16-2. Note that these are the suggestions for optimizing your web app for desktop browsers.

9. **Click the mobile link in the upper-right corner of the page.**

   After a moment, the mobile optimization results screen appears, as shown in Figure 16-3.

**Figure 16-2:** By default, Google's Page Speed shows suggestions for improving your web-app's performance on desktop browsers.

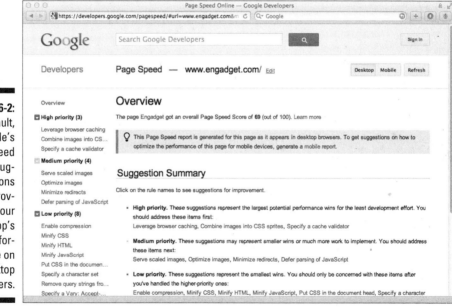

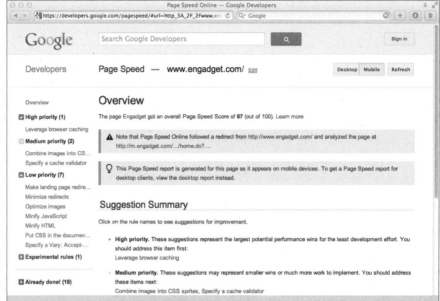

**Figure 16-3:**
Google's
Page Speed
gives you
tips for how
to make
your Mobile
Web app
faster.

# Page Speed Service

If you're not interested in doing the hard work of optimizing your site based on Page Speed's recommendation, you might consider using the Page Speed Service (`http://code.google.com/speed/pss/index.html`). Page Speed Service downloads your site, applies best practices for speeding it up, and then hosts it on Google's servers.

You can get an idea of how fast a site can potentially be by testing it at `www.webpagetest.org`. Here's how you do it:

1. **Go to the Page Speed Service homepage at** `http://code.google.com/speed/pss/index.html`.

   You should see a screen similar to Figure 16-4.

2. **Click the Check It Out link.**

   You're taken to a page containing a lot of information about how the Page Speed Service works and what it does.

3. **On the linked paged, find the link to** `www.webpagetest.org/compare`.

   You see a screen similar to the one in Figure 16-5.

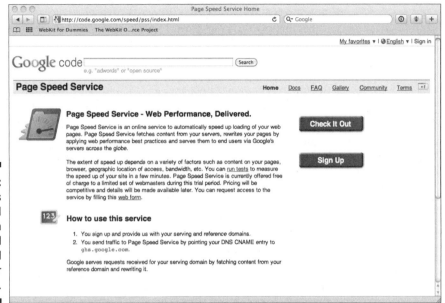

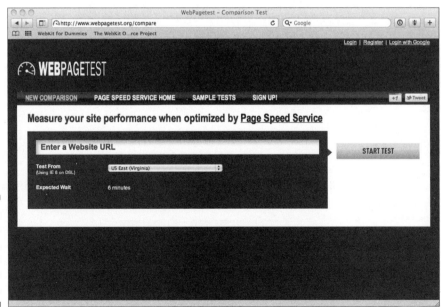

4. **Enter a website URL into the Enter a Website URL field.**

   If you're at a loss for what to do, try our good old cookbook app at www. dummies.com/go/webkit.

5. **Select a data center.**

   The distance of the data center from the actual server that's running the site makes a difference in performance. For your purposes, however, it's really not important which one you choose right now.

6. **Click the Start Test button.**

   At this point, the waiting begins. If you're running a test during a particularly busy time, you'll need to wait longer. I've run a couple of tests and haven't run into any major bandwidth problems.

7. **At some point, your results will pop up, as shown in Figure 16-6.**

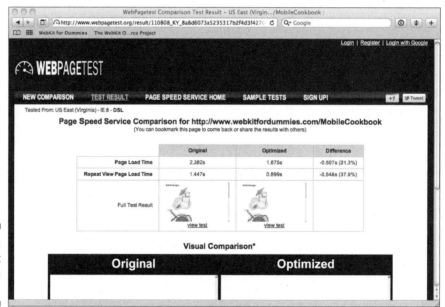

**Figure 16-6:** The moment you've been waiting for!

# mobiReady

mobiReady is a service from mobeForge that tests web pages by using a number of different criteria and assigns them a score between 1 and 5 to indicate how optimized they are for the Mobile Web.

To use mobiReady, go to `http://ready.mobi/launch.jsp?locale=en_EN` and enter a web page address into the form. When you click the Go button, a report will be generated for that URL.

Figure 16-7 shows a typical mobiReady results page. Note that the first test on the page shows a graph of the web page's size, along with a graph showing what a download of that size may cost a user in different countries. Note that these numbers may not be up to date or accurate; nonetheless, always remember that many mobile users pay for bandwidth.

Another useful feature of mobiReady is the visualization test. This test displays your web page in simulations of the browsers on several different phones, as shown in Figure 16-8. Note that simulated browsers are all typical "feature phone" browsers with limited capabilities, not smartphone browsers.

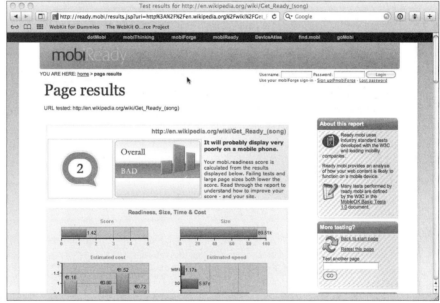

**Figure 16-7:**
The first mobiReady test result reminds us that size matters much more on the Mobile Web.

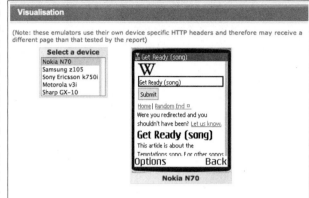

**Figure 16-8:**
Seeing how your app looks on older feature phones can be helpful in resolving performance problems and improving accessibility.

# Controlling Latency

*Latency* is the amount of downtime when web browsers, web apps, and servers are waiting for each other. It's completely unproductive, but it's unavoidable. There will always be some amount of time between when your browser requests a file when the server sends it back, and this amount of time will probably take longer than transferring the same amount of data within your computer.

A large amount of latency will ruin your app's user experience.

## Reducing real latency

If you optimize your app using Google Page Speed and the WebKit Web Inspector Audits tool, it's likely that you've done pretty much everything you can do to reduce the actual latency of your app.

Common techniques for reducing latency include

✔ **Use faster devices, networks, and servers.** Perhaps the best ways to reduce latency may be largely out of your control. With a large budget, you may be able to increase the speed of the computers hosting your web app. With an unlimited budget, you can make sure that all your users have the latest and greatest smart phones with the best browsers and the fastest possible wireless network connects. Chances are good that you don't have much control over at least two of these factors. The good news, however, is that the situation is getting better as technology improves and users upgrade.

✓ **Cache data locally.** Making use of the HTML5 application cache can make your app available offline while dramatically reducing latency after the initial download.

✓ **Use compression and minimize kilobytes.** Transferring less data is always an important strategy for reducing latency.

✓ **Minimize the number of files.** Transferring 10 files with a total size of 100KB takes longer than transferring 2 files with the same combined size.

## *Reducing perceived latency*

Users don't really care about latency. What they care about is whether the app they're using *feels* slow. If you have high latency but the user doesn't notice it because he's busy looking at something else, it's not such a big deal. If you have high latency and it impacts the user experience, though — that's a big problem.

There's a huge difference between actual latency and what the user perceives.

You have a number of options for reducing the perceived latency. Depending on the specifics of you app, you may choose to use any one, or even all, of these:

✓ **Load JavaScript incrementally.** The most common way of implementing this recommendation is to put your JavaScript includes at the bottom of the page, rather that in the `<head>`. What this does is that it causes something to be shown to the user sooner, rather than forcing them to wait until all of the JavaScript includes have loaded before they see anything. The downside of this technique is that the user will see that the browser is still loading something even after the page appears. Users tend to wait until the page is completely loaded before they use it — regardless of what the screen looks like.

✓ **Defer JavaScript evaluation.** This technique uses a clever trick to download all the JavaScript code at once, but then to run it only when it's needed. The result is much faster page load times because the browser doesn't need to pause to interpret the JavaScript, and improved perceived load times over loading the JavaScript at the bottom of the page.

✓ **Preload commonly used data.** If there are parts of your app, or pages in your app, that users are highly likely to view, you should be proactive in loading them.

# Part V
# Advanced Topics

The 5th Wave                    By Rich Tennant

"It was supposed to be a simple sleep potion. That's why you can't always trust the information you get off of 'Wiccapedia.'"

# In this part . . .

With a new build containing new bug fixes and features released every day, WebKit is changing and improving fast. Mobile browsers based on WebKit are generally only updated when a new version of the underlying operating system is released. As a result, you can be positive that the browser on your smartphone doesn't do everything that the latest build of WebKit can do. However, you can also be sure that the latest technologies will be coming to your smartphone eventually.

This part deals with topics and standards that are not well supported in every mobile browser yet, but that are coming soon. Learn about these things and you'll be ahead of the curve when they arrive.

# Chapter 17

# Converting from Web to Native

· · · · · · · · · · · · · · · · · · · · · · · · · · · · · · · · · · · · · · · · · · · · · · · · · ·

· · · · · · · · · · · · · · · · · · · · · · · · · · · · · · · · · · · · · · · · · · · · · · · · · ·

*T*he reality today is that native apps have an advantage in terms of marketing and distribution over web apps — particularly on iOS and Android. App stores get a lot of attention from their prominent location on the user's device, and comparably popular markets for web apps have yet to spring up.

At least for the time being, there are plenty of times when a web app will accomplish your goals for an app, but you may not be able to reach your audience without a native app unless you already have a large audience — like Google or Facebook.

The perfect solution to this problem is to build your app as a web app and then convert it into a native app. The technology for doing this exists today, and is widely used to convert web apps to iOS, Android, and more and to distribute them via the respective app stores: a *bridging framework*.

# Introducing PhoneGap

"Bridging framework" is the name given to code libraries that can be used to make web apps runnable as native apps, thus giving you the benefits of web apps while giving you access to the capabilities of native apps, such as the ability to get your app into app stores.

PhoneGap allows you to write mobile apps using HTML5 technologies and then compile them into native apps for all the major mobile platforms, including iOS, Android, BlackBerry, webOS, and Symbian.

Any time you're working with creating native apps, even if you're building them using web technologies, things get a bit complicated. Every mobile operating system has a different way to build and deploy native apps.

Two versions of PhoneGap are currently available: PhoneGap 1.0 and PhoneGap Build.

## PhoneGap 1.0

PhoneGap 1.0 is a downloadable framework that works with the APIs and SDKs for the various supported platforms to generate native apps from HTML5 web apps.

If your app is complicated or needs to interface with device hardware, PhoneGap 1.0 is the way to go. It does a great job of reducing the complexity, but you still need to do some installing and configuring to convert your Mobile Web app into a native app.

## PhoneGap Build

A new service from PhoneGap promises to make generating native apps as simple as uploading HTML files to the web. For individual developers who have only one app, this service is free to try. Teams of developers, or people with multiple apps, need to pay a monthly fee to use it.

PhoneGap Build is very new. The user interface may be different from what I'm describing here by the time you get your hands on this book. However, I can say with some certainty that a service very much like this one will exist as long as people are still making native apps.

# Converting the Mobile Cookbook with PhoneGap Build

As I mention earlier, PhoneGap Build is a service that allows you to simply upload your HTML5 app to have it converted into all the different types of native apps that PhoneGap supports. To create a native app with PhoneGap build, you first need to sign up with the service at `http://build.phonegap.com`.

After you sign up, click the New App button to start entering some information about your app and uploading the HTML pages.

## Preparing your app for PhoneGap Build

There are several ways to get your app to PhoneGap. Perhaps the easiest way for novice developers is to create a `.zip` file that contains all the HTML, CSS, and JavaScript files that make up your app.

Because the Mobile Cookbook uses mostly linked JavaScript code (the jQuery mobile framework), the actual number of files needed to make the native version is pretty minimal.

I already did this work for you (I'm so nice) and uploaded the `.zip` file to `www.dummies.com/go/webkit`. Go to this URL to download the file you'll need for the next step. Alternatively, you can create your own `.zip` file containing the following files from Chapter 4:

- `index.html`
- `conversions.html`
- `images/lemonade.jpg`
- `soup.jpg`
- `tortilla.jpg`

PhoneGap Build will download the necessary jQuery mobile files to make the app work, so you don't need to worry about including those in your `.zip` file.

## Uploading your app

Here's how to use PhoneGap Build to create native apps for several different platforms.

1. **Go to** `http://build.phonegap.com` **and sign up for an account.**

   After you sign up, you'll see the new app form, as shown in Figure 17-1.

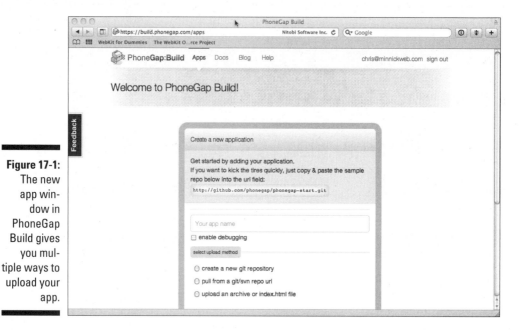

**Figure 17-1:**
The new app window in PhoneGap Build gives you multiple ways to upload your app.

2. **Fill out the new app form, as shown in Figure 17-2, and choose the Upload an Archive or Index.html File option.**

   The other two options (Create a New GIT Repository and Pull from a GIT/SVN Repo URL) involve a couple additional steps and an understanding of revision control and repositories. Revision control software helps you manage software projects by keeping track of every change you and your co-developers make. When multiple people are working on the same files, it's an indispensible tool.

   I highly recommend that anyone who is going to develop any sort of app learns about and uses git or svn for every project. You can get started with git or svn by going to `https://github.com` or `http://svnbook.red-bean.com`.

3. **Click the Create button.**

   Your PhoneGap Build home screen will look similar to Figure 17-3, with clock icons under each of the platforms except iOS.

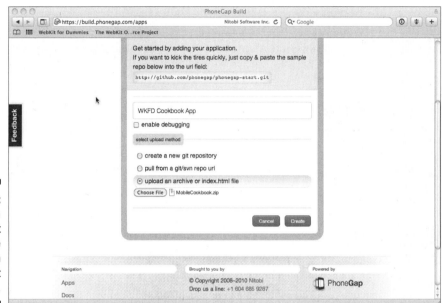

**Figure 17-2:**
To upload a
zip file, just
check the
right button
and select
the file.

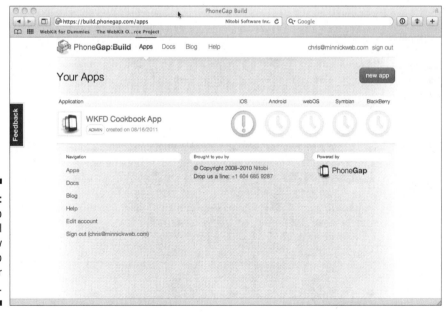

**Figure 17-3:**
PhoneGap
Build will
take a few
minutes to
convert your
app.

4. **Wait a couple minutes, and then reload the page.**

   You should see that some or all of the native apps have been created, as shown in Figure 17-4. The blue boxes indicate each of the file extensions of the native apps, and there are links to download an installable app.

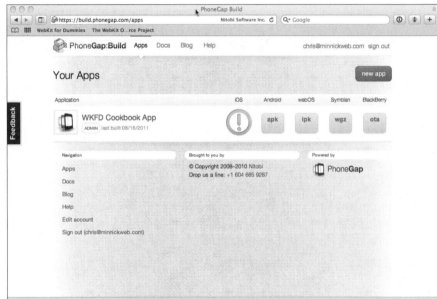

**Figure 17-4:** When the apps are completed, a blue box with the file type for the platform appears.

That's it! The next step is to get these native apps onto devices so we can test them. Fortunately, we have emulators!

## Converting to an iOS native app

To create native iOS apps, you need to sign up and pay to become a registered Apple developer so that you can digitally sign your app and associate it with your developer profile. You can become an Apple developer by going to `http://developer.apple.com/programs/register`.

## Installing the Cookbook on Android

The file type for Android native apps is `.apk`. Follow these steps to install the `.apk` file on Android or the Android emulator.

If you're going to install the app on the Android emulator, make sure that the virtual machine you're going to use has a virtual SD card. You can give your device an SD card by editing the device using the AVD Manager.

1. **Choose Settings⇨Applications on your Android device and then enable Unknown Sources, as shown in Figure 17-5.**

    This step allows you to install apps from some location other than the Android Market.

2. **Close the Settings and then launch the Android browser.**

    In the emulator, you can close Settings by clicking the home icon on the right.

3. **Go to** `http://build.phonegap.com` **in the Android browser and sign in.**

    Figure 17-5 shows the mobile version of the PhoneGap home screen.

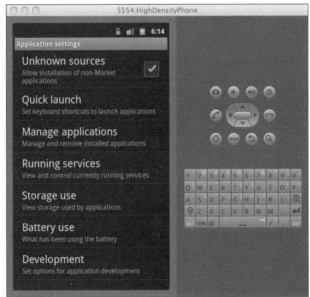

**Figure 17-5:**
The PhoneGap home screen looks and works slightly differently on small screens.

4. **Click the WKFD Cookbook App to go to a list of the different versions PhoneGap built of your app, as shown in Figure 17-6.**

    Each of the apps that was successfully built has a mobile barcode next to it. If your device supports opening URLs using mobile barcodes (also known as "QR codes"), you can take a picture of each barcode to download apps in the future.

**Figure 17-6:**
Mobile bar-
codes are
provided so
you don't
have to
enter full
URLs in the
browser to
download
apps.

5. **Click the apk icon using your Android device.**

   The file will begin downloading, as indicated by the download icon at the top of the Android screen.

6. **After the file downloads, open your notifications window by clicking and dragging down the top menu (in the emulator) or touching and dragging it (on a physical device).**

   You'll see a message, as shown in Figure 17-7, indicating that the download is complete.

7. **Click the download-complete notification.**

   A message appears asking whether you want to install the app and indicating the different permissions that the app is requesting, as shown in Figure 17-8.

8. **Click Install.**

   After a short time, installation will complete.

9. **Click the Open button to launch the app.**

   The Mobile Cookbook appears on your screen as a native app, as shown in Figure 17-9.

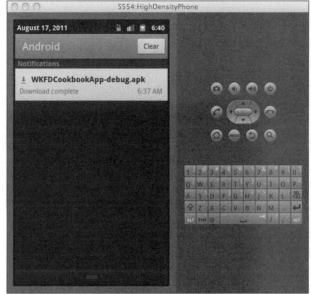

**Figure 17-7:**
The notifications window will indicate when the download is finished.

**Figure 17-8:**
It's installing just like a native app! It is a native app!

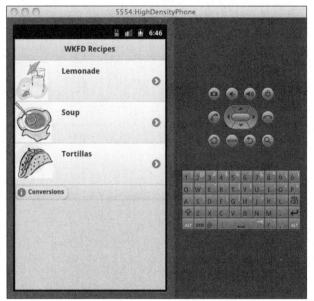

**Figure 17-9:**
Just like
that, the
Mobile
Cookbook is
a native app
running on
Android.

# Chapter 18

# Accessing Phone Features

● ● ● ● ● ● ● ● ● ● ● ● ● ● ● ● ● ● ● ● ● ● ● ● ● ● ● ● ● ● ● ● ● ● ● ● ● ● ● ● ● ● ● ● ● ● ● ● ● ● ●

● ● ● ● ● ● ● ● ● ● ● ● ● ● ● ● ● ● ● ● ● ● ● ● ● ● ● ● ● ● ● ● ● ● ● ● ● ● ● ● ● ● ● ● ● ● ● ● ● ● ●

*A*s mobile phones and tablets become more powerful, they are also packing more types of sensors and cameras. In addition to the microphone, speaker and camera, the mobile device you're using today may also contain an accelerometer, a light sensor, a temperature sensor, a barometer, an altimeter, a compass, a gyroscope, and GPS capabilities. Each device's operating system implements these features differently — and provides its own native APIs for accessing and controlling them.

You can currently access most of the underlying device and operating system functionality by converting your web app into a native app, as you can read about in Chapter 17. This approach still requires you to create a native app, though. Wouldn't it be great if you could access device functionality and data such as contacts and calendar items directly from the phone's WebKit browser? No to worry: You will.

No widely implemented standard currently exists for how to do things like capture a photo or video from within the browser, or use calendar or contacts data from within a web app. You can access some native device functions by using device-specific code in some browsers, but these don't work in every mobile browser, so they're not yet very useful for cross-platform developers. However, the companies and organizations that are shaping the Mobile Web envision much more and are working to create and implement these standards.

# W3C Device APIs Working Group

The W3C Device APIs Working Group is tasked with defining the ways that web apps should be able to access native device hardware and software. While still in the early phases of development, the outline of a plan is coming together now, and mobile vendors have already implemented parts of it.

Device APIs come in two types:

✔ Sensors, such as a camera and an accelerometer

✔ Data, such as contacts and a calendar

In this section, I introduce you to some of the device APIs and tell you about the current state of browser support for each.

## Contacts API

The goal of the Contacts API is to specify how a web app should be able to obtain read access to a user's contacts lists. You can use the Contacts API to choose someone from your contacts to send a link to, for example.

Clearly, as is the case with several of the Device APIs, the Contacts API must be very sensitive to privacy and security concerns. A large portion of the actual API deals with privacy and security.

The specification envisions that when browsers begin to support the API, they will notify you and specifically ask users whether they want to share their contacts. Figure 18-1 shows what this may look like.

**Figure 18-1:**
Web browsers must notify you when a website attempts to access your contacts.

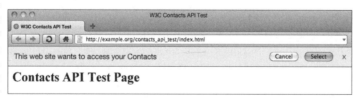

As of this writing, WebKit has begun to support the Contacts API. It's just a matter of time until it comes to the browsers on mobile devices.

## Calendar

The Calendar API aims to give mobile browsers access to calendar data. Using the Calendar API, a web app can check your schedule on your phone prior to you making a dinner reservation and alert you if you seem to have a conflict.

Like the Contacts API, it's still a work in progress, and no browsers have implemented it yet.

## Media Capture API

*Media capture* refers to the ability of a device to take pictures, record video, and record audio. Android 3.0 has implemented parts of the Media Capture API to allow web apps to access the camera and microphone. Look at Listing 18-1 to see how you can create HTML input fields to capture media from your phone.

**Listing 18-1:    Capturing Various Types of Data with the Media Capture API**

```
<form enctype="multipart/form-data" method="post">
<div>
  <label for="file">Get a file</label>
  <input type="file" id="file" name="yourfile"></input>
</div>
<div>
  <label for="picture">Take a picture</label>
  <input type="file" id="picture" name="yourpicture" accept="image/*;capture=cam
          era"></input>
</div>
<div>
  <label for="video">Shoot some video</label>
  <input type="file" id="video" name="yourvideo" accept="video/*;capture=camcor
          der"></input>
</div>
<div>
  <label for="audio">Record some audio</label>
  <input type="file" id="audio" name="youraudio" accept="audio/*;capture=microph
          one"></input>
</div>
</form>
```

Figure 18-2 shows what this form looks like on an Android 3.2 emulator. It looks pretty much like an ordinary form. However, it's actually a portal for bringing all the media-capture capabilities of the modern smartphone into the browser.

**Figure 18-2:**
Media Capture API specifies how forms capture pictures, video, and audio.

Now, check out Figure 18-3, which shows what happens when I click the Choose file button for the picture input. Not surprisingly, the camera opens.

I'm using an emulator here; this device has no actual camera. In the interest of making this figure more visually interesting, I simulated what the picture-capture area of the camera would look like if this were an actual front-facing camera on my Android tablet.

## Battery Status

The idea behind the Battery Status Event Specification is to allow web apps to find out several things about the device's battery, such as whether the device is currently running on battery power and how much charge is left.

This information would be useful so that (for example) web apps that consume a large amount of power could warn the user or put off doing background tasks until the device is plugged in.

**Figure 18-3:**
Clicking an input with the capture parameter set to camera brings up the device camera.

No browsers currently have support for this API, as far as I know.

## Network Information API

The Network Information API gives web applications access to your device's network connection info. When web browsers implement this API, it will be able to tell a web application the device's current online status (online or offline) as well as the type of network connection the device currently has (such as Ethernet, 3G, 4G, Wi-Fi, and so forth).

This API will be useful for web apps that can operate in both an online and offline mode, or for apps that require large data downloads that should be done when there's a faster internet connection.

# Giving Permission for Device and Feature Access

Imagine what would happen to the Web if it were possible for any website you visited to take a picture of you or record video of you without your permission. It wouldn't take long before we started disabling webcams and putting our phones in the sock drawer. Clearly, browser manufacturers need to prohibit this sort of invasion from happening.

With web browsers and web applications gaining greater access to the features and functions of users' computers, very real privacy concerns arise.

## Preventing Peeping Tom apps

If you look at how native apps on iOS work, you'll notice that after you install them and agree to give them access to certain data once or twice, they can pretty much do as they please with your phone, data, and devices.

Part of the reason for Apple's process of approving apps is to make sure those apps don't misbehave. When a developer modifies an app, Apple must verify that no new features have been added that will violate user privacy or seek to grab sensitive data.

Android native apps ask for your permission to access device features when you download them, as shown in Figure 18-4. After the initial request, you don't need to give permission again. The app installs on your device and has these certain permissions every time it runs unless you specifically modify them or install an update to the app.

**Figure 18-4:** Android apps ask for necessary permissions upon installation.

Web apps, on the other hand, can change at any time. Even if the creator of a web app has the best of intentions, some bit of code on the page can introduce a back door through which hackers can exploit sensitive user data or the functions of the device.

Because web apps are very different from native apps, the standards for web-app access to device features must be different from those that govern native apps.

## Balancing usability and security

The authors of device access standards, and those of us who work with these standards, must make tradeoffs between ease of use, functionality, and security. This is set to become one of the most difficult hurdles for web-app developers over the next few years.

Permission to access device features and functions can be given in two ways: implicitly or explicitly. When you click a button on a web page to activate the camera, this is considered implicate permission for the browser to access your device camera. When you go to a web page and it wants to use your current location, a dialog box will pop up and ask you for explicit permission.

Today, although standards exist for when browsers must ask for permission to access device features, *how* they ask is inconsistent. One suggestion from the W3C for how browsers should ask is shown in a demo web page (see Figure 18-5) at

```
http://dev.w3.org/2009/dap/docs/feat-perms/feat-perms.
         html
```

This demonstration shows how the different permissions that a web app requests can be combined into a single toolbar. This approach may be a good way to make the permissions process as painless as possible.

Contrast the previous Figure with how permissions for using geolocation currently work in the WebKit nightly build, shown in Figure 18-6. In my opinion, this approach is much more intrusive and less elegant than the demonstration from the W3C.

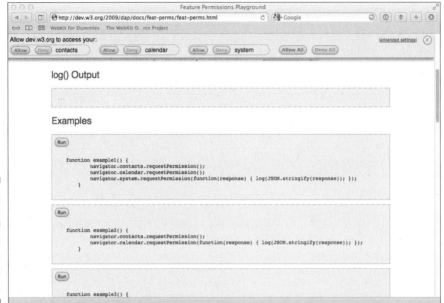

**Figure 18-5:**
A demonstration of how feature permissions can work in browsers.

**Figure 18-6:**
WebKit's method of asking for permissions feels a bit clunky.

## Using device features with PhoneGap

The PhoneGap framework has a unique place in the world of mobile apps. The basic way it works is that it sits between the device's native operating system and the web browser, translating back and forth from one to the other.

Because of this unique vantage point, PhoneGap is able to add native functionality onto web apps. The way it does this is by imple-

menting Device APIs that aren't yet supported by the browser on the device. It's really quite ingenious!

So, even though the Contacts API doesn't yet work in WebKit browsers, you can write Contacts API code in your app, compile it with PhoneGap, and make full use of device contacts.

# Geolocation API

*Geolocation* is a fancy word for figuring out where on Earth you (or, more precisely, your computer) may be. The satellites are watching and will tell you.

The Geolocation API allows your browser to share your location with websites that you trust. The location is given in the form of latitude and longitude; the device may determine this information by using any of several techniques or a combination of them. These techniques include

- GPS
- Your computer's IP address
- Which cellphone tower your device is connected to
- The location of your wireless router

The API doesn't actually care how the device detects your location. What the API cares about is longitude, latitude, and the accuracy (in meters) of the device's estimate. Additional information may be available from the device, but it's not guaranteed to be available, including:

- **Altitude:** How high is your present location?
- **Altitude accuracy:** How sure is the browser of that altitude?
- **Heading:** Which direction are you moving?
- **Speed:** How fast are you moving?
- **Timestamp:** When, exactly was this information determined?

The Geolocation API is one of the coolest APIs around, and it's widely deployed on desktop browsers as well as mobile browsers. Although not technically part of the W3C Device API working group, they are closely related.

To see an example of the Geolocation API in action, visit `http://html5demos.com/geo`. As you see in Figure 18-7, the app opens a default Google map and asks your permission to get your location.

At the very top of your browser viewport, you'll see a dialog box asking if you'd like to share your location with the website. Click Share Location. The map should adjust to show your current location, or at least an approximation of your current location.

My dream "current location" is shown in Figure 18-8. Too bad there isn't a transporter API just yet.

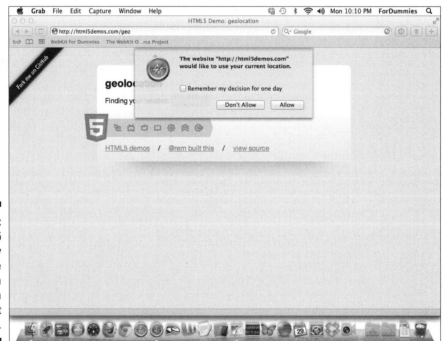

**Figure 18-7:**
The HTML5 Laboratory example opens a map to a default location.

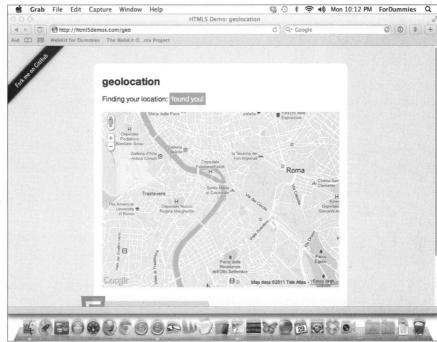

**Figure 18-8:**
If you share
your loca-
tion, the
map can
adjust (wish
I were
here).

# Getting your location with getCurrentPosition

The Geolocation API is surprisingly simple to use. To get the computer's current location (in longitude and latitude), all you need to do is use the following JavaScript API:

```
navigator.geolocation.getCurrentPosition(successCallback, errorCallback,
          options);
```

Listing 18-2 shows a real-life example that you can try in your WebKit
browser today. When you load this page, it will print your current latitude
and longitude.

**Listing 18-2:** **Getting Your Current Position**

```
<!DOCTYPE html>
<html>

  <head>

  <meta name = "viewport" content = "width = device-width"/>
  <title>Know Your Geolocation</title>
  </head>

  <body>
    <script>
      if (navigator.geolocation) {
      /* geolocation is available */

      var gps = navigator.geolocation.getCurrentPosition(tellme);

      } else {
        alert("Your browser doesn't support geolocation.");
      }

      function tellme(position) {

        var latitude = position.coords.latitude;

        var longitude = position.coords.longitude;

        document.write ('latitude: '+latitude+'<br />');

        document.write ('longitude: '+longitude+'<br />');

      }

  </script>



  </body>

</html>
```

So there you have it. With just a couple lines of code, you know the exact
location of your computer or mobile device. Here's how this code works:

1. You start, of course, with declaring that this is an HTML5 document and
   doing the normal things that you always do to set up the viewport for
   mobile devices and so forth.

```
<!DOCTYPE html>
<html>

  <head>

  <meta name = "viewport" content = "width = device-width"/>
  <title>Know Your Geolocation</title>
  </head>

  <body>
    <script>
```

2. Do a quick test to see whether the browser supports geolocation (if it does, you'll move forward).

```
if (navigator.geolocation) {
  /* geolocation is available */
```

3. The next line is where you do the real work of this app:

```
var gps = navigator.geolocation.getCurrentPosition(tellme);
```

This line of code uses a technique called a *callback,* in which you pass executable code to another function as a parameter.

Without going into the nitty-gritty details, this line first tells the browser to query the device's positioning hardware for the current location. When that information is ready, the code sends it to a function called `tellme` for further processing.

4. If geolocation isn't available, the `else` portion of the `if/else` test will run, which will display a message to the user.

```
} else {
  alert("Your browser doesn't support geolocation.");
}
```

5. The next few lines define the function that makes use of the positioning data, and that is called when `getCurrentPosition` returns its results.

```
function tellme(position) {

    var latitude = position.coords.latitude;

    var longitude = position.coords.longitude;

    document.write ('latitude: '+latitude+'<br />');

    document.write ('longitude: '+longitude+'<br />');

    }
```

The `gps` object that you created and packed with location information is brought into this function and given the new name `position`. The next two lines create new variables to hold the values of the `latitude` and `longitude` properties. Then, finally, use the `write` method of the `document` object to print these values to the web page.

6. Wrap up everything by closing all the tags you opened.

```
</script>



   </body>

</html>
```

# Mashing up with geolocation

Knowing your exact latitude and longitude is fun and everything, but it's hardly the sort of app anyone is going to get excited about (except for you and me, maybe). Where some exciting stuff starts to happen is when you use geolocation along with web APIs, such as Google Maps, to create mash-ups.

I'll finish this chapter with a somewhat more complicated example. Some of the techniques used in this example are beyond the scope of this book, but you can learn a lot about how the app works just by tinkering with it.

The app in Listing 18-3 takes your position information and uses it to show your current location on a Google map.

**Listing 18-3:    Showing Your Location on a Map**

```
<!DOCTYPE html>
<html>

<head>

<meta name="viewport" content="initial-scale=1.0, user-scalable=no" />

<meta http-equiv="content-type" content="text/html; charset=UTF-8" />

<title>Map Me!</title>

<script src="http://maps.google.com/maps/api/js?sensor=true"></script>

<script>

function $(id){

  return document.getElementById(id);

}
```

```
var you = {};

var map = {};


function initialize() {

if (navigator.geolocation){

  var gps = navigator.geolocation;

  gps.getCurrentPosition(function(position){

    var latLng = new google.maps.
             LatLng(position.coords.latitude,position.coords.longitude);

    var opts = {zoom:6, center:latLng, mapTypeId: google.maps.MapTypeId.
             ROADMAP};

    map = new google.maps.Map($("map_canvas"), opts);

    you = new google.maps.Marker({

      position: latLng,

      map: map,

      title: "There you are!"

      });
    var infowindow = new google.maps.InfoWindow({

      map: map,

      position: latLng,

      content: 'Location found using HTML5.'

      });


  showLocation(position);

  });

  } else {

    alert("Your browser doesn't support geolocation.");

  }
```

*(continued)*

**Listing 18-3** *(continued)*

```
}


function showLocation(position){

  var latLng = new google.maps.
            LatLng(position.coords.latitude,position.coords.longitude);
  }



</script>

</head>

<body style="margin: 0px; padding: 0px;" onload="initialize()">


  <div id="map_canvas"
            style="width: 100%; height: 100%; float: left; border: 1px solid
            black;"></div>

</body>

</html>
```

This example makes use of Google Maps API, which Google allows any web-site to use at no cost so long as the website is free for consumers. The Google Maps API license agreement makes a special exception to this "free" rule for mobile apps. You can use the Maps API in a mobile application that you charge a fee for and that is downloaded from an app store.

The confusing part of the special "mobile" exception relates to Mobile Web apps that are sold and accessed via the web, rather than from an app store. In this case, the Mobile Web app is essentially a website that's restricted to paying customers, and this would be forbidden by Google. If you want to sell a web app that uses the Google Maps API, you should check with Google and your lawyer. The safest bet may be to package it as a native app (using PhoneGap or another bridging framework) first.

Figure 18-9 shows the results of running this app in iOS. Notice that all of the regular functionality that you're used to having with Google Maps is available to you — including zooming, satellite view, and (if you zoom in close enough) street-level view.

**Figure 18-9:**
Using the
Geolocation
API with
Google
Maps API
to produce
a useful app
with minimal
code.

This example shows off the primary benefit of using web APIs such as Google Maps in your apps: It allows you to do amazing things that most of us would otherwise have no idea how to do, and to do them while writing only a minimal amount of code yourself.

# Chapter 19

# Graphics and Animation

*W*ithout graphics, the Web would be a dull place. Imagine what the web would be like if we didn't have LOLcats, FAIL Blog, or viral videos.

Fortunately, we don't live in that lifeless universe. Graphics are everywhere, and video currently accounts for the majority of the growth in web traffic. Networking equipment maker Cisco Systems has estimated that by 2013, video will make up 90 percent of consumer traffic on the Internet.

Two pages of text, or about 1,000 words, can be stored in about 4K. An image of that text, in 10-point (pt) Times New Roman, takes up about 400KB of disk space. In this case, a picture is worth 10,000 words, at least in terms of bandwidth.

If you have a powerful desktop computer and a broadband Internet connection, you're unlikely to notice too much if a web app makes less-than-optimal use of graphics. On mobile devices, however, graphics and video will be two of the most important factors determining whether your app will feel sluggish or slick to your users.

Today, web browsers are increasingly including support for two newer and much more flexible and lightweight types of graphics: Scalable Vector Graphics (SVG) and HTML5 `canvas` graphics. Support for these newer formats promises to enable a new, and much more flexible, generation of graphical web applications both on the desktop and on mobile devices.

# Understanding Computer Graphic Formats

Computer graphics are just dots of different-colored light arranged in a certain way onscreen. A graphics format's job is to store the information about where to put these dots so computers can reproduce the image.

Dozens of graphics formats are available to choose from, including GIF, PNG, JPEG, TIFF, AI, PSD, BMP, EPS, and many others. Each format serves a different purpose, and your choice of format depends on where the graphic will be used (on the Web, printed, onscreen), how high its quality is, how photorealistic it is, and other factors.

Computer graphics formats can be divided into two basic types: raster graphics and vector graphics.

## Raster graphics

*Raster graphic formats* store information images in a set of instructions that specify where to locate pixels on a rectangular grid. Another name for raster graphics is "bitmap" graphics.

When you take a picture, your digital camera stores the image as a raster graphic. The resulting JPEG file (or other format) contains encoded data about the color and position on a grid of each pixel in the image. This grid is the size of your photo and contains a defined number of pixels. For example, if an image has a size of 640 x 480 pixels (px), it contains $640 \times 480$ pixels (or 307,200 pixels).

If you zoom in on that picture, however, you're seeing the same number of pixels in a larger area, which is why the image quality degrades as you zoom in on a raster image.

Raster graphics are great for photographs, where a large amount of detail is necessary.

## Vector graphics

Vector graphics store the information about an image using lines, shapes, and colors represented as mathematical equations. The benefit of using vector graphics, when possible, is that they can be scaled infinitely larger or smaller without any change in resolution or file size.

Vector graphics work like telling a person to draw shapes. You may say something like, "Draw a circle with a diameter of five inches." It wouldn't take any longer to tell someone to draw a circle with a diameter of ten kilometers (although it would take longer to draw it, of course!).

When you're dealing with lines and shapes, vector graphics are much more succinct than raster graphics. As a result, they have much less of an impact on performance.

# Reducing File Size with Compression

If graphics and video are important to the look or functionality of your app, you should use them. However, if you're optimizing a web app for mobile devices, you need to be very aware of the tradeoffs between conserving limited bandwidth and compromising the look of your app.

This brings me to the topic of *compression,* which is reducing the size of a file using some sort of digital trickery. Merely using compression doesn't guarantee that your file will be optimized, though. If you misuse compression, it can have but a slight impact on the size of your file, or it can have a major (negative) impact on the look of your graphics.

Fortunately, the basics are easy to understand. Depending on the type of graphic, you can use one of two types of compression: lossy or lossless. Details coming right up. . . .

## Lossy compression

*Lossy* compression works by strategically throwing away parts of an image that you probably won't miss all that much. The human eye can distinguish among only so many shades of black, for example. A lossy compression format simplifies an image by reducing this sort of complexity in less-important details of an image.

The most popular example of a lossy compression format is JPEG, which does a very good job of compressing photographic images. When you create a JPEG image, you can select the image quality you want. What you're actually selecting is the level of compression. A higher level of compression means a smaller file size, but it also means a lower-quality image with more noticeable "artifacts" from the compression process.

## Lossless compression

*Lossless* compression works by using statistical models to replace the pixel-by-pixel representation of an image with information about how each pixel is different from the last.

Lossless compression works because images, especially those created using a drawing program, often contain areas of identical pixels. The image in Figure 19-1 can be highly compressed using lossless compression. (This PNG image is 11K.) It has only two colors, and large contiguous portions of the image are solid blocks of white or black.

**Figure 19-1:**
Simple
graphics
can be
highly com-
pressed.

Figure 19-2 shows an image with exactly the same dimensions as Figure 19-1 but that can't be compressed very much at all because it doesn't contain any large, predictable, blocks of color.

**Figure 19-2:**
Lossless
compres-
sion doesn't
work
well with
complex
graphics.

Figure 19-3 shows the same image as in Figure 19-2, but compressed using JPEG (a lossy compression format). This graphic doesn't look noticeably different from the PNG file, but the file size has gone from 547 KB (in the PNG) to 91 KB (in the JPEG).

**Figure 19-3:**
JPEG compression for complex images reduces the file size without much reduction in image quality.

At typical 3G wireless speeds, this simple change to use the correct file format for the job will reduce the download time of this image by at least several seconds.

Use lossy compression formats (such as JPEG) when you're working with highly complex images, such as photographs. Use lossless compression formats (such as GIF or PNG) when you're dealing with simpler graphics, such as icons.

# Drawing with SVG

Scalable Vector Graphics (SVG) is the W3C specification for vector graphics. SVG graphics are created by using XML in text files. For example, here's the code for drawing a circle using SVG:

```
<svg xmlns="http://www.w3.org/2000/svg" version="1.1">
  <circle cx="175" cy="60" r="40" stroke="black"
  stroke-width="4" fill="yellow"/>
</svg>
```

To see this circle rendered in your WebKit browser, follow these steps:

1. **Open your WebKit browser.**

2. **Choose Develop⇨Snippet Editor to open the Snippet Editor.**

3. **Paste or type the SVG code into the top window.**

   When you finish entering the code, a yellow circle with a black border should appear in the lower frame of the Snippet Editor, as shown in Figure 19-4.

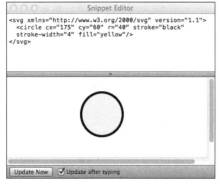

**Figure 19-4:** You can try SVG graphics in WebKit by using the Snippet Editor.

The only information SVG needs to draw a circle is the starting location of the center of the circle and the radius of the circle. The starting location is specified by using the cx and cy attributes, and the radius is specified by using the r attribute. To actually make the circle visible, you need to at least add either a fill attribute or a stroke attribute.

SVG can also be used to draw other shapes and lines. By using multiple shapes in combination, you can create any image you want, but the XML code for highly complex images can get to be way more than you could possibly create by hand.

For this reason, most people create SVG graphics with the help of an SVG editor.

## Making graphics with SVG-edit

SVG-edit is a free, browser-based SVG editor. To get started creating some SVG graphics that you can use in WebKit, follow these steps:

1. **Go to** `http://code.google.com/p/svg-edit/` **and click the link to open the latest version.**

   You see a blank canvas, similar to the one shown in Figure 19-5. Notice that the toolbar has all the tools that you expect from a simple drawing program.

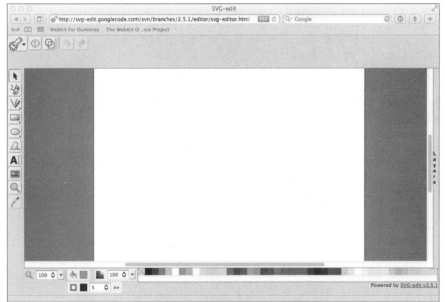

**Figure 19-5:**
SVG-edit is a full-featured drawing program.

2. **Select the Oval tool from the left-hand toolbar.**

   If you click and hold the Oval tool, you see three sub-items. The first one enables you to draw an oval of any size and shape. The second one is for drawing circles only. And the third allows you draw freehand shapes with the Pencil tool and then turn them into ovals.

3. **Draw some ovals (or anything you want, really).**

   Try using the color picker to change the fill and border colors.

4. **Experiment with the different tools and come up with your masterpiece.**

   Figure 19-6 shows my (ahem) awesome work of art.

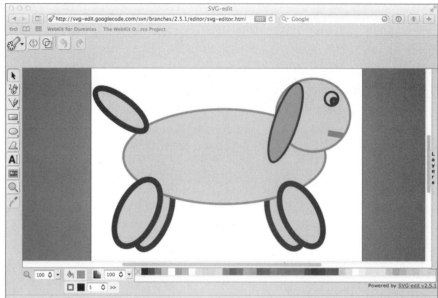

**Figure 19-6:**
Draw some-
thing and
then peek
at the code
beneath.

**5. Click the SVG source button near the top.**

A window opens to show you the generated SVG code, as shown in
Figure 19-7. If you didn't use many complicated shapes in your drawing,
notice how little code it takes to create your drawing.

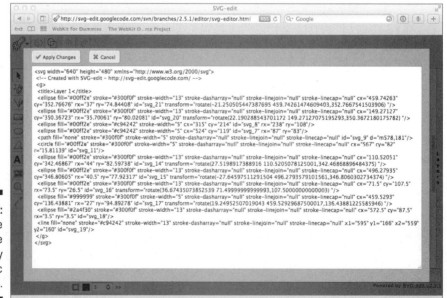

**Figure 19-7:**
A little code
can produce
a stunningly
realistic
image.

6. **Make some changes to the SVG code and then click Apply Changes.**

   See what the change did, and then try something else.

   You're completely free to change anything in the SVG code. However, if you change something that generates a syntax error, your drawing may not display correctly or at all. No problem, though! Just use the Undo button, or start a new drawing.

## Finding SVG graphics

Because SVG Graphics are XML, search engines can index them just like any other text content on the Web. Google Image Search does just this, and even makes it possible for you to search for just SVG graphics. Being able to search for SVG graphics makes learning more about SVG — and seeing great examples of what it can do — much easier.

Here's how you can do searches on Google for just SVG graphics:

1. **Open your WebKit browser and go to** `http://images.google.com`.
2. **Click the Advanced Image Search link to the right of the Search Images button.**
3. **On the Advanced Images Search form, enter a keyword, such as** animal.
4. **Select SVG Files from the File Type drop-down menu.**
5. **Click Search Images.**

   Your results appear.
6. **Browse through the pages of search results.**

   Click a few to see them up close.

## Embedding SVG graphics in HTML

To use SVG graphics in HTML5 documents, do the following:

1. **Save the SVG document in its own file with a `.svg` extension.**

   SVG is written in XML, so the rules are a little different for how SVG code is written when that code has to be in the `.svg` file. Make sure that your SVG file has an XML document type declaration and also that the SVG element contains the `xmlns` attribute.

**2. Use the HTML `<object>` element to include the contents of the `.svg` file.**

There are actually a couple other ways to include SVG files in HTML, but the use of the `<object>` element is the most widely supported by browsers.

Listing 19-1 shows a valid SVG document.

Pay special attention to the following differences with HTML5 syntax:

✔ The XML document type declaration is required to be at the beginning of the file.

✔ The `<svg>` element should contain an `xmlns` attribute.

✔ XML is case sensitive. To reduce mistakes, good practice is to simply make all your markup code lowercase.

### Listing 19-1: An SVG Document

```
<?xml version="1.0"?>
<svg xmlns="http://www.w3.org/2000/svg">
  <circle cx="175" cy="60" r="40" stroke="black"
                     stroke-width="4" fill="yellow">
  </circle>
</svg>
```

Listing 19-2 shows what the HTML document that displays this SVG image should look like.

### Listing 19-2: Including SVG in HTML

```
<!DOCTYPE HTML>
<html>
<head>
  <meta name="viewport" content="initial-scale=1.0, user-scalable=no" />
  <title>Yellow Circle</title>
</head>
<body>
```

```
   <object data="animationfun.svg" type="image/svg+xml"></object>
</body>
</html>
```

Piece of cake, right? But wait — it gets even better with HTML5. Listing 19-3 shows the new and improved method of writing SVG directly into HTML5 documents.

**Listing 19-3:   HTML5 SVG Element**

```
<!DOCTYPE HTML>
<html>
<head>
  <meta name="viewport" content="initial-scale=1.0, user-scalable=no" />
  <title>Yellow Circle</title>
</head>
<body>
  <svg xmlns="http://www.w3.org/2000/svg">
  <circle cx="175" cy="60" r="40" stroke="black"
                        stroke-width="4" fill="yellow">
  </circle>
  </svg>
</body>
</html>
```

This method works now in WebKit and in most web browsers, and is useful for simple graphics that don't require a lot of code and that you don't need to reuse on other pages.

Clearly, this inline embedding method wouldn't be as useful if you wanted to embed a very complex graphic on multiple pages.

# Animating SVG with SMIL

SVG is great for creating and displaying static graphics, but things start getting fun when you start animating vector graphics with SVG. There are actually three different ways to animate SVG:

- ✔ JavaScript
- ✔ CSS
- ✔ Synchronized Multimedia Integration Language (SMIL)

WebKit supports all three of these methods for animating SVG, but I'm going to focus on SMIL because it's the standard, and perhaps simplest, method.

To animate an object with SMIL, you use the `<animate>` element. Listing 19-4 shows how to animate the movement of a yellow circle from left to right on your screen — and to repeat that movement ten times.

### Listing 19-4:   Moving a Yellow Circle across the Screen

```
<svg xmlns="http://www.w3.org/2000/svg">
  <circle cx="175" cy="60" r="40" stroke="black"
                    stroke-width="4" fill="yellow">
  <animate attributeName="cx" to="0" dur="3s" repeatCount="10" />
  </circle>
</svg>
```

Take a closer look at the `animate` element. This example uses four different attributes:

- ✔ `attributeName` is where you specify what property of the object you want to change over time. In this case, I set it to `cx`, which represents the horizontal position of the circle's center.

- ✔ `to` indicates the end goal of the animation. Because the `cx` property of the circle is initially set at `175`, the animation being created will adjust that number step by step until it gets to `0`.

- ✔ `dur` is short for duration. In this case, it's set to 3 seconds (`3s`). This animation will take exactly 3 seconds to move the circle from a `cx` of `175` to `0`. If you want the circle to move faster or slower, you can change the value of the `dur` attribute.

- ✔ `repeatCount` does exactly what you would think: It tells the browser to start the animation over when it's done and repeat the action this many times.

In addition to moving objects, you can use SMIL to animate the colors of an object, cause the object to move along a path, or to animate rotation and transformation of objects.

# Scripting Graphics with the Canvas Element

New to HTML is the `canvas` element that creates a "draw-able" region in an HTML document. Like SVG, `canvas` allows you to draw graphics in the browser, but it's different from SVG in a number of important ways.

- ✔ **SVG creates vector graphics, while `canvas` creates raster (or, bitmap) graphics.** So, even though you can use `canvas` to draw shapes, these shapes are rendered in the browser as pixels, rather than as mathematical shapes.

- ✔ **Drawings on `canvas` aren't accessible with the DOM, whereas SVG objects are.** SVG objects are created with XML markup. So, with SVG, you can assign event handlers, such as `onclick`, to objects. Inside a `canvas`, you're actually drawing pixels, with no connection to the DOM.

- ✔ **The `canvas` element creates graphics; SVG creates objects.** Because `canvas` is just drawing graphics to the screen with JavaScript, it runs much faster than SVG, which is creating actual objects in the browser.

Both `canvas` and SVG have their places:

- ✔ If you need high-performance graphics — when you're creating games, for instance — `canvas` is the way to go.

- ✔ If you need objects that can be scaled to fit different screen resolutions and if you need to work with your drawings through the DOM (for animation or interactivity purposes, for example), SVG is the way to go.

## Creating a canvas

The code for creating a canvas looks like this:

```
<canvas id="mycanvas" width="300" height="300">
This is a canvas. Your browser will display this text if it doesn't support the
            canvas element.
</canvas>
```

The `canvas` element takes just two attributes — `height` and `width` — in addition to the global HTML attributes, such as `id` and `title`. The `canvas` element just creates the blank sheet of virtual paper for you to draw upon.

## Drawing on the canvas

After you have a canvas, you can use the canvas API to draw 2-D graphics on the canvas with JavaScript. For example, the following code will draw a yellow rectangle (a square, to be precise):

```
var mycanvas = document.getElementById('mycanvas');
var context = mycanvas.getContext('2d');
context.fillStyle = "rgb(255,255,0)";
context.fillRect(10, 10, 50, 50);
```

Take this example apart, line by line, to get a better understanding of what's going on before moving on to more advanced canvas topics.

This first line of JavaScript code locates the canvas in the DOM, using the value of its id attribute (mycanvas).

```
var mycanvas = document.getElementById('mycanvas');
```

After it locates the canvas, it can assign it to a variable (mycanvas) that you'll use as a shortcut later.

This next line is required before you do any drawing on the canvas. It defines the object on which your drawing actually appears. In this case, it's the two-dimensional square defined by your HTML5 canvas element.

```
var context = mycanvas.getContext('2d');
```

At this point, 2d is really the only valid parameter to use here. 3-D canvases will be supported in the future, but they aren't yet, so don't worry about it.

The fillStyle property is used to set the fill color for any shape. I haven't yet created this shape in this running example, but the next shape to create (and any shapes created after that) will use this style — until the value of fillStyle is changed, of course.

```
context.fillStyle = "rgb(255,255,0)";
```

In this case, I'm setting the fill style to yellow, using RGB color values.

The following is where you actually create the rectangle. The fillRect method takes four parameters. These are (in order) x (horizontal) start point, y (vertical) start point, width, and height.

```
context.fillRect(10, 10, 50, 50);
```

The x and y values are based on the upper-left corner of the canvas. So, with a 300 x 300 canvas, this square will begin 10 pixels (px) in from the left side of the canvas and 10px down from the top. Listing 19-5 shows a complete HTML document with the canvas and JavaScript for drawing this lovely square.

**Listing 19-5:   Using canvas to Draw a Square**

```
<!DOCTYPE HTML>
<html>
<head>
<title>a square</title>
</head>
<body bgcolor="#dadada">
  <canvas id="mycanvas" width="300" height="300">
  This is a canvas. Your browser will display this text if it doesn't support
            the canvas element.
  </canvas>
  <script>
    var mycanvas = document.getElementById('mycanvas');
    var context = mycanvas.getContext('2d');
    context.fillStyle = "rgb(255,255,0)";
    context.fillRect(10, 10, 50, 50);
  </script>
</body>
</html>
```

Figure 19-8 shows what this canvas looks like rendered in a web browser.

## Animating with canvas

Because canvas draws pixels, rather than shape objects, animation works very differently from the way it works with SVG. In SVG, you'll recall, you can move an object by specifying a starting location, an ending location, and the amount of time the object should take to get from point A to point B. The canvas element, on the other hand, works like a flipbook: Erasing the previous drawing, and then drawing a new shape in a slightly different location creates the animation.

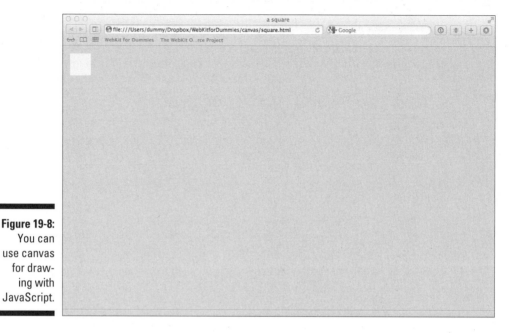

**Figure 19-8:**
You can
use canvas
for draw-
ing with
JavaScript.

So, to animate the yellow square in the previous example, you first specify how often it will refresh (using `setInterval`). Then you create a function that actually does the drawing — and that makes the drawing slightly differently each time it's run.

You can modify the previous example, as shown in Listing 19-6, to make the yellow square move across the screen.

### Listing 19-6: Moving the Square

```
<!DOCTYPE HTML>
<html>
<head>
  <title>an animated square</title>
</head>
<body>
  <canvas id="mycanvas" width="600" height="400" style="border:1px
           dotted;float:left">
  This is a canvas. Your browser will display this text if it doesn't support
             the canvas element.
```

```
</canvas>
<script>
/*first, set some initial values and declare global variables*/
var x = 10;
var y = 10;
var dx = 3;
var dy = 4;
var w = 50;
var h = 50;
var mycanvas;
var context;
var WIDTH = 600;
var HEIGHT = 400;
function rect(x,y,w,h) {
  /*draws a rectangle of the specified size, at the specified location */
  context.fillStyle = "rgb(255,0,0)";
  context.fillRect(x, y, w, h);
  }
function clear() {
  /*erases the canvas*/
  context.clearRect(0, 0, WIDTH, HEIGHT);
  }
function init() {
  /*initializes the canvas and sets the refresh interval*/
  mycanvas = document.getElementById('mycanvas');
  context = mycanvas.getContext('2d');
  return setInterval(draw, 10);
  }
function draw() {
  /*draws a shape, then calculates the position of the next shape*/
  clear();
  rect(x, y, w, h);
  /*test for whether any part of the shape is over a horizontal edge and change
            directions if so*/
  if (x + dx > (WIDTH - w) || x + dx < 0) {
            dx = -dx;
            }
  /*test for whether any part of the shape is over a vertical edge and change
            directions if so*/
  if (y + dy > (HEIGHT - h) || y + dy < 0) {
            dy = -dy;
            }
  /*calculate the position of the next shape*/
  x += dx;
  y += dy;
  }
  init();
</script>
</body>
</html>
```

I added some comments to this listing to help explain what's going on. Here are a few of the sticky bits in more detail.

All the code in this listing is contained within functions, except for two things:

✔ **The variables at the beginning of the `<script>` block:** These variables are set outside any function (instead of within the curly braces of a function) so that they can be used inside any of the functions. Variables defined in this way are *global variables.* In JavaScript, as is the case with most programming languages, when a variable is declared inside a function, the variable can be used only inside that function.

✔ **The call to the `init()` function at the end of the `<script>` block:** This is the function call that sets off the whole chain of events that makes this animation work.

Functions don't do anything until they are invoked by other code. So, even though all the functions in this JavaScript program are already created and read by the browser, nothing actually happens until one of them is specifically called.

The `init()` function call sets off a chain of events that will go on forever, or until you close your browser. Here's the `init()` function again.

```
function init() {
  /*initializes the canvas and sets the refresh interval*/
  mycanvas = document.getElementById('mycanvas');
  context = mycanvas.getContext('2d');
  return setInterval(draw, 10);
  }
```

This code is the standard code for configuring a new canvas with JavaScript. The one addition I made is to call the `setInterval` method. The `setInterval` method takes two parameters: what to do and how often (in milliseconds; ms) to do it. So, in this case, `setInterval` calls the `draw` function every 10 ms.

Setting the interval to a longer time (such as 20 or 30 ms or more) is like reducing the frames per second of a movie camera: It has the effect of slowing down the action and of creating less-smooth animation. On the other hand, if you're animating many objects simultaneously, you'll likely need to use a higher interval time to avoid bringing the computer's CPU to a grinding halt.

Now focus on the `draw` function.

```
function draw() {
  /*draws a shape, then calculates the position of the next shape*/
  clear();
  rect(x, y, w, h);
  /*test for whether any part of the shape is over a horizontal edge and change
          directions if so*/
  if (x + dx > (WIDTH - w) || x + dx < 0) {
          dx = -dx;
          }
  /*test for whether any part of the shape is over a vertical edge and change
          directions if so*/
  if (y + dy > (HEIGHT - h) || y + dy < 0) {
          dy = -dy;
          }
  /*calculate the position of the next shape*/
  x += dx;
  y += dy;
  }
```

The first line of code in the `draw` function is a call to a function called `clear`. Allow me to take a quick detour to the `clear` function and talk about what that does.

The `clear` function simply erases everything on the canvas within the rectangle that you define. In this case, I'm clearing everything within a rectangle that's the same size as the canvas.

```
function clear() {
  /*erases the canvas*/
  context.clearRect(0, 0, WIDTH, HEIGHT);
  }
```

To see why this is necessary, look at Figure 19-9, which shows what happens when I remove the call to the `clear` function from the `draw` function. Instead of moving the rectangle, the code just draws a thick line that will eventually fill the entire canvas.

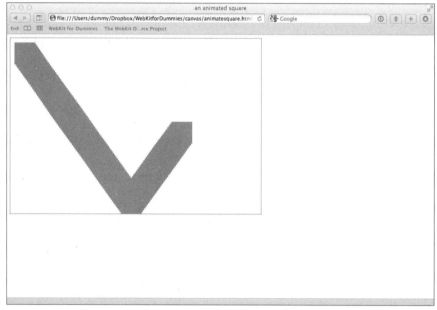

**Figure 19-9:**
Unless this
is what you
want, clear
the canvas
after each
frame.

Immediately after the script clears the canvas by using the `clear` function, it calls the `rect` function.

```
rect(x, y, w, h);
```

This function takes four parameters. The first time it's called, each of the parameters has the default values that were set at the top of the `<script>` block. Execution of the code takes a detour to inside the `rect` function now.

```
function rect(x,y,w,h) {
    /*draws a rectangle of the specified size, at the specified location */
    context.fillStyle = "rgb(255,0,0)";
    context.fillRect(x, y, w, h);
}
```

This function simply takes the parameters passed to it by the `draw` function and draws a square of the specified size, at the specified location. If you wanted, you could also dynamically set the color of the rectangle at this point, perhaps by passing in additional parameters. In the interest of simplicity, though, just change the location for now.

After the browser draws the rectangle, execution of the code returns to the next line in the `draw` function.

```
if (x + dx > (WIDTH - w) || x + dx < 0) {
        dx = -dx;
        }
```

The function of this line is to test the location of the next rectangle to be drawn as well as reverse the direction of the animation if drawing another one going in the current direction will put it over the horizontal boundary of the canvas.

This code may look indecipherable to you if you're not used to thinking like a computer, so I'll break it down:

```
if (x + dx > (WIDTH - w)
```

Remember that `x` is the horizontal location of the last rectangle to be drawn. The `dx` variable is used to specify how far the rectangle will move with each frame of the animation. The width of the `canvas` is set with the `WIDTH` variable, and `w` is equal to the width of the rectangle.

So, what this is saying, in English, is, "If moving the rectangle horizontally by 3 pixels will cause the new location of the rectangle to be greater than the width of the `canvas` minus the width of the rectangle. . . ."

The reason for subtracting the width of the rectangle from the width of the canvas here is that the `x` location of a rectangle is specified as its upper-left corner. If the `x` location of a 50px-wide rectangle is `580`, and the `canvas` is 600px wide, then 30px of the rectangle will be outside the canvas.

So, to simplify even further, this code is really saying, "If moving the rectangle will put it over the right edge of the canvas. . . ."

Okay, good, you tested for the right edge. Immediately after the right-edge test are two vertical lines (||). In JavaScript, this means "or."

Now, move on to the rest of this line:

```
x + dx < 0
```

Here, you're testing for the left edge of the canvas by checking whether the x position of the next rectangle will be less than 0 (zero). Note that you don't subtract the width of the rectangle here because the x position of the rectangle is on the left.

The next part of the line of code says what to do if either test evaluates as true:

```
dx = -dx;
```

What you're saying here is to change the value of dx to a negative number. The effect this change has is to avoid going over the canvas boundary by moving the rectangle in the opposite direction.

The next line in the script does the same test and reversal for the y-axis:

```
if (y + dy > (HEIGHT - h) || y + dy < 0) {
        dy = -dy;
        }
```

The final two lines calculate the position of the next rectangle by adding the values of dx and dy to the current values of x and y.

```
x += dx;
```

```
y += dy;
```

After this is done, the next frame of the animation will start, back up at the top of the draw function, with new values for x and y.

The result produced by this script is an animation of a red rectangle that appears to be bouncing off the border of the canvas at 90-degree angles. You can adjust the different starting variables such as the canvas size, rectangle size, movement increments (dx and dy), and animation speed to customize the script. You may even want to try adding another rectangle or other shape that moves differently from the first.

WebKit-based mobile browsers also feature support for `canvas`. Figure 19-10 shows this animation running in iOS.

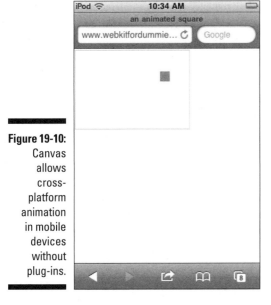

**Figure 19-10:**
Canvas
allows
cross-
platform
animation
in mobile
devices
without
plug-ins.

Using the `canvas` element, you can create complex cross-platform drawings and animation that will work in both desktop and mobile browsers. In this chapter, I just scratched the surface of what's possible.

# Chapter 20

# The Future of WebKit and HTML5

*W*ebKit is large and complex, and it keeps getting larger and more complex — but also better. The same can be said for HTML5. In this chapter, I show you a few of the newest things coming to a browser near you and explain why they're so significant.

## WebKit2

What's better than WebKit? WebKit2, of course!

WebKit2 is the name used to describe the latest re-engineering of the WebKit structure. The point of WebKit2 is to increase the stability and speed of WebKit rather than to give you any new functionality.

The WebKit nightly build that you've been working with is WebKit2, and the version of Safari that's included with Mac OS X starting with version 10.7 (Lion) is also based on WebKit2.

The different between WebKit and WebKit2 is that WebKit2 has more separation between web content (such as JavaScript, CSS, HTML, and so forth) and the application (meaning everything else that makes up the browser). The reason for making this division stronger is to increase both the speed and stability of the browser.

In WebKit, which uses a single process model, one crashed browser tab can bring down everything. With WebKit2, if a web app in one tab happens to become unresponsive for some reason, it shouldn't affect your ability to use web apps in the other tabs.

# Getting Input with Web Forms

For years, HTML forms have been completely inadequate to the task of gathering data for web applications. Ingenious web developers have relied on tricks and JavaScript to make up for what HTML lacked, but these solutions have always been inconsistently applied.

With HTML5, HTML forms are getting a major overhaul — and some long-overdue new powers.

## Placeholder text

*Placeholder text* is text that displays in an input field until you click in the field. It often gives some instructions or hints about the type of information the form author is looking for, or how you should format your input. To create placeholder text with HTML5, just use the `placeholder` attribute like this:

```
<input type="text" name="fav_icecream" placeholder="Strawberry or vanilla, for
          example">
```

## Autofocus

*Autofocus* is the technique of putting the cursor into a certain field when the page first loads. For example, if you visit Google.com, you can start typing your search query right away without having to first click in the search form.

To enable autofocus for a form field in an HTML5 document, put the `autofocus` attribute in the `input` element. It looks like this:

```
<input type="text" name="search" autofocus>
```

If your browser doesn't understand the `autofocus` attribute, it will just ignore it.

## New field types

HTML5 has a slew of new field types. If you've worked with previous versions of HTML, you know that the standard input types have always been pretty vague: `text`, `select`, `textarea`, `hidden`, `checkbox`, `radio`, `submit`, `reset`. What HTML5 has done is create input types for the types of data that web-app developers actually gather.

HTML5 contains new input types, such as the following:

```
url         search
tel         email
datetimee   date
time        color
```

The Forms section of the HTML5 specification defines parameters for what sort of data can be entered into may of these new input types. For example, a URL or an e-mail address needs to be in a standard URL or e-mail address format in order for input to be valid.

The result of all these new input types is that it will be easier for web-app developers to gather useful data from users, and fewer users will be frustrated by having their data rejected by a server for being in the wrong format. Enforcing formatting and syntax rules for input types can also make it easier for the user to input data, by allowing the browser to display input fields using controls that make sense for the particular type of data.

Take a closer look at some of the new input types and how they're currently implemented (or not) in WebKit.

## Number sliders

When users are expected to choose from a range of numbers, it may be easier on them to use a slider control rather than typing in a number. This is especially true when the range of values controls something that users don't really think about or care about numerically — say, volume or brightness. Users don't care whether the volume is 5 or 7 (or, okay, 11). What they care about is whether it's loud enough.

To create a slider in HTML5, use the following markup:

```
<input type="range"
       min="0"
       max="11"
       step="1"
       value="5">
```

A value of "range" in the type attribute tells the browser to render this control as a slider. Figure 20-1 shows what this slider control looks like in WebKit.

Figure 20-1:
A volume
slider can
go up to any
number in
HTML5.

## Color

The `color input type` is used for when you'd like a user to select a color. As of today, the only browser that actually supports this input type is Opera. Eventually, however, you'll be able to use this input type anywhere that you'd like users to choose a color, and some sort of a color picker will appear when the user clicks the input field.

```
<input type="color" name="pickacolor">
```

As shown in Figure 20-2, here's how Opera displays color input fields.

Figure 20-2:
Opera
browser
supports
color picker
inputs.

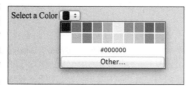

## Date pickers

Like color pickers, date pickers are also not yet supported by WebKit. The Opera browser does support date pickers, however.

```
<input type="date" name="pickadate">
```

As shown in Figure 20-3, here's how Opera displays the date input field.

**Figure 20-3:**
Date pick-
ers make
choosing a
date easier.

# Creating 3-D Scenes with WebGL

Web-based Graphics Library (WebGL) is one of the most exciting new Web technologies to look forward to enjoying in the coming years. It allows JavaScript access to your computer's graphics card directly to speed up rendering 3-D graphics.

## Enabling WebGL in WebKit

WebGL support is built in to the latest versions of WebKit. However, it's not enabled by default. To turn on WebGL support in your WebKit browser, just select Enable WebGL from the Develop menu.

After that, your WebKit browser suddenly becomes a 3-D rendering powerhouse. It's capable of displaying interactive 3-D models, taking you into 3-D worlds using nothing but HTML5 code and enabling you to play some great HTML5 games.

## Taking WebGL for a spin

WebGL isn't yet as fast as native graphics libraries. But, there have been many very impressive apps and demonstrations created with it that all point toward the web of the future being much more graphically rich and exciting. The most famous demo of WebGL is the version of the first-person shooter game, *Quake 2,* that runs entirely in your web browser.

Google currently hosts the WebGL Quake 2 project at `http://code.google.com/p/quake2-gwt-port/`. To try it, you can download the code and install it on your own server, or you can try searching for someone else who has installed it so you can play her version.

If you don't have the patience to install all the various requirements and you don't care enough to find and visit a site where it's been previously installed, you can turn to YouTube. Several great videos of people playing Quake 2 in the browser have been made. Figure 20-4 shows a still from one of these videos.

**Figure 20-4:** WebGL permits an interactive web graphics first: the first-person shooter.

The exciting thing about WebGL isn't that it makes your computer able to display 3-D graphics or a game from 1997. If that's all there were to it, it wouldn't be noteworthy at all.

What *is* so great about WebGL is that it makes a merger between the vast resources of the Web and 3-D graphics possible, and it does it all with no plug-ins and nothing to install — except a browser, of course. The other very exciting thing about WebGL is that it's getting better and faster as web browsers progress and as JavaScript execution gets faster.

Google has really been at the forefront of demonstrating the power of WebGL and pushing its limits. To see (yet another) mind-blowing demonstration, visit www.ro.me.

Figure 20-5 shows a still from this 3-D interactive music video that merges video with interactivity and graphics that are generated as the video plays.

**Figure 20-5:**
Ro.me
shows the
power of
WebGL.

# Chrome OS

In 2009, Google announced that it was working on an operating system based on its WebKit browser, Chrome, and that the operating system would be called Chrome OS. In 2011, the first netbooks with Chrome OS installed shipped. All apps that run on Chrome OS are web apps, and Google has built a store (the Chrome Web Store) where you can browse both paid and free web apps and add them to Chrome.

When you choose an app from the Chrome Web Store, a verification window confirms that you want to install it, and informs you of the permissions that the app requires (such as access to your Clipboard or location data) and then adds the app to your desktop.

The experience of using Chrome OS is very much like using a large mobile device or tablet computer, except that everything happens in the browser. In addition to all the apps available through the Chrome Web Store, hundreds of extensions are available to add functionality to Chrome (and, therefore, to Chrome OS).

Chrome OS has a user interface that is essentially the Chrome web browser, as you can see in Figure 20-6. I'm preparing to install one of my favorite old arcade games, Lunar Lander.

**Figure 20-6:**
Chrome OS
is based, in
large part,
on WebKit.

Currently, only a limited number of manufacturers are offering netbooks with Chrome OS (called "Chromebooks"). You can try Chrome OS by downloading the source code from Google, compiling it, and running it in a virtual-machine environment such as VirtualBox.

Of course, if you don't have the patience for compiling source code, you can find and download a nightly build of Chrome OS on the web. One such source for downloading the latest version of Chrome OS (actually, Chromium OS, the open source version) is from Liam McLoughlin at `hexxeh.net`.

To try Chrome OS using a virtual machine downloaded from hexxeh.net, follow these steps:

1. **Go to** `http://chromeos.hexxeh.net/vanilla.php` **and download the most recent VirtualBox image.**

   The file will download to your computer with a `.tar.gz` extension.

2. **Uncompress the downloaded file.**

   - *Mac OS X:* Double-click it and use the Archive Utility to uncompress it.

- *Windows:* You may need to download a separate program, such as WinRAR, to uncompress it. When it's uncompressed, you'll have a file with a `.vdi` extension. This is a VirtualBox disk image.

3. **Download and install VirtualBox from** `www.virtualbox.org`.

   VirtualBox software creates a *virtual machine* — a window that runs operating systems within your computer's primary operating system.

4. **Start VirtualBox.**

5. **Choose Machine⇨New from the main menu.**

   The New Virtual Machine Wizard opens.

6. **Click Continue to move past the introductory screen of the wizard.**

7. **Give your new virtual machine a name.**

   Something like Chrome OS Nightly may be appropriate.

8. **Select Linux from the Operating System drop-down menu and then Other Linux from the Version drop-down menu; then click Continue.**

9. **Select the amount of RAM to allocate to the virtual machine.**

   Chrome OS requires a large amount of RAM, especially when it's running in a virtual machine. Select at least 1GB (1024MB), or else the virtual machine will run extremely slowly.

10. **Click Continue to advance to the next step of the wizard.**

11. **Choose the Use Existing Hard Disk option and then click the folder icon to the right of the drop-down menu.**

12. **Locate and select the `.vdi` file that you downloaded and uncompressed.**

13. **Click Continue and then Create to confirm and create your new virtual machine.**

14. **Select your new virtual machine from the VirtualBox home screen and click start to crank it up.**

    After a short while (depending on how fast your computer is and how much RAM you allocated to the virtual machine), you'll see the initial configuration wizard for Chrome OS, as shown in Figure 20-7.

15. **A touchpad tutorial appears onscreen, which you may not be able to get through by using a mouse.**

    If this is the case, close the window containing the tutorial.

    You're brought to a default screen similar to the one shown in Figure 20-8.

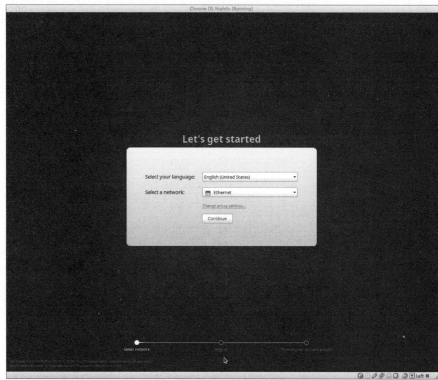

**Figure 20-7:**
The virtual
machine
that's
running
Chrome OS.

Chrome OS is still in its infancy, but it's already showing just how capable and useful a browser can be (and specifically, a WebKit browser). In the same way that Mobile Web apps are the next step in the development of mobile apps, some people are already predicting that Chrome OS, or some web-based operating system such as Chrome OS, is the next step in the evolution of computing on desktops, laptops, and netbooks.

# Part VI
# The Part of Tens

**Permissions**

- **Phone calls**
  Read phone state and identity

- **System tools**
  Prevent phone from sleeping

- **Network communication**
  Full Internet access

- **Your location**
  Coarse (network-based) location, fine

# In this part . . .

The best advice I can give anyone who wants to get a leg up in the new world of HTML5 and the mobile Web is to spend time every day finding out what's new and what other people are doing.

In this part I show you some of the less-known features of WebKit. These are the sorts of things that don't make the headlines and that you might have to dig pretty deep to even know they exist. Then, you'll see some more cutting-edge Web apps that take advantage of features built in to WebKit. Creating and viewing demonstration apps is a fantastic way to learn a new skill. Perhaps you'll even be inspired to try your hand at some demo apps yourself. Finally, I'll tip you off to some of the tools that you can add on to your WebKit/Safari browser to make your life just a bit easier.

# Chapter 21

# Ten Cool WebKit Tricks

*T*his book presents the many things that WebKit is capable of. In this chapter, I show you some features and capabilities that you may not have known about, along with some tools that you can use in conjunction with WebKit to do some things that go beyond your normal browser functions.

## HTML Editor

One component of WebKit that you don't often get to see when you're just browsing the web is its HTML Editor. Currently, the WebKit HTML editor is mostly used for enabling HTML editing in desktop applications, such as Apple's Mail and iChat.

The WebKit HTML editor can also be used for online editing of web pages by using the HTML5 `contentEditable` attribute. Figure 21-1 shows a simple HTML editor demo from the WebKit website. You can try this demo for yourself at `www.webkit.org/demos/editingToolbar`.

The text on this page looks normal, but when you click it, a WYSIWYG editor appears, and you can start editing the content.

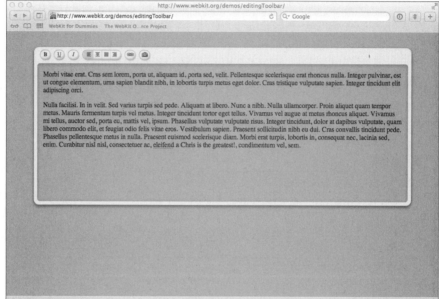

**Figure 21-1:**
WebKit
and HTML5
enable
WYSIWYG
editing
of HTML
pages.

The changes you're making to this page are made only on your local copy. When you reload the page, WebKit will download the content from the server again, and your changes will be gone.

# Alternate WebKit Applications

You've heard of Apple Safari, Google Chrome, and the BlackBerry browser, but do you know about the Flock browser? How about the Surf browser?

Because WebKit is open source, and because it can do so much, a lot of people and companies have used it as the basis for all sorts of applications. The WebKit project keeps track of these applications at the following URL:

```
http://trac.webkit.org/wiki/Applications%20using%20WebKit
```

Just a few of the applications that use WebKit are

- ✔ **Flock:** Flock (www.flock.com) is a browser for people who spend a lot of time with social networking sites such as Facebook and Twitter.

✔ **Sunrise Browser:** Sunrise Browser (http://www.sunrisebrowser.com/) is a browser for web developers. It has developer-friendly features, such as source code tabs that are paired with the web page tab (for easily comparing and finding code), and a URL downloader that allows you to put in the URL to a file you want to download rather than open.

✔ **eCrisper:** eCrisper (http://ecrisper.com) turns your Mac OS X computer into a secure pubic access kiosk. With eCrisper, you can prevent users from accessing the underlying operating system and restrict them just to the task at hand, which may be a presentation at a tradeshow, an exhibit at a museum, or a library book catalog, for example.

# Remote Debugging

*Remote debugging,* the capability to control and analyze web apps remotely by using Web Inspector, is pretty much the dream feature if you're developing for the Mobile Web. RIM Playbook already supports remote debugging today (as you can see in Chapter 14); I expect other mobile devices to implement it in the not-too-distant future.

Until that day comes, however, we have Weinre (which, according to its creator, is pronounced either "winery" or "weiner," as in "hot dog"). Weinre makes a subset of Web Inspector's features available remotely for iOS, Android, BlackBerry, and webOS.

Weinre has three parts:

✔ The *server* is a specialized web server that's used for communication between the client and the target.

✔ The *client* is your desktop browser, where you'll be running the Web Inspector interface.

✔ The *target* is the browser or device that's viewing the web page you'll be debugging.

Installing and running Weinre on Mac OS X is easy:

1. **Download the Mac OS X application from** https://github.com/phonegap/weinre/archives/master.

2. **Open the downloaded archive and drag the Weinre.app file into your Applications folder.**

3. **Launch Weinre.app by double-clicking its file.**

   The server and client parts of the application start; you see the remote debugger appear (as shown in Figure 21-2), which indicates that you're not yet connected to any targets.

To connect the client to a target, you have to take one of two actions:

- Insert a piece of code into the web app that you want to debug.

- Run a bit of JavaScript to insert the code into your target that will connect it to the server.

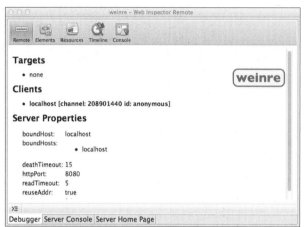

Figure 21-2:
Wienre isn't
connected
to targets
when it
launches.

4. **Open your target device.**

   For now, just use your WebKit nightly browser.

5. **Click the Server Homepage tab at the bottom of the Wienre window.**

   In this window, you can find instructions for connecting to a target.

6. **Drag the `bookmarklet` URL from Weinre to the Bookmarks bar in your WebKit browser.**

   A *bookmarklet* is a small application stored as a bookmark in your browser. In this case, Weinre is using a bookmarklet to insert JavaScript code into any web page running in the browser.

7. **WebKit asks you to name the bookmarklet.**

   After you do that, a new link appears on your bookmarks bar that connects the current page to the Weinre application.

8. **Open several tabs in your WebKit browser, and click the Weinre `target debug` bookmark in each.**

9. **Return to Weinre and refresh the debugger window.**

   Your target web pages are listed onscreen under the targets header, as shown in Figure 21-3.

**Figure 21-3:**
Targets
must be
connected
to the client
for remote
debugging.

10. **To start debugging, click any of the targets, and then click the Element, Resources, Timeline, or Console panels.**

    Try using the elements panel to highlight code and modify styles. The actions you take in the Wienre debugger are instantly reflected in the target web page, as shown in Figure 21-4.

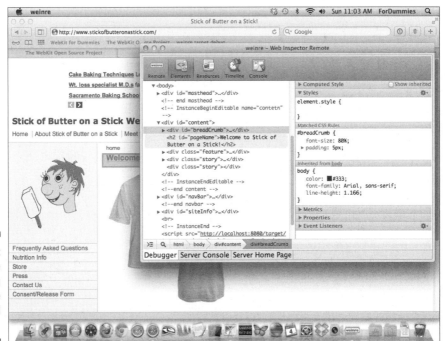

**Figure 21-4:**
Remote
debugging
with Wienre
is good
for you!

# Simulating Touch Events

It's difficult to know exactly how a web app will work on a mobile device without actually loading it onto that device. With apps that use touch input, it's even more difficult. Mouse clicks and touch events are fundamentally different things.

Phantom Limb is a JavaScript library that translates mouse clicks into touch events. Figure 21-5 shows Phantom Hand in action. As a bonus, it changes your cursor into a giant floating hand!

You can start using Phantom Limb by going to the homepage at www. vodori.com/blog/phantom-limb.html and grabbing the code for the JavaScript bookmarklet.

After you install the bookmark in your browser, all you need to do to start touching things is to go to a web app that's touch-enabled and click the bookmarklet. If the page you're on doesn't support touch events, your mouse clicks will be interpreted as just standard mouse clicks — but with a floating hand doing the clicking. (That can be fun, too.)

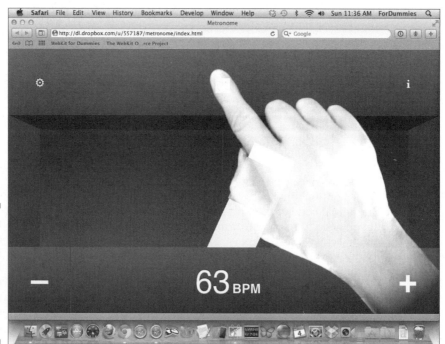

**Figure 21-5:**
The
Phantom
Hand
homepage
links to a
demo metro-
nome app.

# Web Inspector Settings

If you sometimes get frustrated and confused by what the WebKit Inspector is trying to tell you (or isn't telling you), you may find some relief in the Web Inspector Settings screen.

To open the Web Inspector settings, click the gear icon in the lower-right corner of Web Inspector. A semi-opaque overlay appears over Web Inspector, as shown in Figure 21-6, offering several options that you can adjust.

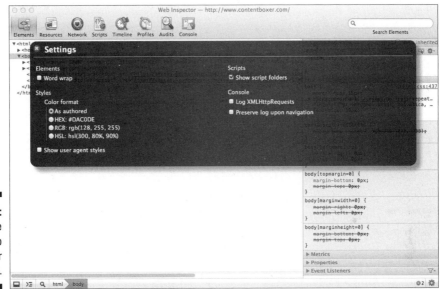

**Figure 21-6:** Customize your Web Inspector experience.

 Based on my experience, I would recommend turning off Word Wrap, changing the color format to As Authored, and deselecting the Show User Agent Styles option. Then what you see in Web Inspector more accurately reflects the actual code of the web app, which can often make debugging a bit easier. If you need to re-enable or modify these features, you can always return to the settings and change them again.

# MathML

I'm no mathematician, but I can appreciate the beauty and logic of mathematical expressions as much as the next person can. MathML is a W3C specification for including mathematical expressions in HTML without the use of images.

WebKit supports MathML although not completely. For most folks, however, this incomplete support will likely be enough. If you're the type of person who regularly uses mathematical expressions in your web pages, you can use a plug-in to provide complete support for MathML.

Figure 21-7 shows a demo of MathML, which is located at

```
http://www.webkit.org/demos/mathml/MathMLDemo.xhtml
```

Make sure that you're visiting this web page using the latest WebKit nightly build.

All those fancy characters (almost none of which I understand) are rendered by using markup language.

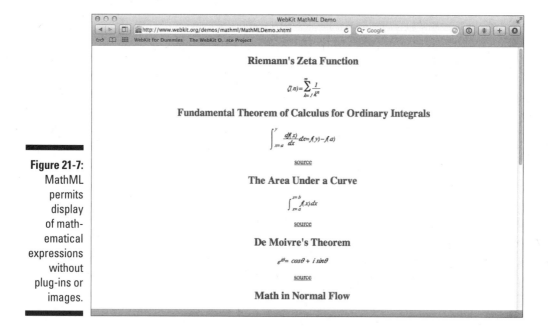

**Figure 21-7:**
MathML
permits
display
of math-
ematical
expressions
without
plug-ins or
images.

# Create Folders on the Bookmarks Bar

If, like me, you have a tendency to add bookmarks to the Bookmarks bar so that you won't forget about them, you probably have a completely disorganized list of bookmarks that run off the side of the browser and make it impossible for you to find anything at all.

Fortunately, it's possible — and very easy — to create folders and to drag bookmarks into those folders.

To create a new Bookmark bar folder, just right-click a blank space on the bookmarks bar and select New Folder. You can then right-click the new folder and select Edit Contents to begin adding items to it.

# Using the Activity Window

The Activity window can be opened by choosing Window⇨Activity from the main menu of WebKit or Safari. The purpose of the activity window is to show you what web pages are open in every window and tab of the browser, what files make up those web pages, and how long each file took to download.

Figure 21-8 shows the Activity window in action.

One of the uses for the Activity view is to quickly access or download a resource that's part of a web page. If a particular graphic or file that's part of a web page isn't loading or is causing problems, for example, you will see that in the Activity window. By double-clicking any line of text in window, you can isolate and open just that file in a new browser window. Often, just isolating the problem in this way makes the solution obvious.

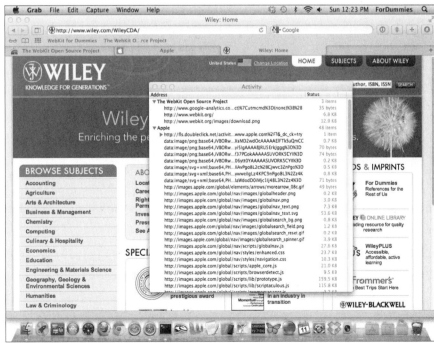

**Figure 21-8:** The Activity window shows a bird's-eye view of activity in your browser.

# Title Bar Site Navigation

Many websites organize content hierarchically with directories. For example, the WebKit homepage is `http://www.webkit.org`. Several paths branch off the main page, including one called Projects. After you're inside the Projects area, you can make several more choices, including the CSS branch. The URL to the CSS project, for example, is `http://www.webkit.org/projects/css`.

Safari contains a hidden trick for navigating this type of site, using the page title. If you're at a URL such as `http://www.webkit.org/projects/css`, you can click the page title while holding down the Command key (⌘; Mac OS) or the Ctrl key (Windows) to get links to and to open any of the directories at a "higher" level than the current one, as shown in Figure 21-9.

**Figure 21-9:**
The title link shortcut jumps to higher levels of site hierarchy.

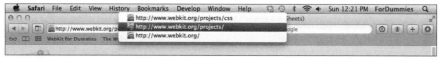

# Open Links in New Tabs

When I do a web search, I often need to check out several the results before I'm satisfied that I have the answer I'm looking for. Usually, I'll open one result, look over the page, and then use the Back button to return to the search results so that I can try the next one.

With Safari, however, you can quickly open several results in new tabs while remaining on the page you opened the links from. You can do this by holding down the Command key (⌘; Mac OS) or the Ctrl key (Windows) while clicking the links.

# Chapter 22

# Ten Amazing HTML5 Demos

So you think you know what HTML and the web can do, huh? Maybe you've been around the web and the Mobile Web a few times, and you've seen it all and done it all. You know what a website is and what it isn't.

This chapter is going to blow your mind and show you some demos of pure HTML5 technologies — using no plug-ins — that you probably never imagined to be possible to create with just a text editor and some design skills.

Time to get the show on the road: Fire up the latest nightly build of WebKit, and read on.

## Exploding Video

Start with something extremely cool, but almost completely useless. Point your WebKit browser at the following URL:

```
http://craftymind.com/factory/html5video/CanvasVideo.html
```

You'll see a cute little video with some furry woodland creatures, as shown in Figure 22-1. Aren't they sweet?

Now click the video. Pow! Your mouse must be made of dynamite because you just blew a gigantic hole in that video, as shown in Figure 22-2. Notice that each piece of the blown-up video keeps on playing after you explode it!

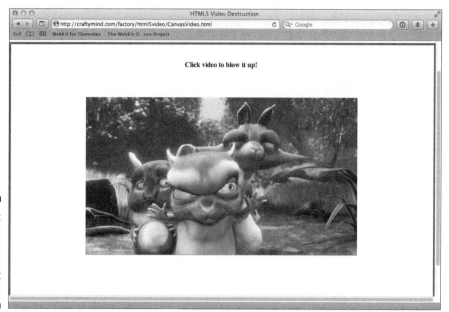

**Figure 22-1:**
Here's an entertaining little cartoon with forest creatures.

**Figure 22-2:**
Sorry, little critters! This mouse and this WebKit browser are too powerful!

Now right-click somewhere outside the video and choose View Page Source from the contextual menu. What you'll see is a bunch of JavaScript code that controls an HTML5 `<canvas>` element and an HTML5 `<video>` element. There are no fancy plug-ins, and there are also no external files at all (except for the Google Analytics code at the bottom that's just used to track the page traffic).

# Virtually Like Being There

Apple has a demo of HTML5, CSS3, and JavaScript being used together to present a 3-D view of the Apple Store in San Francisco. You can check it out at

```
www.apple.com/html5/showcase/vr
```

Use your mouse to move around in the scene. Look up! Look down! Spin around! Are those real live geniuses from the genius bar? Wow. Figure 22-3 does a poor job of re-creating a 360-degree virtual reality scene, but you can imagine the rest, or check it out online.

**Figure 22-3:** Here's the virtual view of the lobby of the San Fran Apple Store.

# The Wilderness Downtown

www.thewildernessdowntown.com

This has to be one of the cooler things on the web. You really have to see this interactive music video created by the band The Arcade Fire and Google to believe it. It's processor intensive and cutting edge in a number of ways — and it's all HTML5.

Figure 22-4 shows the homepage of the app. This is one demo that won't be running on your smartphone anytime soon. When you see it, you'll understand why.

**Figure 22-4:** The Wilderness Downtown.

# Agent 008 Ball

http://www.agent8ball.com

At Agent 008 Ball, a weak back-story about a billiards tournament that's been infiltrated by a terrorist organization somehow means that you need to play a lightning round of no-rules pool by yourself — and some of the balls are bombs.

The graphics look great, as you can see in Figure 22-5, the game play is really smooth, and the game is actually pretty addictive.

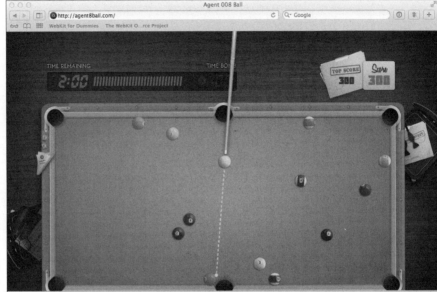

**Figure 22-5:**
Don't try to understand why you're doing this. Just have fun.

# Solar System Explorer

www.solar-system-explorer.com

Solar System Explorer shows a live 3-D model of the solar system, with all eight (or nine) planets and the largest moons shown. You can speed up or slow down time and see how the planets move around the sun and in relation to each other.

If you zoom in on a planet, you'll see textures and an approximation of how the planet actually looks, as shown in Figure 22-6. Each planet has some additional information available when you zoom in.

The site uses WebGL, so you may need to enable it before you can view this app. Choose Develop↪Enable WebGL from the main menu of WebKit.

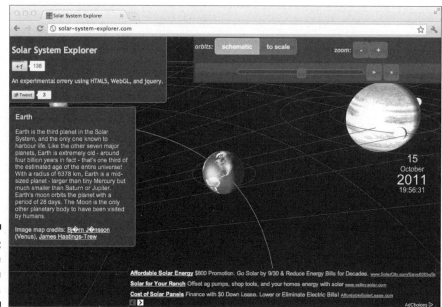

**Figure 22-6:**
Explore the solar system with HTML5.

# Art of Stars

www.nakshart.com

Continuing with the astronomical theme, look a little farther out. Art of Stars is an HTML5 web app that uses geolocation to figure out your position and then show what the night sky looks like above you right now, complete with constellations, planets, stars, and galaxies.

Sit back and enjoy the night sky in your computer, because, as we all know, the ambient light where most of us live pretty much destroys any hope of doing any real stargazing. My personal favorite feature of this app is that you can change the observer location, as shown in Figure 22-7, and see what the night sky looks like right now in other places.

# Aviary Photo Editor

```
www.aviary.com
```

Aviary Photo Editor is a photo editor created using HTML5. Anyone can go to the site, upload a photo, and start touching it up for free. Options for editing include: sharpen, whiten teeth, rotate, resize, adjust colors, add drawings and text, and more.

When you're done editing your photo, you can save it, download it, and share it on social networking sites. It's the perfect solution for making a quick fix to the lighting or to remove someone from a picture before uploading it to Facebook. Figure 22-8 shows my creation.

# Canvas Rider

```
http://canvasrider.com
```

Canvas Rider, shown in Figure 22-9, is a black-and-white horizontal-scrolling game where you're a stick figure riding a bike over maps that are drawn by users. You must hit the right speed to make it over ramps, bumps, and valleys to land upright after jumps — or meet a grisly stick-person demise.

**Figure 22-8:** Use Aviary Photo Editor to fix photos before posting them.

**Figure 22-9:** Canvas Rider features user-drawn maps for riding your virtual bike.

The game uses HTML5 Canvas to draw and animate the rider and the course. It's a very addictive game, so watch out if you're trying to get anything done today!

# Every Time Zone

```
http://everytimezone.com
```

Every Time Zone is a simple HTML5 app for seeing what day and time it is in various timezones, as shown in Figure 22-10. Its purpose is simple, but the way it works is ingenious.

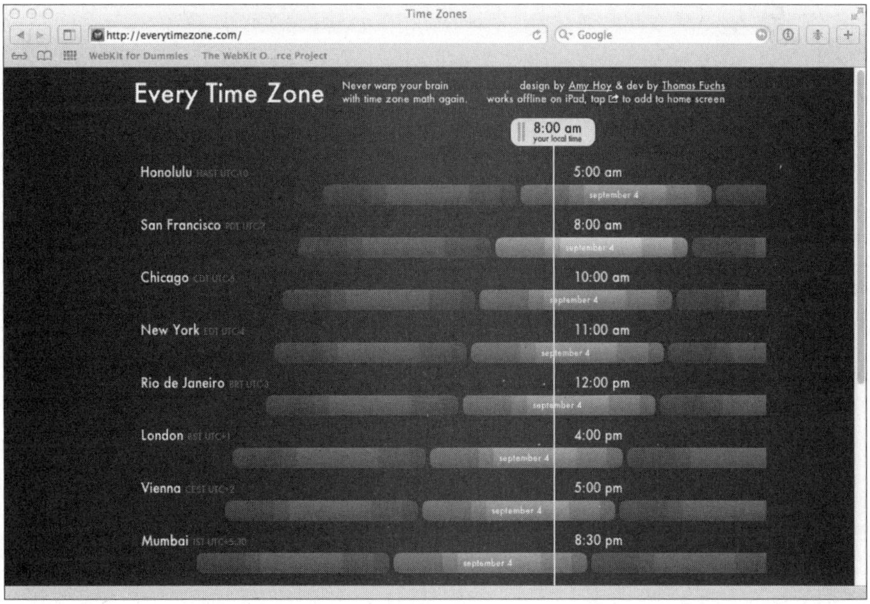

**Figure 22-10:**
Every Time
Zone.

The interface is so simple and intuitive that you hardly think about the cool technologies that make it work. It's optimized for the iPad, and it responds to touch events, works offline, and loads very quickly.

Every Time Zone doesn't explain to me why Mumbai has that half-hour thing, but at least I don't have to figure out timezones by counting on my fingers anymore.

## 20 Things I Learned about Browsers and the Web

www.20thingsilearned.com

20 Things I Learned about Browsers and the Web, shown in Figure 22-11, is a guide to some basics about how the Web works. It covers topics such as cookies, TCP/IP, and cloud computing in a friendly, attractive, HTML5 flip-book format.

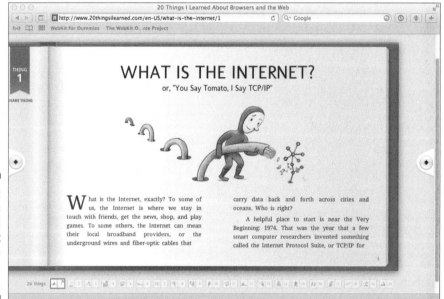

**Figure 22-11:** 20 Things I Learned about Browsers and the Web.

# Chapter 23

# Ten Useful Safari Extensions

*In This Chapter*

▶ Teaching Safari new tricks

▶ Boosting your productivity with extensions

*T*he functionality that's included with WebKit browsers is pretty impressive by itself. Sometimes, though, it becomes necessary or helpful to add to those powers. Most browsers (desktop browsers, anyway) allow two methods of adding new functionality: plug-ins and extensions (sometimes also called *add-ons*).

The terms are sometimes confused and misunderstood, so allow me to get clear what I'm talking about before going any further.

A *plug-in* is a code library that "plugs in" to the browser to allow it to handle a new type of content. Examples of plug-ins include

- ✔ Adobe Flash Player
- ✔ Microsoft Silverlight
- ✔ Adobe Reader
- ✔ Apple QuickTime
- ✔ Java
- ✔ Windows Media Player

A plug-in doesn't create a toolbar or add items to menus. It just sits there and waits to be called by a web page (using an `<object>` or `<embed>` tag) and then it springs into action to handle a piece of content.

One of the goals of HTML5 is to make plug-ins unnecessary — or, at least, much less necessary — by building the ability to handle audio, video, and other types of nontext content right into the browser.

 *Extensions,* on the other hand, actually beef up ("extend") the functionality of the browser so it can do more things, do new things, or work better. They can add toolbars and menu items, do cool things to the pages loaded by the browser, and much more. Safari's Extension Builder (which you can access from the Develop menu) allows you to write your own extensions if you're so inclined. Hundreds of people have done just that, and Apple publishes a directory of extensions at `http://extensions.apple.com`.

In this chapter, I focus mostly on extensions that can help you be more productive or a better web developer, but plenty of extensions are just for fun. Without further ado, here are some of my favorite Safari extensions.

# BetterSource

`www.awarepixel.com/safari/bettersource`

Anyone who regularly makes use of the View Source feature in Safari can benefit from using the BetterSource extension. It adds two buttons to your toolbar. One shows you the source code for the current HTML page, and the other shows you the generated HTML source — what the browser is actually using to display the current page after any changes that have been made by client-side JavaScript.

Perhaps best of all, however, is that BetterSource adds line numbers and color-coding to its views of the source code, making them much easier to read than the bland, regular old Source View source code. Figure 23-1 shows the output of View Source without BetterSource enabled; Figure 23-2 shows the output of BetterSource.

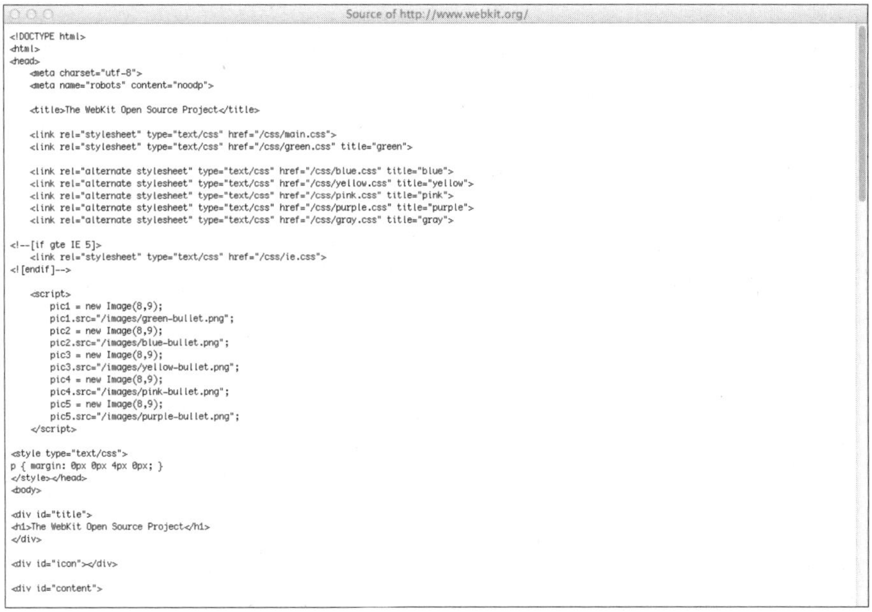

**Figure 23-1:**
The standard View Source output omits colors and line numbers.

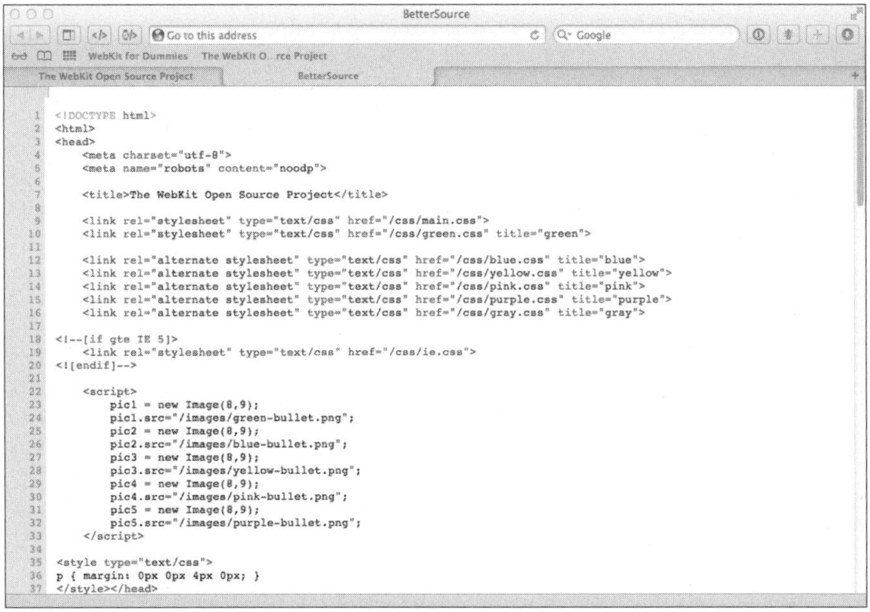

**Figure 23-2:**
BetterSource makes your browser's source code easier on the eye.

# Glims

www.machangout.com

Glims is like the Swiss Army Knife of extensions. It adds a plethora of new features to Safari. Many of these are nice, user interface enhancements, such as adding icons to tabs, and putting a separator between items in the bookmarks toolbar.

Other features modify web pages in useful ways: for example, adding thumbnail images to Google, Yahoo!, and Bing search results.

But one feature in particular makes installing Glims worth it for me: keyword search in the address bar. Ever since Google Chrome came out with this feature, I've been trying to do it (with no luck) in all my browsers. An extension that enables that feature in Safari absolutely makes my list of the ten most useful extensions.

After Glims is installed, you can access its preferences and turn features on and off from the Safari Preferences panel, as shown in Figure 23-3.

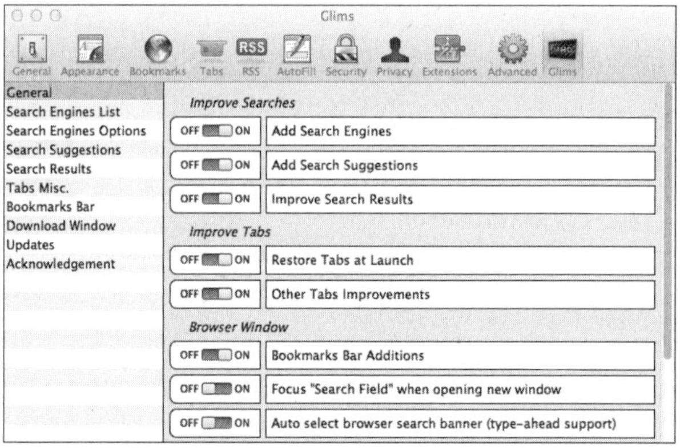

**Figure 23-3:**
Set Glims
preferences.

# Exposer

http://maypril.se/safariextensions/

By the end of my workday, I often have 20 to 30 tabs open in each of three or four browser windows. When you get past a certain point, there's really no hope of figuring out what's on each of those tabs without clicking a tab to see.

Exposer adds a new button (just to the left of the Safari address bar) that you can click to bring up a small picture of each open tab. As you can see from Figure 23-4, this set of pictures can be a real time-saver if you're prone to opening so many tabs that you can no longer read labels on them.

**Figure 23-4:**
Exposer shows you what's on your tabs.

# TabLock

```
www.fuzzycloud.co.uk/tablock
```

One downside of having so many tabs open at the same time is that my computer starts to get slow, and I need to start closing tabs like crazy to get things back to normal. Inevitably, I close the most important tab . . . maybe the one where I was filling out a complicated form. And after I close that tab, there's no getting it back. Sure, I can reopen the tab, but the data I entered into that form is probably gone forever.

The purpose of TabLock is to protect you from yourself. When you're in a tab that you want to make sure you don't accidentally close, just click the lock icon in the toolbar. Now, when you try to close that tab, you'll get a warning message that you locked it using TabLock.

# WasteNoTime

http://bumblebeesystems.dyndns.org/wastenotime/

WasteNoTime lets you create a list of websites where you're likely to waste time, along with the maximum amount of time you want to be able to use that site per day. When your limit for the site is reached, you'll be cut off and reprimanded for wasting time.

You probably owe the fact that you're reading this book to this extension.

# BuiltWith

http://blog.builtwith.com/2010/06/08/builtwith-safari-
            extension/

Have you ever visited a website and wondered how it did something? As a web developer, this is pretty much half your job. BuiltWith will analyze the code of the site you're visiting and report everything that it finds about the server-side and client-side languages and technologies that were used to create the site.

# Unicorn

http://archives.grincheux.be/validator-safari-extension

This extension validates web pages using the W3C code validator, Unicorn. Because it's faster for web browsers to render valid code, a simple way to test a page is very important in tuning the user experience of your site.

# True Knowledge Search Enhancer

http://blog.trueknowledge.com/2010/07/true-knowledge-
            search-enhancer-now-available-for-safari.html

This extension will insert a direct answer into your search results, if it can find one. For example, say you search for "What is the population of New York State?" using Google. True Knowledge will insert its best answer above the search results and will ask you whether this is a good answer. (Hmm. If I knew, I wouldn't have asked in the first place, but that's another matter.)

# Google Fonts in Safari

www.juliodinicola.es/safari

This extension lets you change the default font of any web page you're viewing to use any fonts from Google's font directory. This is especially handy for seeing how a site you're working on will look with different fonts.

# Comic Sans Be Gone

www.sitharus.com/comic-sans-be-gone.html

Speaking of fonts: If you're the type to get upset, annoyed, or overly excited when you see the Comic Sans font, this is just the extension for you. When it encounters a website that uses Comic Sans, it just replaces it with good ol' Helvetica. No muss, no fuss. If you're a web developer trying to fix up a site that someone else built, however, it's best to have this extension disabled so as to not get a false sense of everything being just fine while all the time, Comic Sans lurks in the background for everyone who doesn't have this extension installed to see.

# Index

# • *H* •

**• X •**

**• Y •**

**• Z •**

## Apple & Mac

iPad 2 For Dummies,
3rd Edition
978-1-118-17679-5

iPhone 4S For Dummies,
5th Edition
978-1-118-03671-6

iPod touch For Dummies,
3rd Edition
978-1-118-12960-9

Mac OS X Lion
For Dummies
978-1-118-02205-4

## Blogging & Social Media

CityVille For Dummies
978-1-118-08337-6

Facebook For Dummies,
4th Edition
978-1-118-09562-1

Mom Blogging
For Dummies
978-1-118-03843-7

Twitter For Dummies,
2nd Edition
978-0-470-76879-2

WordPress For Dummies,
4th Edition
978-1-118-07342-1

## Business

Cash Flow For Dummies
978-1-118-01850-7

Investing For Dummies,
6th Edition
978-0-470-90545-6

Job Searching with Social
Media For Dummies
978-0-470-93072-4

QuickBooks 2012
For Dummies
978-1-118-09120-3

Resumes For Dummies,
6th Edition
978-0-470-87361-8

Starting an Etsy Business
For Dummies
978-0-470-93067-0

## Cooking & Entertaining

Cooking Basics
For Dummies, 4th Edition
978-0-470-91388-8

Wine For Dummies,
4th Edition
978-0-470-04579-4

## Diet & Nutrition

Kettlebells For Dummies
978-0-470-59929-7

Nutrition For Dummies,
5th Edition
978-0-470-93231-5

Restaurant Calorie Counter
For Dummies,
2nd Edition
978-0-470-64405-8

## Digital Photography

Digital SLR Cameras &
Photography For Dummies,
4th Edition
978-1-118-14489-3

Digital SLR Settings
& Shortcuts
For Dummies
978-0-470-91763-3

Photoshop Elements 10
For Dummies
978-1-118-10742-3

## Gardening

Gardening Basics
For Dummies
978-0-470-03749-2

Vegetable Gardening
For Dummies,
2nd Edition
978-0-470-49870-5

## Green/Sustainable

Raising Chickens
For Dummies
978-0-470-46544-8

Green Cleaning
For Dummies
978-0-470-39106-8

## Health

Diabetes For Dummies,
3rd Edition
978-0-470-27086-8

Food Allergies
For Dummies
978-0-470-09584-3

Living Gluten-Free
For Dummies,
2nd Edition
978-0-470-58589-4

## Hobbies

Beekeeping
For Dummies,
2nd Edition
978-0-470-43065-1

Chess For Dummies,
3rd Edition
978-1-118-01695-4

Drawing For Dummies,
2nd Edition
978-0-470-61842-4

eBay For Dummies,
7th Edition
978-1-118-09806-6

Knitting For Dummies,
2nd Edition
978-0-470-28747-7

## Language &
## Foreign Language

English Grammar
For Dummies,
2nd Edition
978-0-470-54664-2

French For Dummies,
2nd Edition
978-1-118-00464-7

German For Dummies,
2nd Edition
978-0-470-90101-4

Spanish Essentials
For Dummies
978-0-470-63751-7

Spanish For Dummies,
2nd Edition
978-0-470-87855-2

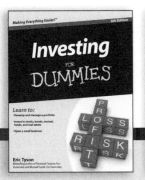
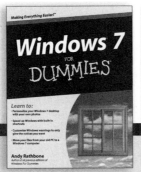

## Math & Science

Algebra I For Dummies,
2nd Edition
978-0-470-55964-2

Biology For Dummies,
2nd Edition
978-0-470-59875-7

Chemistry For Dummies,
2nd Edition
978-1-1180-0730-3

Geometry For Dummies,
2nd Edition
978-0-470-08946-0

Pre-Algebra Essentials
For Dummies
978-0-470-61838-7

## Microsoft Office

Excel 2010 For Dummies
978-0-470-48953-6

Office 2010 All-in-One
For Dummies
978-0-470-49748-7

Office 2011 for Mac
For Dummies
978-0-470-87869-9

Word 2010
For Dummies
978-0-470-48772-3

## Music

Guitar For Dummies,
2nd Edition
978-0-7645-9904-0

Clarinet For Dummies
978-0-470-58477-4

iPod & iTunes
For Dummies,
9th Edition
978-1-118-13060-5

## Pets

Cats For Dummies,
2nd Edition
978-0-7645-5275-5

Dogs All-in One
For Dummies
978-0470-52978-2

Saltwater Aquariums
For Dummies
978-0-470-06805-2

## Religion & Inspiration

The Bible For Dummies
978-0-7645-5296-0

Catholicism For Dummies,
2nd Edition
978-1-118-07778-8

Spirituality For Dummies,
2nd Edition
978-0-470-19142-2

## Self-Help & Relationships

Happiness For Dummies
978-0-470-28171-0

Overcoming Anxiety
For Dummies,
2nd Edition
978-0-470-57441-6

## Seniors

Crosswords For Seniors
For Dummies
978-0-470-49157-7

iPad 2 For Seniors
For Dummies, 3rd Edition
978-1-118-17678-8

Laptops & Tablets
For Seniors For Dummies,
2nd Edition
978-1-118-09596-6

## Smartphones & Tablets

BlackBerry For Dummies,
5th Edition
978-1-118-10035-6

Droid X2 For Dummies
978-1-118-14864-8

HTC ThunderBolt
For Dummies
978-1-118-07601-9

MOTOROLA XOOM
For Dummies
978-1-118-08835-7

## Sports

Basketball For Dummies,
3rd Edition
978-1-118-07374-2

Football For Dummies,
2nd Edition
978-1-118-01261-1

Golf For Dummies,
4th Edition
978-0-470-88279-5

## Test Prep

ACT For Dummies,
5th Edition
978-1-118-01259-8

ASVAB For Dummies,
3rd Edition
978-0-470-63760-9

The GRE Test For
Dummies, 7th Edition
978-0-470-00919-2

Police Officer Exam
For Dummies
978-0-470-88724-0

Series 7 Exam
For Dummies
978-0-470-09932-2

## Web Development

HTML, CSS, & XHTML
For Dummies, 7th Edition
978-0-470-91659-9

Drupal For Dummies,
2nd Edition
978-1-118-08348-2

## Windows 7

Windows 7
For Dummies
978-0-470-49743-2

Windows 7
For Dummies,
Book + DVD Bundle
978-0-470-52398-8

Windows 7 All-in-One
For Dummies
978-0-470-48763-1